ALFALFA BILL MURRAY

William H. Murray, 1930

ALFALFA BILL MURRAY

BY KEITH L. BRYANT, JR.

UNIVERSITY OF OKLAHOMA PRESS : NORMAN

LIBRARY OF CONGRESS CATALOG CARD NUMBER: 68–10299

Copyright 1968 by the University of Oklahoma Press, Publishing Division of the University. Composed and printed at Norman, Oklahoma, U.S.A., by the University of Oklahoma Press. First edition.

FK

To Margaret

✪

PREFACE

To many Americans, the name "Alfalfa Bill" Murray conjures up an image of a seedy old man, wearing a wrinkled white cotton suit covered with cigar ashes, his face distinguished by an untrimmed walrus mustache, his head covered with an unkempt tassel of gray hair protruding from under a battered hat, and his always short trouser legs raised above his shoes, revealing bony legs, run-down white socks, and six inches of long underwear. To the author, as to other Oklahomans, Alfalfa Bill became a living legend in his own time. Virtually every resident of the Sooner State has at least one story, true or apocryphal, about Murray, and everyone has an opinion of him. William Henry David Murray's personality generated controversy, and people either loved or hated him; there was no indifference.

Murray's life extended from Reconstruction to the first administration of Dwight D. Eisenhower, and he became a part of the political history of Oklahoma, Texas, and the nation during those years. Although he reached maturity in the middle of the farmers' revolts of the 1890's, he was not a Populist; he rejected the third party and most of its platform. Neither was he a dedicated Progressive in the years after 1900; he accepted and worked to enact measures of political and economic reform advocated by those in the Progressive movement but refused to countenance many social aspects of progressivism.

Alfalfa Bill stood with a small and dwindling body of men who could be called "Agrarians." The meaning of this term has been so misconstrued that the definition as used in this volume must be made clear. The word has been applied to "Pitchfork Ben" Tillman,

Tom Watson, Ignatius Donnelly, and other political leaders, and it has been used to describe the farm organizations of the 1890's. This is a perversion of the definition of the word as it was originally understood and used by eighteenth-century Americans. An Agrarian was one who advocated the equal, or a more equitable, distribution of the cultivated land. The term relates to land tenure and utilization, and this is the definition used in this volume. Murray advocated state and national laws to provide land for the landless and to prevent ownership of large tracts by aliens or corporations. He idealized rural America and all the virtues which this mystique has captured. For him, the only true Americans were Thomas Jefferson's yeoman farmers, living on 160-acre farms, tilling the good earth, and voting the Democratic ticket. Murray was the product of the environment of central Texas in the last quarter of the nineteenth century. His commitment to this way of life so constricted his vision that he rejected industrialization, urbanization, and centralization of governmental power.

The "Sage of Tishomingo" supported those policies and programs which he deemed beneficial to the preservation of rural America. By this criterion he judged all proposals, whether they were of Populist, Progressive, or New Deal origin. He defended and worked to preserve a way of life that was disappearing even as he labored to maintain it. As late as the 1940's Murray wrote that the only way to save the country, which he claimed was still basically agricultural, was the extension of the family farm.

The tactics Alfalfa Bill adopted in his fight to prevent large-scale landowning and to protect the yeoman farmer often caused his political opponents, the metropolitan press, and some historians to label him a demagogue. As C. Vann Woodward has written, the word "demagogue" should be acknowledged for what it is, a political epithet. From definitions found in standard dictionaries, the word describes a popular leader or orator who makes use of social discontent to gain political office. By this definition nearly every aspirant to an elective position becomes a demagogue. If, however, the word is used to describe a politician who lacks scruples and attempts to gain popular acclaim by flattery or false promises and who appeals to racial or religious prejudices, then Bill Murray could never be so labeled. He campaigned on platforms that dealt with real issues and did not engage in the Negro baiting generally attributed to southern "demagogues." Unlike Tom Watson, Coleman Blease, and James K. Vardaman, he refused to use the Negro as an issue to win the votes of white Oklahomans. The key to the use of the word "demagogue" seems to be the intentions of the politician, and Murray's sincerity on the vast majority of issues cannot be questioned, even if one does not agree with the positions he took. Some of his methods were questionable; his objectives usually were not. He contended that it was often necessary to appeal to the emotions of the voters as well as to their intellect and that this was not demagoguery. It was not.

There are two major themes in this book, one positive, the other negative. Alfalfa Bill was an Agrarian in the original sense of the word; he was not a southern demagogue. He spent his life desperately trying to arrest the forces that were changing the nation from a land of family farmers to an urban industrial giant. This is the story of a man's frustrated but absolutely determined efforts to preserve agricultural America as it existed in the nineteenth century.

The author of any volume such as this acquires innumerable debts to individuals and institutions. Two former teachers provided the stimulation that led to the writing of this book. The author's interest in the history of Oklahoma developed in the classroom of Professor Charles C. Bush, Jr., of the University of Oklahoma. Professor Lewis E. Atherton, of the University of Missouri, suggested Alfalfa Bill as the subject of a biography and provided helpful guidance in its development.

The librarians and archivists of the University of Texas, the State Historical Society of Missouri, the Library of Congress, the National Archives, the Oklahoma Historical Society, the Franklin D. Roosevelt Library, and the University of Oklahoma Library, Division of Manuscripts, graciously aided me in my research. A grant from the University of Missouri Alumni Achievement Fund and a reduced teaching assignment and research grant from the University of Wisconsin—Milwaukee helped defray travel expenses and provided time for writing.

A number of individuals have read different versions of this manuscript, and their comments have been deeply appreciated. John Lankford, Richard A. Watson, Richard S. Kirkendall, and Gilbert C. Fite contributed in many ways to its improvement. The author, of course, is alone responsible for any errors. The completion of this book would have been impossible without the aid and encouragement of my wife, Margaret, who served as research assistant, typist, and critic.

KEITH L. BRYANT, JR.

Milwaukee, Wisconsin
January 8, 1968

★

CONTENTS

✪

ILLUSTRATIONS

ALFALFA BILL MURRAY

✪

THE FORMATIVE YEARS

I

Some politicians prefer to have been born in log cabins. William Henry David Murray had to settle for a crude, one-room, slab-sided house of undressed pine. The future governor, congressman, and Presidential candidate was born on November 21, 1869, in the Texas frontier village of Toadsuck. The third son of Uriah Dow Thomas Murray and Bertha Elizabeth Jones Murray would be known as "Alfalfa Bill" during most of his adult years. The environment in which this child was born and reached maturity shaped the man who would become a leading figure in his adopted state of Oklahoma.

In the years before his birth, north central Texas was changing from an Indian-harassed frontier to an agricultural region, and the vast acres of black-dirt prairie beckoned settlers like Uriah Murray. A Scotsman, Uriah had left his native Tennessee to seek opportunity in the West.[1] He arrived in Texas in 1852 and several years later married Elizabeth Jones. Uriah worked for his father-in-law at a gristmill in the town of Collinsville, a few miles from Toadsuck. Economic advancement eluded Uriah, but his family grew with the arrival of John Shade in 1862, George Thomas in 1867, and William two years later. Sorrow came to the family in 1871, when Elizabeth died in childbirth.[2]

After the death of his wife Uriah took his sons to Collinsville to live with their maternal grandparents. William Henry would remember the next few years as a happy time, and he expressed great devotion to the Jones family. Yet he missed the maternal love and

[1] William H. Murray, *Memoirs of Governor Murray and True History of Oklahoma* (Boston, Meador Publishing Company, 1945), I, 64–104. Murray's memoirs contain long passages about his genealogy.
[2] Gordon Hines, *Alfalfa Bill: An Intimate Biography* (Oklahoma City, Oklahoma Press, 1932), 2–9.

care that he lost so very young, and when the quiet interlude with his grandparents ended, four-year-old William's world was further disrupted.

The three Murray brothers were taken from the love and security of their grandparents' home in February, 1873, when Uriah married the widow Mollie Green, of Montague. The Murrays moved to Montague, where Uriah worked in a mill and farmed a few acres. Something of a ne'er-do-well, Uriah became a sawyer and then a butcher and grocer.[3]

The boys resented Mollie from the beginning. A deeply religious woman, she also believed in strong punishment for her undisciplined stepsons. She restricted their activities and often whipped them. These whippings were among William's most enduring memories of his boyhood.[4] Uriah and Mollie ultimately had seven children of their own. Displaced by stepsisters and stepbrothers, William later recalled his early years as an unhappy time. He remembered pretending to be lost and having "stomach worms."

The only education the boys received at this time was their father's efforts to teach them their letters and numbers. Many years later William would speak often of his father and would tell his own sons how his respect for their grandfather grew after he left home.[5] His view of his stepmother never changed, and their relationship was, at best, one of mutual toleration.

In 1880 John Shade, the oldest son, left home to escape the unpleasantness of the household. Upon his return a year later he found his younger brothers extremely restive under Mollie's domination. On the evening of September 18, 1881, after telling Uriah they were going to church, the three boys ran away.[6] Alienated from his family, William Henry would now try to find a place in the world and the acceptance and acclaim he so desperately needed. He would eagerly search for a substitute for the close family relationship he had been denied.

At first, running away was a great adventure for the twelve-year-

[3] *Ibid.*, 15; Murray, *Memoirs*, I, 123–24.

[4] Murray, *Memoirs*, I, 125–26; Johnston Murray, interview of Dec. 29, 1965.

[5] Murray, *Memoirs*, I, 135–36; Johnston Murray, interview of Dec. 29, 1965.

[6] Murray, *Memoirs*, I, 147.

old boy. Henry, as he was generally known, and his two brothers rode their pony and an old horse a few miles south to Wise County. There they picked cotton, felled trees, and wandered from place to place seeking employment. They obtained work from Ed Loper and his family, and here for a time young Henry had a home. Mrs. Loper became the only mother he was to know.[7] After a few months with the Lopers he left to work in the brickyard at the nearby town of Aurora. He was dismayed to discover that some of the workmen were horse thieves. He decided to move on to Keeter, where he cut wood for a cotton-gin furnace.

While living at Keeter, he attended the local one-room school and lived with the teacher, Mr. Merrill. William Henry struggled to overcome the deficiencies in his education and took part in the literary society and its debates; oratory and debate appealed to a boy seeking acceptance and praise. His early education was quite limited. He skipped *McGuffey's First Reader* and failed to finish the *Second* or *Third*. The school terms were erratic, and he could attend only between crops or during the summer months. Much of Henry's education was received in Sunday School, where a *McGuffey* or a *Blueback Speller* was used as the text.[8] Longing for family life, he returned occasionally to the Loper home, where Ed Loper urged Henry to "pay your debts, treat your neighbors right, tell the truth, vote the Democratic ticket, and drink your whiskey straight."[9]

Then Henry heard of a new school at Springtown, about ten miles from Keeter. He sold his few possessions and departed to enroll at College Hill Institute. The institute had been founded in 1884 by John McCracken and D. P. Hurley. By present standards it was a country high school.[10] Built through donations of money and labor, the school afforded Henry his longest period of formal education. McCracken took the awkward backwoods boy into his home. The ragged student did not impress his classmates. They

[7] Hines, *Alfalfa Bill*, 36.

[8] Murray, *Memoirs*, III, 283–84; I, 134.

[9] Hines, *Alfalfa Bill*, 45.

[10] John W. Nix, *A Tale of Two Schools and Springtown, Parker County* (Fort Worth, Thomason and Morrow, 1945), 61–65.

ridiculed his manners, his clothing, and his poverty. Encouraged by his teachers, William Henry studied, read, and absorbed as much learning as he could.

At the end of the school term Henry and John Shade became traveling salesmen, selling books and atlases to the farmers of central Texas.[11] The Murray boys could speak the language of the poor farmers they called upon and yet present themselves as "college men." After saving a little money, Henry returned to the Loper home, where he spent most of his time reading; the habit of voracious reading would continue throughout his life. Two and one-half years would pass before he returned to College Hill.

The Loper family now resided at Buffalo, in Leon County, and it was here that Henry Murray first entered practical politics. He joined the Farmers' Alliance, a movement which was protesting the economic conditions of Texas farmers. The farmers were unhappy about usurious interest rates, low prices for agricultural products, and high railroad rates. In 1888 the state of Texas witnessed an intensive effort by the Farmers' Alliance to defeat the entrenched Democratic party structure, which refused to respond to their needs. The Leon County alliance was endeavoring to oust the local officeholders, and young Henry attended the meetings of the Farmers' Political Club at Sand Hill Church. In his political debut he became one of the club's leaders.[12] Even though, at nineteen, he was still ineligible to vote, Murray was elected by the Buffalo caucus as a delegate to the Leon County Democratic convention.[13] He gained a reputation as a speaker and scholar among the farmers, many of whom had had no formal education and therefore respected a man who had spent a year in college.

After this initial flirtation with politics Henry returned to College Hill with his brothers John Shade and George. His instructors, Hurley and McCracken, made a profound impression on him. Years later Murray wrote that McCracken taught him to reason but

[11] Hines, *Alfalfa Bill*, 51.
[12] Murray, *Memoirs*, I, 168; Hines, *Alfalfa Bill*, 59.
[13] "Murray on Cause of Defeat," Nov. 12, 1920, broadside, William H. Murray Collection (Norman, University of Oklahoma Library, Division of Manuscripts). Hereafter cited as Murray Coll., Univ. of Okla. Library.

Hurley taught him how to teach himself.[14] Henry called his teacher "Old Hundred and Plus," in honor of a grade he had received on an examination. While in school Murray became a local correspondent for the *Fort Worth Gazette*. He signed his copy "W. H. Murray" or "William Henry Murray."

At the end of the school year he looked for employment. After another brief stint as a book salesman he took the teacher's examination at College Hill and secured a teaching position at Millsap, in western Parker County. Armed with his teaching certificate and some stout switches, he presided over the rough one-room school for the next year.[15]

During this time he made his first trip out of north central Texas, when he accompanied Hurley and McCracken to the state teachers' convention at Galveston.[16] Both men continued to take an interest in their backwoods prodigy, and Murray repaid them with intense loyalty. For the rest of his life he used College Hill as a measuring rod to evaluate higher education.

Murray returned to Springtown in 1890 and entered politics again. He was elected by the district Democratic convention at Weatherford to serve as a Parker County delegate to the state convention in San Antonio. He won minor recognition at the meeting when he nominated Hurley for superintendent of schools.[17] The *San Antonio Daily Express* and the *Dallas Morning News* reported that Murray stressed Hurley's principles and complete candor with the public. The young orator castigated the *Express* for refusing to publish Hurley's views—the first but certainly not the last time the metropolitan press would rouse Murray's ire. Despite Murray's eloquent plea Hurley received only a small vote.[18]

Far more significant than Murray's speech was his meeting with

[14] William H. Murray, *The Finished Scholar* (Philadelphia, Dorrance & Company, 1941), 12.

[15] Teaching certificate issued by Judge I. N. Rouch, June 10, 1889, William H. Murray Collection (Oklahoma City, Oklahoma Historical Society Library). Hereafter cited as Murray Coll., OHS Library.

[16] Hines, *Alfalfa Bill*, 68; Murray, *Memoirs*, I, 140–41.

[17] *Austin Statesman*, Aug. 15, 1890.

[18] *San Antonio Daily Express*, Aug. 15, 1890; *Dallas Morning News*, Aug. 15, 1890; *Austin Statesman*, Aug. 15, 1890.

James S. Hogg, the man who became his political idol. From this meeting until he left Texas in 1898, Murray campaigned for Hogg and the reform faction of the Democratic party. Throughout his political career in Oklahoma he repeatedly referred to Hogg, maintaining his hero worship for more than fifty years.

After the convention Murray accepted a position at County Line School at Cade, on the Navarro-Limestone county line.[19] He soon acquired a reputation as a teacher and was invited to present his philosophy of education in the columns of the local press. In an editorial for the *Messenger*, the Jewett paper, he wrote that teaching was based entirely on the definition of the word "education."[20] Though lacking in profundity, the article apparently impressed the local readers.

While living in this community, Murray joined the Campbellite church. Although he remained a member of this denomination, he would never attend any church regularly. He had a deep and abiding interest in religion and kept three sacred books close at hand throughout his life: the King James Version of the Bible, the Roman Catholic Vulgate, and the Koran. Refusing to accept any single interpretation of religious questions, he consulted all three. His independent approach to theology meant that he would never find a minister or a church with which he could completely agree. Yet, while his religious convictions prevented him from becoming a regular churchgoer, they did not prevent him from giving his children a strong religious faith.[21] He gave to his political life some measure of the dedication that other men give to organized religion.

In 1890 Murray began to satisfy his ambitions when he entered the turbulent political life of central Texas. The first People's party or Populist organization in Texas had been formed in Navarro County, and the third party soon rivaled the Democrats in strength.[22] Murray's oratorical abilities were tested in a series of

---

[19] Teaching certificate issued by County Superintendent Howard, Oct. 25, 1890, Murray Coll., OHS Library.

[20] Newspaper clipping, *Messenger* (Jewett), June 6, 1890, Murray Coll., Univ. of Okla. Library.

[21] Johnston Murray, interview of Dec. 29, 1965.

[22] Hines, *Alfalfa Bill*, 72–73; Roscoe C. Martin, *The People's Party in Texas: A*

debates with Populist speakers. He opposed the Populist sub-treasury scheme, which called for action by the federal government to meet the needs of the farmers. The plan proposed for subtreasury offices to be established in every agricultural county. These offices would accept farm commodities as collateral for low-interest loans. The farm products could be redeemed by the farmers within a year, but if they were not, they would be sold by the subtreasury office.[23] The Populists claimed that the plan would provide farm loans at low interest rates, lower elevator and warehouse costs, support farm prices, and stimulate currency inflation. Murray debated the subtreasury proposals with the leading third-party orator in Texas, Harry Tracy.

Their debates became the main event in the Populist-Democratic campaign in Navarro County. The budding politician must have presented a stirring case to the gatherings of farmers and their families. One reporter wrote that "for two long hours [Murray] held the audience spellbound, frequently bringing forth an ava-lanche of applause." The story referred to Murray as "Roger Q. No. 2," comparing him to Congressman Roger Q. Mills, the local Democratic leader. Murray put down Tracy at a picnic by endors-ing free and unlimited coinage of gold and silver, reduced govern-mental expenditures, elimination of national banks, and tariff reform. Another newspaperman commented, "[Murray is] a tal-ented young man and is a fluent speaker, and is, I think about the best material the opposition could get up." A local editor wrote, "If Mr. Murray were not too young he would be good timber out of which to construct a state senator."[24] The young orator extended his speaking engagements from the small communities to the county seat of Corsicana. There, in the city park, he warned voters against third-party schemes and attacked the subtreasury plan.[25]

At last William Murray was receiving the attention he needed.

Study in Third Party Politics, Bulletin of the University of Texas Bureau of Research in the Social Sciences, Study No. 4, 1933, 33, 61.

[23] John D. Hicks, *The Populist Revolt* (Minneapolis, University of Minnesota Press, 1931), 186–204.

[24] Undated newspaper clippings, Murray Coll., Univ. of Okla. Library.

[25] Newspaper clipping, *Corsicana Light*, Murray Coll., Univ. of Okla. Library.

Not yet a voter, he had taken on the best Populist speaker and won public acclaim. Heady with success, the young man began to over-estimate his political prowess and his qualifications for public service. He had accomplished much in a very short time, but in the next few years he would learn the lessons of humility and patience and recognize the need for further education. Rising from poverty and insecurity, Murray would later romanticize these years as a time of idyllic bliss.

Murray began to devote more time to politics, but he continued to teach in one of the rural schools. The local people expressed satisfaction with his position on the leading political issues of the day as well as his classroom performance.[26] John McCracken admired Murray and asked him to speak at a College Hill commencement exercise.[27] After College Hill was destroyed by fire, McCracken established a new school at Mineral Wells, which awarded Murray the degree of bachelor of science.[28] Although he achieved success in the classroom, public life seems to have fascinated the young teacher even more, causing him to abandon the rural schools temporarily and return to the robust personal politics of the 1890's.

Like other states of the South and Middle West during the summer of 1891, Texas was the scene of a desperate battle among the farmers. Both the Farmers' Alliance and the Democratic party were sorely divided by the subtreasury question and by the alliance platforms adopted at Ocala, Florida, in December, 1890, and at Omaha, Nebraska, in January, 1891. The alliance Democrats of Texas, led by Jim Hogg, bitterly attacked the entrenched oligarchy, which opposed the reforms advocated by the insurgents.[29]

Murray stood with Hogg against the People's party on the left and the Bourbon Democrats on the right. On June 23, 1891, he spoke to the "grand rally" of the alliance and defended his views.

[26] Newspaper clipping, Murray Coll., Univ. of Okla. Library.

[27] Jno. W. McCracken to Murray, n.d., Murray Coll., Univ. of Okla. Library.

[28] Bachelor of Science Diploma from Mineral Wells College, May 19, 1893, Murray Coll., OHS Library. Murray always claimed to have graduated from College Hill Institute.

[29] For details of this political strife see Robert C. Cotner, *James Stephen Hogg: A Biography* (Austin, University of Texas Press, 1959).

At this all-day picnic in Thornton, the twenty-one-year-old speaker addressed his audience at length, arguing that he could be both an alliance member and an opponent of the subtreasury. He and other Hogg Democrats had been attacked as traitors to the alliance and had been threatened with expulsion. The alliance was a nonpolitical organization, and Murray took the position of Leonidas Polk, the national alliance leader, that members were free to support any political party or take any position on an issue.[30]

The pro-Hogg faction of the Farmers' Alliance organized a convention of anti-subtreasury men, which met in Fort Worth on July 10, 1891. The *Fort Worth Gazette* reported the activities of the meeting and printed biographical sketches of the leaders. One sketch described Murray as a self-made man who left home at the age of twelve, illiterate and penniless. The paper described him as a staunch Democrat: "He is true as steel to his convictions and has the reputation of being a fine speaker who always 'hits the nail on the head'; and is always ready to support any parliamentary position he takes on any question." The convention elected Murray its secretary, and he urged the alliance men to "let their successes be achieved only under the shield of honor."[31]

At the meeting Murray met Sam Dickson, publisher of the *Farmer's World*, who asked him to become a reporter for the paper. In his first major journalistic venture Murray contributed to the August 1 issue a front-page editorial six columns wide. This exposition, entitled "Democracy Defined," set forth his economic and political beliefs, and the contents reveal the sources of his views. Murray accepted the views of Hogg on the means to control railroads and the prohibition of farmland ownership by aliens and corporations. He agreed with the Texas Democrats on states' rights, tariff reductions, and opposition to federal aid to railroads. The alliance platforms adopted at St. Louis in 1889, Ocala in 1890, and Omaha in 1891 were also part of his beliefs, with two important exceptions. Unlike the Populist leaders Tom Watson, Ignatius Donnelly, and Leonidas Polk, he absolutely opposed the subtreasury

[30] *Farmer's World* (Dallas), July 4, 1891.
[31] *Fort Worth Gazette*, July 10–12, 1891.

plan and federal ownership of the railroads. Murray could never accept the two principal solutions to the farm problem presented by the Populist party.

The article argued that the farmers could achieve their goals within the Democratic party and need not form a third party. Like Democrats Ben Tillman and William Jennings Bryan, Murray accepted the goals of the Farmers' Alliance, but he asserted that he was a "strict party man":

> Parties, like governments and taxes are necessary evils. . . . No man joins any party because there is a single individual in it. He does so on account of its principles. . . . He that opposes political parties is a confirmed anarchist.[32]

According to Murray, the alliance should not become a separate political party but should seize control of the Democratic party. He was a Democrat, he asserted, because that party advocated local self-government, strict adherence to the Constitution, the reserved rights of the states, and the supremacy of the federal government only as defined by the Constitution.

The editorial reflected the influence of Hogg, the party, the alliance, and rural Texas. Murray advocated an immigration law to exclude both nonwhite immigrants and "pauper labor even of Aryan countries of Europe." He favored a drastic reduction in federal expenditures. He opposed federal subsidies for business but contended that the nation should have a policy of free ships, free seas, and free trade. The federal government should enforce the anti-monopoly laws but should not operate the railroads, telegraph companies, or steamship lines. He wanted all national banks abolished to divorce government from finance. He concluded the lengthy editorial with a flourish: "Hurrah for democracy!"

Murray's philosophy was so close to the Populist platform that he was often accused of being a member of the third party. He did adopt those planks of the Populist platform which buttressed his agrarian proposals; he was for alien land laws, agricultural education, graduated income taxes, and federal land loans, and he was

32 *Farmer's World*, Aug. 1, 1891.

opposed to all dealings in agricultural futures. His attitude was remarkably similar to that of William Jennings Bryan in Nebraska.[33] The positions taken by Alfalfa Bill in 1891 would dominate his thinking throughout his life.

In September Murray had his first opportunity to grace a national platform. He took an active role in a meeting of the Interstate Convention of the Anti-Sub-Treasury Farmers' Alliance, held in St. Louis. The delegates elected him secretary, and he demonstrated his forensic skills for them:

> He alluded to the sub-treasury proposition as a "lightening scheme." The honest farmers of the country would meet the advocates of the scheme "from Cape Cod to Kalamazoo, and from hell to breakfast," and would "snow them so deep that hell couldn't melt it in forty generations."[34]

The convention resolved to oppose the subtreasury and government ownership of the railroads.

After this meeting Murray returned to Corsicana to make arrangements for an anti-subtreasury convention which was to convene there. Before the meeting he had to face strong opposition within the Texas alliance, which had acted to remove him as a member because of his opposition to the subtreasury. The Cade County Line Alliance defied the parent organization and denied that Murray's activities were grounds for removal. Murray's friends and neighbors voted to acquit him of all charges.[35]

He reported the deliberations of the Corsicana meeting for the *Farmer's World*. When the body voted to form a new organization, the Farmers' Grand Alliance, he declared, "God bless the farmers, they need no eulogy." Murray helped write the constitution of the new organization. As chairman of the constitution committee he refused to give the document to anyone but the newly elected president. His zeal to protect the charter was to be repeated at the Oklahoma constitution convention in 1907. Before the meeting

[33] Paolo E. Colletta, *William Jennings Bryan* (Lincoln, University of Nebraska Press, 1964), I, 39–41, 51, 67, 399.
[34] *St. Louis Post-Dispatch*, Sept. 15, 1891.
[35] *Farmer's World*, Oct. 31, 1891.

13

adjourned, Murray was appointed state organizer for the Grand Alliance.[36]

He worked for the alliance only a short time, quitting on March 14, 1892, to become a correspondent for the *Fort Worth Gazette*. He covered a special session of the legislature in Austin, and during the assignment became even more devoted to Governor Hogg. After the legislative session ended, he sold books as a traveling salesman and then returned to Navarro County.

In 1892, having reached the age of twenty-three, Murray was eligible to enter the political wars as a candidate. He continued to speak throughout central Texas, advocating free and unlimited coinage of gold and silver, reduction of the tariff, and adherence to the national Democratic platform. After he appeared in Henderson, the local editor wrote, "Mr. Murray is an eloquent and fluent speaker, and his speech was well received."[37]

The rising politician formally announced in June that he was a candidate for the state senate from the district comprising Navarro, Kaufman, and Henderson counties. His friends in rural Navarro County endorsed him immediately. The communities of Richland and Cade pledged him their votes at the county Democratic convention, and the Cade Democrats resolved, "We recognize him as a safe exponent of pure democracy, handed down to us by our fathers."[38] An "Old Soldier" sent the *Mexia Democrat* a letter urging Murray's nomination. The letter said, "If it is necessary we can get up a petition signed by all the people except the republicans and sub-treasuryites in this section requesting him to run."[39] Murray circulated a political broadside containing letters from John McCracken, Monte Walker, and Tom Gilbert. McCracken wrote highly of Murray's intellectual ability, and Walker, an old friend from Buffalo, praised the candidate's appearance before the Leon County Democratic convention. Gilbert, a Cade farmer, wrote that

[36] *Ibid.*, Dec. 5, 1891.

[37] *Henderson County Times*, Apr. 28, 1892; newspaper clipping, Murray Coll., Univ. of Okla. Library.

[38] *Dallas Morning News*, June 26, 1892, July 17, 1892; newspaper clipping, Murray Coll., Univ. of Okla. Library.

[39] Newspaper clipping, *Mexia Democrat*, Murray Coll., Univ. of Okla. Library.

Murray's nomination would keep the young men in the district from voting for the Populists.[40] Murray's first campaign for public office established a pattern which continued for the next fifty years; his chief source of strength would be the small farmers, who saw him as their champion.

The contest for the 1892 senatorial nomination was decided by a district convention. The convention had to resolve a three-way contest among O. B. Colquitt, George Jester, and Murray. Murray's opponents would later serve Texas in high office, Colquitt as governor and Jester as lieutenant governor. Murray ran a poor third in the three county conventions, and the district meeting finally nominated Jester after 136 ballots.[41] Young Murray was jolted by the defeat but later admitted that he was a spoiled boy who should never have run.[42] He was not qualified to serve and was too inexperienced to win. This was one of the few times he was completely candid about his headlong rush to achieve political recognition.

Defeat failed to cool Murray's ardor for politics, and he joined Governor Hogg's campaign for re-election. The Texas Democratic convention was to be held in Houston in August, and Murray asked prominent political figures to support him for the position of convention secretary. The Hogg forces caucused on August 15 and nominated him for the office. The Democratic party was torn asunder by Hogg's supporters and those of George Clark, a conservative. When Clark saw that the Governor's men were in the majority, he bolted and held a rump convention with his supporters.[43] Meeting in a large car shed, the Hogg convention adopted a reform program. Murray served as secretary and presented a resolution authorizing a committee of fifteen to investigate the Clark bolt.[44] After the "car-shed convention" Murray campaigned

[40] Broadside, Murray Coll., Univ. of Okla. Library.

[41] *Dallas Morning News*, July 10, 23, 27, 1892; newspaper clipping, Murray Coll., Univ. of Okla. Library.

[42] Murray, *Memoirs*, I, 188. The interpretation of the 1892 senatorial race presented here is antipodal to Murray's. See Murray, *Memoirs*, I, 188; Hines, *Alfalfa Bill*, 76–77.

[43] *Dallas Morning News*, Aug. 16, 1892; *Houston Daily Post*, Aug. 18, 1892.

[44] *Austin Statesman*, Aug. 19, 1892.

for Hogg, who had both the Democrat Clark and the Populist Thomas Nugent as opponents.

Murray's enthusiasm for Hogg jeopardized the Governor's re-election and embarrassed Grover Cleveland, the Democratic Presidential nominee. The young campaigner wrote to Cleveland on August 31, 1892, to give his version of the division among the Texas Democrats. The former President responded on September 18, saying only that he applauded Murray's zeal for the party. The latter then publicly claimed that Cleveland had endorsed Hogg against Clark. Cleveland immediately issued a denial, saying he refused to be a party to a factional fight, and the Clark men seized upon Murray's rash statement to attack the Governor.[45] After Cleveland again stated that he did not know of Murray's role in the split, Murray sent a long letter to the *Fort Worth Gazette*. From the "Headquarters of the Democratic Campaign Committee of Navarro County at Richland" Murray wrote that after the debacle in Houston he decided to obtain Cleveland's opinion of the bolters. Since Cleveland had commended his work for the party, he construed this as an endorsement of Hogg.[46] The rebuttal he offered demonstrated either great naïveté or political immaturity, or perhaps both. His defeat for the legislature and embroilment in the gubernatorial campaign had been bitter lessons, but he was learning about the ofttimes humiliating vagaries of politics.

After the political campaign ended in November with victories for Hogg and Cleveland, Murray returned to the schoolroom. He accepted an offer to teach at the Prairie Hill school near Mexia. He was constantly organizing and joining groups. He served as president of the Camp Stonewall Jackson chapter of the United Sons of the Confederate Veterans and the Navarro Educator's Library Association.[47] Political reversals seemed only to whet his appetite for leadership and recognition.

[45] Newspaper clippings, Murray Coll., Univ. of Okla. Library.

[46] Grover Cleveland to Thomas Finley, Jr., Sept. 27, 1892, reprinted in "A Campaign Lie Nailed," broadside, Murray Coll., Univ. of Okla. Library; *Fort Worth Gazette*, Sept. 30, 1892.

[47] Newspaper clipping, Murray Coll., Univ. of Okla. Library; Murray to Governor James S. Hogg, Mar. 27, 1894, James Stephen Hogg Collection (Austin, University of Texas Archives). Hereafter cited as Hogg Coll., Univ. of Texas Archives.

While William Murray was outspoken as a politician and as a teacher, he approached the opposite sex with reluctance and timidity. Homeless in adolescence, he had lacked the opportunity to court girls. At last a romance developed between Murray and one of the belles of Corsicana, Lita Rakestraw. After a summer courtship they agreed to be married as soon as Murray could support a wife. But some members of the Rakestraw family, which was related to the Jester family, objected to the engagement. The objections led to a quarrel, the return of love letters, and the end of the romance. Having lost his first sweetheart, Murray decided to devote all his time to his career.[48]

In spite of the controversy that Murray created during the campaign, Governor Hogg sent him an invitation to the inaugural ball at Austin. Murray apparently felt that all was forgiven, for in his reply to the Governor he suggested the name of a Corsicana man for a position in the Cleveland administration.[49]

Murray lived with the Tom Gilbert family at Cade during the summer of 1893. He left in the fall to teach at the Midway school near Mexia and later at Mount Nebo. Like most of the schoolteachers of the time, he lived with local families. He complained about the sparse fare on their tables and their reluctance to furnish light and heat when he wanted to read late into the night.

Now that Murray had tasted the excitement of politics, presiding over a one-room school held little appeal for him. He decided to broaden his political experience. In August, 1893, he had asked Governor Hogg to appoint him a delegate to the Pan American Bi-Metallic Congress, which was to meet in St. Louis in October. Hogg complied with the request, and Murray departed for the meeting.[50] This convention, like others organized in the 1890's, was sponsored by the American Bi-Metallic League to encourage the use of silver. Though it was primarily a free-silver meeting, it also urged increased trade with Latin America. Present at the congress

[48] Hines, *Alfalfa Bill*, 47–48, 83–84, 93–94; Murray, *Memoirs*, I, 191–92.

[49] Ticket, Murray Coll., Univ. of Okla. Library; Murray to Hogg, Feb. 21, 1893, Hogg Coll., Univ. of Texas Archives.

[50] Murray to Hogg, Aug. 19, 1893; Hogg to Murray, Sept. 6, 1893; Hogg Coll., Univ. of Texas Archives; Certificate of Appointment, Murray Coll., OHS Library.

were Governor Ben Tillman of South Carolina; the Populist governor of Kansas, James Lewelling; Mary E. Lease, the fiery Kansas Populist who advocated "raising less corn and more hell"; and General James B. Weaver, the Populist candidate for President in 1892.[51] Undoubtedly meeting with such a group as this re-enforced Murray's belief in free and unlimited coinage of gold and silver.

When Murray returned to Corsicana, he persuaded his brother George to join him in a new venture, newspaper publishing. Like Bryan, Polk, Tom Watson, and Ignatius Donnelly, Murray had decided to turn to journalism to further his political ambitions and fatten his purse. The brothers rented the back room of a barbershop from Foster Nelson, a Negro barber, and purchased a press and type. Jim Garrity, a local businessman, provided the capital. With their small press they began publishing a daily, the *Corsicana Daily News*, and, for the farm population, a weekly, the *Navarro County News*. William was editor, and George was the business manager and advertising solicitor. Small businessmen in Corsicana purchased advertising, though the larger firms in Corsicana boycotted them, and the papers became moderately successful.[52] William apparently reported the local news and provided editorials.[53]

In 1894 the Murray papers became involved in the election campaign. In his editorials William urged the Democrats of Navarro County to adopt the primary system to nominate their candidates. He claimed that the primary system would assure nomination of the popular candidate rather than a hand-picked candidate selected by a few men who could control the convention. Evidently Murray thought he had a better chance in an open primary, for he had decided to run again for the state senate. In March he wrote to Governor Hogg, asking for information and advice about the problems facing the state.[54] He borrowed $500 from the City National Bank and, aided by Foster Nelson, who controlled the local Negro vote, put on a spirited campaign.

[51] *St. Louis Post-Dispatch*, Oct. 1–3, 1893.

[52] Murray, *Memoirs*, I, 183–84; Hines, *Alfalfa Bill*, 81–91.

[53] Mrs. George Jester to Murray, Mar. 25, 1894, Murray Coll., Univ. of Okla. Library.

[54] Murray to Hogg, Mar. 27, 1894, Hogg Coll., Univ. of Texas Archives.

Murray's opponent for the office was O. B. Colquitt, a rival Corsicana editor. The campaign was conducted on a high level, and Murray proved a serious challenge in the district, which was now confined to Navarro County. He carried the rural precincts of Cade, Richland, Dawson, Rabbit Hill, Spring Hill, and Pisgah, but Colquitt carried Corsicana and defeated him, 1,441 votes to 1,232.[55] In Texas, and later in Oklahoma, Murray was to learn that most people in the larger towns and cities refused to vote for a man whose main concern was the small farmer and whose platform, manners, and speech were directed toward his rural constituents.

Stung by his second defeat and needing money to repay his campaign loan, Murray returned to the school at County Line. He resigned after an altercation with one of the older boys, taught briefly in Hill County, and then returned to Corsicana.[56] The newspapers had continued publication in his absence.

The papers constantly attacked the conservative gold Democrats and the Populists. One of the Populists often singled out for criticism was Thomas Pryor Gore, a Mississippian who had moved to Corsicana. Gore later served as United States senator from Oklahoma, and one day he and Murray would join forces in their adopted state. The Democratic triumph of 1896 in Texas almost eliminated the Populists in Navarro County, but Murray took a fateful step by endorsing for district judge a Populist candidate rather than a gold Democrat. No one had been more enthusiastic than Murray for William Jennings Bryan and the Democratic ticket, but Corsicana Democrats attacked Murray for defecting in the judgeship contest. He contended that gold Democrats were not representative of his party.[57] Because of his forthright stand the newspapers' advertising revenues and circulation declined, and the papers, already on shaky financial ground, began to sink.

Even as his journalism venture was collapsing, Murray was studying for a new profession. He had been reading law at night with Judge John Rice, and after several months of concentrated

[55] *Dallas Morning News*, June 17, 18, 21, 1894.

[56] Hines, *Alfalfa Bill*, 87, 92–93.

[57] Newspaper fragment, Murray Coll., Univ. of Okla. Library. This fragment is the only copy the author was able to find from either newspaper published by Murray.

effort he appeared for his bar examination before a three-man committee of lawyers. By Murray's own admission the examination was a farce.[58] After passing the bar on April 10, 1897, he decided to sell the papers. His brother concurred, the equipment was sold, and the fledgling lawyer left Corsicana for Fort Worth. In his efforts to achieve success Murray had farmed, taught, worked as a reporter, sold books, organized alliances, run for office, and edited newspapers. Now he would try his luck as a member of the legal profession.

To the former resident of Cade and Corsicana, Fort Worth seemed a large metropolis. It had a population of 25,000 people, and it was a bustling livestock and trading center. It seemed to offer a lawyer golden opportunities. However, Murray's practice proved to be unsuccessful. He formed a partnership with two former College Hill classmates, Albert Baskin and Less L. Hudson. He practiced general law, but when he found it less than lucrative, he became an installment collector.[59] Continuing his quest for knowledge, he studied municipal law with Judge W. D. Harris. After Murray won a suit for a Negro widow, a number of Fort Worth Negroes came to him with damage cases. Living on strong black coffee and five-cent fruit pies, he broadened his legal experience.

In August, 1897, he went to Marlow, in Indian Territory, to visit his father, who had moved there some time earlier. Impressed by the territory, Murray decided it held a promising future. Returning to Fort Worth, he borrowed some money from friends, paid his debts, packed his belongings, and purchased a train ticket. In March, 1898, armed with letters of recommendation from Judge Harris and other friends, he left to seek his fortune in the Indian Territory.[60] He went first to Ardmore and then to Pauls Valley, in the Chickasaw Nation. There W. B. Johnston, the United States attorney, suggested that he might find Tishomingo, the capital of

[58] Murray, *Memoirs*, I, 184–85.
[59] Letterhead, Murray Coll., Univ. of Okla. Library.
[60] Judge W. D. Harris to "To Whom It May Concern," Mar. 16, 1898; A. L. Matlock to "To Whom It May Concern," Mar. 19, 1898; Murray Coll., Univ. of Okla. Library.

the Chickasaws, a good place to practice.[61] Murray arrived in that small town on March 28, 1898, to begin a new life.

For twenty-eight years Murray had been meeting adversity in his struggle for public recognition. Deprived of the home life he so eagerly sought, he turned to the Loper and Gilbert families as substitutes. His extremely modest education became, in his mind, the best possible type of academic training and a yard stick to measure all schools and colleges. Modest political success had encouraged him to grasp at higher goals, only to see them pass beyond his reach. Even when he turned to journalism and law he had failed to find the rewards he needed. A lesser man would have become bitter and cynical, but not Bill Murray. Defeat meant only that he needed to study more, to read more, to try something new. From his first speech at Sand Hill Church to the election of 1896 he had been learning the lessons of politics. The trials of his youth had formed Murray's political commitment in a significant way. As he wrote in later life:

> When I came to the Indian Country and began to meditate on my career in Texas, and there was no politics, except in the Indian Government, I decided as I had suspected before, that the Populists, in part, and in fact largely, were right, with only minor errors in their platform. Then I vowed I would never again study a public question from the standpoint of any party or any group; That I would endeavor to find the *"truth"* irrespective of its popularity.[62]

Murray would always be a Democrat and would fight the Socialist party as hard as he fought the Populists, but no longer would he be bound by the position of his party. Throughout his political career in Oklahoma he would pursue a course independent of the tack taken by the Democratic party. The experiences of his formative years had shaped and molded Alfalfa Bill. From now on he was to dedicate himself to the preservation of the family farm and the way of life he had known in central Texas, which he came to glorify beyond recognition.

[61] Murray, *Memoirs*, I, 199.
[62] *Ibid.*, I, 308.

LAWYER IN THE CHICKASAW NATION

II

WHEN WILLIAM H. MURRAY stepped from Bud Bowen's hack on March 28, 1898, the residents of Tishomingo probably observed this gaunt young man with deep reservation. Wearing a Prince Albert coat and a derby hat and carrying a carpetbag containing a few collars, a suit, and copies of Peter Parley's *History of the World* and the United States Constitution, Murray arrived penniless and owing Bowen a dollar for his fare. Never lost for words, however, the destitute lawyer had become acquainted with Jewel Boyd during the trip from Ardmore, and since her father operated the Poyner Hotel, he soon had a place to stay.[1] Despite this inauspicious beginning, the former Texan would find his years in the Chickasaw Nation among the most pleasant of his life. Here he would find fame, fortune, family, and friends—the foundation from which to launch a tempestuous political career in a state not yet in existence.

If the people of Tishomingo were skeptical of Bill Murray, he probably had similar reservations about Tishomingo. The capital of the Chickasaw Nation consisted of a few frame buildings on a flat area next to Pennington Creek. It had five hundred residents, two hotels, and the federal commissioner's court. It was thirty-two miles from the nearest railroad. Hogs and cattle roamed the streets leading from the creek to the hill where workmen were erecting a new limestone capitol. Numerically the smallest tribe of the Five Civilized Tribes, the Chickasaws occupied the area of Indian Territory north from the Red River to the South Canadian River and from the Choctaw Nation on the east to Oklahoma Territory on the west. The Chickasaws were proud of their nation, their capital, and the Indian Territory.[2]

---

[1] Hines, *Alfalfa Bill*, 102–12.   [2] *Ibid.*

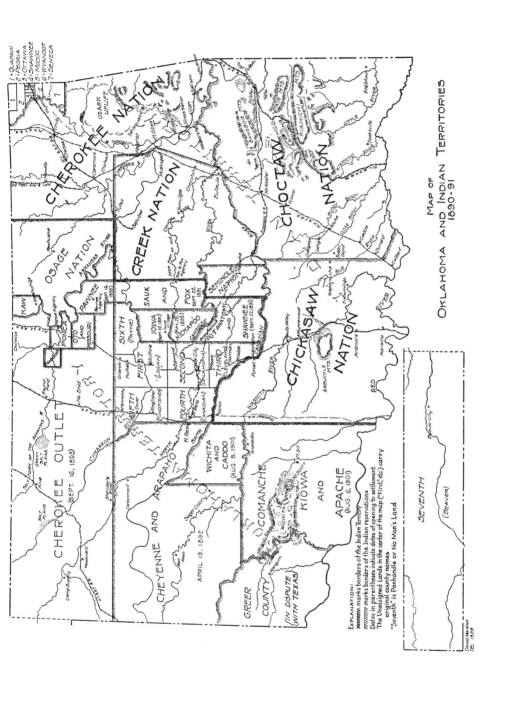

MAP OF
OKLAHOMA AND INDIAN TERRITORIES
1890-91

1. QUAPAW
2. PEORIA
3. OTTAWA
4. SHAWNEE
5. MODOC
6. WYANDOT
7. SENECA

EXPLANATION:
xxxxxxxx marks borders of the Indian Territory
/////////// marks borders of the Indian reservations
Dates in parentheses indicate dates of opening to settlement
The Unassigned Lands in the center of the map ("First", etc.) carry
    original county names
"Seventh" is Panhandle or No Man's Land

The Chickasaw, Creek, Choctaw, Cherokee, and Seminole nations were natives of the southern United States. Totally unlike their counterparts in the plains, the Five Civilized Tribes developed their own schools, newspapers, democratic legislative bodies, and political parties. The Chickasaws were moved from their homes in northern Mississippi in 1837, and by 1860 the federal government had relocated nearly all the members of the Five Tribes in Indian Territory. Related to the Choctaws, who had moved west to the Indian Territory in 1835, the Chickasaws settled on the western lands of their kinsmen. Their tribal governments were merged, and the result was a virtual amalgamation of the two tribes. Outnumbered and dissatisfied, the Chickasaws recreated their own nation in 1855. With the outbreak of the Civil War in 1861, the Choctaws and the Chickasaws allied themselves with the Confederacy because of their southern heritage and their ownership of slaves. After the war the federal government required the Five Civilized Tribes to give up large portions of Indian Territory so that the Plains Indians could be settled there. The lands surrendered in the treaties of 1866 were divided into reservations, and between 1867 and 1883 a large number of plains tribes occupied the western half of the Indian Territory.[3]

The Five Civilized Tribes were fearful of their plains brothers, separated from them by only a treaty line. The brutal Indian wars of the 1860's and 1870's served to re-enforce their fears. But a far greater menace was developing. When the westward march of continental expansion came to an end and the Indian wars ceased, cattlemen, farmers, and businessmen began to look longingly at the Indian Territory, with its well-watered grasslands, large stands of timber, and undeveloped coal deposits. Some cattlemen had already moved into the reservations, leasing large areas from the Indians upon which to graze Texas cattle herds before they were sent to market. Great pressure was brought upon the federal government to open to white settlement a region in the central portion of the ter-

[3] Edward Everett Dale and Morris L. Wardell, *History of Oklahoma* (Englewood Cliffs, Prentice-Hall, Inc., 1948), 126–29, 183–85, 198–99.

ritory known as the Unassigned Lands. On March 4, 1889, President Benjamin Harrison signed a proclamation releasing the area for settlement. This event marked the beginning of rapid change in the western half of Indian Territory, for when the white settlers moved in, they demanded the creation of a territorial government.

The lands of the Plains Indians were gradually opened to the whites in the 1890's and early 1900's. The opportunity to acquire a farm of 160 acres at $1.25 per acre attracted thousands of families from throughout the United States. By land runs, drawings, and auctions the whites obtained title to the Indian reservations and extended their territorial government. The former lands of the Plains Indians were named Oklahoma Territory. Now the area surrounded by Texas, Kansas, Missouri, Arkansas, New Mexico, and Colorado had two governments and became known as the Twin Territories.[4]

The Five Tribes continued to operate under their own tribal governments, but they were not free from the pressures experienced by their plains kinsmen. Many white men entered the nations, and by 1890 they accounted for almost two-thirds of the population. These men married into the tribes, operated businesses, leased lands, and built farms on an ever-increasing scale. The white settlers demanded a voice in the exclusively Indian tribal legislatures and also protested the restrictions against them with regard to land ownership.[5] On March 3, 1893, Congress authorized the President to appoint a three-member commission to negotiate with the Five Civilized Tribes for the purpose of extinguishing tribal titles to their lands and transferring title to the properties to the Indians as individuals.[6] Coal, oil, asphalt, and mineral lands were to be sold or leased to benefit all members of the tribes. Henry L. Dawes, a former senator from Massachusetts, was named chairman of the commission. Throughout the period from 1893 to 1905 the Indians protested the work of the Dawes Commission. The Curtis Act of

[4] *Ibid.*, 225–56.
[5] *Ibid.*, 272–88; Edwin C. McReynolds, *Oklahoma: A History of the Sooner State* (Norman, University of Oklahoma Press, 1954), 277.
[6] Dale and Wardell, *History of Oklahoma*, 288–89.

1898 further extended the powers of the commission and eliminated tribal laws and tribal courts. In their place federal courts were established throughout the territory.

The efforts to extend justice to the Indians and the white settlers in the Indian Territory brought about legal chaos. In the absence of adequate law enforcement or judicial officers, courts were inundated with cases. The efforts of the Dawes Commission to create tribal rolls added to the complexities. All members of the tribes had to be certified legally, but many full-blooded Indians refused to sign the rolls. Thousands of whites tried to enroll in hopes of obtaining a farm or town lot and also a share of the tribal mineral rights. Former slaves had to be enumerated, as did white men who had married Indian women. It was an enormous task that took years to accomplish.[7] Into this legal tangle came the ambitious Texas lawyer, Bill Murray.

One of Murray's first acts was to give away the Prince Albert coat and the derby hat. In a more acceptable white cotton suit, and with ten dollars borrowed from an old Springtown college classmate, he ventured into the legal circles of Tishomingo.[8] There were already seven or eight lawyers in town. After considering a partnership with a future political ally, John McKeel, he joined the firm of Treadwell and Lucas, which then became Treadwell, Murray, and Lucas. Murray began to practice in the federal courts, specializing in criminal law, though he did not receive his license until November 6, 1899.[9]

The Texas dust had hardly settled from his clothes before he entered politics again. He had arrived in Tishomingo in the midst of an election campaign for the office of governor of the Chickasaw Nation. Tribal elections were bitter contests, and the Chickasaws were divided into two brawling parties. The candidate of the National party, Douglas H. Johnston, favored opening the Chickasaw lands to individual ownership. Treadwell, Murray, and Lucas

[7] *Ibid.*, 289–97.
[8] Hines, *Alfalfa Bill*, 118.
[9] License to Practice Law in the Chickasaw Nation, Nov. 6, 1899, Murray Coll., OHS Library.

worked for Johnston. Assuming his favorite political role, Murray served as secretary of the National party. The secretary was actually the manager of the party, and he soon found himself deeply embroiled in tribal affairs.[10]

In August, 1898, Johnston won the race for the governorship, and Murray reaped a harvest of legal work. After the inauguration, for which Murray made the arrangements and gave an address on the Constitution, he received a request from the new Governor to help draft bills for the Chickasaw legislature. The Secretary of the Interior, Ethan A. Hitchcock, had refused to approve some of the statutes passed by the legislature on the grounds that they were poorly constructed.[11] As legal adviser to Governor Johnston, Murray drafted laws providing for an annual tax of $1.00 on every noncitizen, for the creation of a Chickasaw commission to assist the Dawes Commission, and for an appropriation of $30,000 to defend contested citizenship cases in the preparation of tribal rolls. He suggested a new tax structure to free the Chickasaws from a $300,000 tribal debt. The tax plan placed an annual fee of $.25 on every head of livestock owned by white residents in the nation and resulted in increased revenues.[12]

Murray also entered into the polite society of the capital city. Chickasaw young people engaged in a formal social life of dances, readings, and parties. Because of his connections with the Governor, the young lawyer was welcomed by the Chickasaw elite. The Hearrell sisters, Ada and Daisy, often danced with the Governor's assistant, but it was their older sister, Mary Alice, who became the only woman in Murray's life.

Mary Alice Hearrell was the niece of Governor Johnston and was one of the social belles of the tribe. One-sixteenth Chickasaw, the dark-haired beauty was born on January 9, 1875, in a cabin near Ada, Oklahoma. In 1883 she was sent to Bloomfield Academy for girls, in what is now Bryan County, Oklahoma. Her uncle was

[10] Murray, *Memoirs*, I, 239.

[11] Hines, *Alfalfa Bill*, 131–32.

[12] D. C. Gideon, *Indian Territory* (New York, The Lewis Publishing Company, 1901), 865; Hines, *Alfalfa Bill*, 133–34.

superintendent of the academy at the time. The curriculum included music, painting, expression, and the domestic arts—a course for refined young Chickasaw ladies.

Mary Alice was an excellent student, and after graduation she was hired as a teacher by the academy. She had taught there four years when she met Murray.[13] After becoming acquainted with her at several formal social events in Tishomingo, Murray summoned all his courage and sent her a note asking if he might call. Her affirmative reply launched a Victorian courtship of chaperoned visits and formal love letters.

Since Mary Alice lived at the academy and Murray was either in Tishomingo or in nearby towns attending to his law practice, the courtship was largely conducted by mail.[14] Late at night, after long days in court, Murray composed his somewhat stilted but increasingly ardent letters. He asked his "Lady Love" for her picture and pleaded with her to write more often about her "frank, sincere self." As the tempo of the courtship increased, he asked her to set a date for their marriage. Would she agree to the ninth hour of the ninth day of the ninth month of the ninety-ninth year of the nineteenth century when he was in his twenty-ninth year? In his ardor he quoted a passage he attributed to Robert Burns: "Our Heavenly father made me with faults wild and strong, that listening to hot music I often times do wrong." Subsequent letters repeatedly urged her to move the wedding date forward. Mary Alice finally succumbed to his pleadings and in a letter that began, "My dear Mr. Murray," she asked him to agree to an August wedding, adding, "Won't you dearie?" But "Mr. Murray," as she would refer to him for the next thirty-nine years, was not to be denied, and on July 19, 1899, they were married in the home of Governor Johnston at Emet, near Tishomingo.[15]

13 Hines, *Alfalfa Bill*, 120–24.

14 Murray to Mary Alice Hearrell, May 8, May 16, June 13, June 19, 1899, Murray Coll., Univ. of Okla. Library.

15 Certificate of Marriage, District Court Book of Tishomingo County, Chickasaw Nation, July 19, 1899, Indian Archives, Vol. 76 (Oklahoma City, Oklahoma Historical Society). Hereafter cited as Indian Archives, OHS.

The Reverend J. C. W. Jacobs, of the Methodist Episcopal Church, South, officiated at the wedding, which was one of the social events of the year. An Indian Territory newspaper captioned its report of the wedding "Prominent Young Attorney Secures a Chickasaw Queen." Five eminent tribesmen gave the groom the recommendations necessary for marrying into the tribe and becoming one of its intermarried citizens.[16]

At the time of his marriage Murray had the appearance and manner of a gaunt Texas braggadocio, which, of course, he was. He was five feet ten inches tall and weighed 142 pounds. His figure appeared even more elongated because of his long arms and fingers. His lean face was marked by deep-set, steel-blue eyes and a handlebar mustache; it would be a few years before the famous "walrus mustache" would appear.[17] He had a deep voice that boomed forth; he spoke in an accent that could have come only from central Texas. Wearing a flapping white-cotton suit wrapped around his lanky frame, he strode confidently into the courts of the Chickasaw Nation, a notable citizen with significant family and political ties to the government.[18]

In the fall Murray and his bride took up residence in a small house north of Tishomingo. On January 1, 1901, the first son arrived and was named Massena. The names selected for the Murray sons reflected Murray's esteem for men in public life. Massena was named for André Masséna, Marshal of France under Napoleon I. Bill Murray admired the French Emperor, and like some other rural political leaders, such as Ignatius Donnelly and Tom Watson, he considered himself an authority on the subject. He had read a biography of Napoleon and then passed it on to his brother John Shade, who later named one of his sons Clive after the English Lord Clive.[19]

A second son, Johnston, named for Governor Johnston, was born to the Murrays on July 21, 1902. Between the births of the two sons

16 *Daily Ardmoreite*, July 20, 1899.
17 Murray, *Memoirs*, I, 37–38.
18 Hines, *Alfalfa Bill*, 118.
19 Johnston Murray, interview of Dec. 29, 1965.

the Murray family had moved to a farm on Twelve Mile Prairie east of Emet.[20]

The land around Twelve Mile Prairie ranged in quality from sandy, blackjack-covered hills to rich black-dirt bottom lands. Murray went to work to convert his lands into a diversified farm. He was interested in scientific agriculture and bought the most recently developed seeds and used the best methods of cultivation. He began to experiment with alfalfa, a crop new to the area, and finding that it made excellent forage, he extolled its virtues to his neighbors. Meanwhile, to meet the needs of his growing family, he continued his now lucrative law practice.

At about this time the partnership with Lucas and Treadwell was dissolved by mutual agreement. Murray had accused Treadwell of being jealous of his practice. When Treadwell left the firm, Murray and Lucas also split.[21] Murray took a new partner, Martin Cheadle, a Chickasaw lawyer and speaker of the Chickasaw legislature. This partnership was apparently brief. Murray then joined forces with J. B. O'Bryan, a schoolteacher who was reading law. Through its political connections the partnership of Murray and O'Bryan obtained many citizenship cases.

To be listed on the tribal rolls being prepared by the Dawes Commission, residents of the Chickasaw Nation had to prove their affiliation with the tribe. It was often necessary for applicants to hire lawyers to plead their cause. Murray accepted these cases for a fee of 25 per cent of the value of the land the applicants received. These cases brought him a substantial income. In one case his fee came to $7,500, although this was an unusually large amount.[22]

As legal adviser to Governor Johnston, he often received citizenship cases in lieu of fees for drafting laws. He handled other legal work for the tribe, too, such as preparing the incorporation papers for the towns of Tishomingo, Ravia, Oakland, Durwood, and Pontotoc.[23] Murray and Cheadle also handled suits for Indians who had

20 Hines, *Alfalfa Bill*, 145.
21 Murray, *Memoirs*, I, 202.
22 Hines, *Alfalfa Bill*, 140.
23 Murray, *Memoirs*, I, 211.

leased their lands to whites and wanted to regain control of their property. In such cases Murray would agree to manage lands regained in the suits in lieu of a fee. Since Murray could get along with the white tenants better than the landowners could, the Indians were willing to pay him 20 per cent of the rent money to act as their manager. He acquired control of large tracts of land along the Washita River through these agreements.[24]

Murray also continued to practice criminal law. The Chickasaw tribe paid him to defend members accused of crimes, and his law practice expanded rapidly.[25] Murray claimed that the federal judges in the territory were uniformly arbitrary and dictatorial and often prejudiced against the Indians.[26] On one occasion a judge sentenced Murray to three days in jail for contempt, though the sentence was never carried out.[27] Such experiences gave Murray a lasting antipathy for the lower federal courts. He usually referred to them as the "inferior" courts.

From 1900 until 1904 most of Murray's legal practice continued to center around problems of the Chickasaw Nation. The tribe waged a long fight with Secretary of the Interior Hitchcock, whom they accused of encroaching on tribal rights. Murray served on the colored committee of the tribe, which was trying to determine which Negroes were eligible to be placed upon the tribal rolls.[28] The Choctaw and Chickasaw joint holdings of mineral lands created problems in the distribution of royalty payments. Governor Johnston and the Governor of the Choctaws created a Choctaw-Chickasaw coal commission, and Johnston commissioned Murray, J. Wes Parker, and Dave Fulsom to adjust the differences between the two tribes. The commissioners received $7.00 a day for their work, and

---

[24] *Ibid.*, I, 248.

[25] Receipt for $750.00 for defense of Tom Underwood, Chickasaw constable accused of murder, Nov. 3, 1889, Indian Archives, 4557, OHS.

[26] Murray, *Memoirs*, I, 254.

[27] *Ibid.*, I, 254–55.

[28] Receipt for $29.85 paid to Murray for services on the colored committee, Feb. 11, 1899, Indian Archives, 7130, OHS; An Act for the Relief and Pay of William H. Murray for Fifteen Cases Presented in United States Court, Appropriating $800.00, Jan. 12, 1901, Indian Archives, 4564, OHS.

by October, 1905, Murray had been paid $1,290 for his service on the commission.[29] In 1902, a typical year, he earned $4,950 in legal fees, a considerable sum for the period.[30] His efforts for the Chickasaw Nation and Governor Johnston enabled him to earn far more than the average small-town lawyer.

Governor Johnston had won re-election in 1900. In 1902 the National party had to find a new candidate. Governor Johnston had served two terms, the limit under the tribal constitution, and the National party planned to elect Palmer S. Mosley for two years and then re-elect Johnston in 1904. The Curtis Act provided that the last tribal election would be held in 1904; Johnston would then hold office for life. Again serving as party secretary, Murray worked diligently for Mosley.[31] The National party's plan temporarily faltered when William Byrd, Mosley's opponent, claimed that he had won the election. Believing that there had been fraud in both the voting and the counting, Murray managed to have certain returns thrown out and Mosley declared the winner. To repay his efforts for the National party Murray was given still more legal work for the tribe.

The Murray farm at Twelve Mile Prairie also received much attention from its owner. He developed a sizable tract of alfalfa and began to promote its cultivation by giving lectures to local farm organizations. From one of these meetings came his sobriquet. Arthur Sinclair, a visitor to Tishomingo, attended one of Murray's talks and told the editor of the *Tishomingo Capital-Democrat* that he had heard "Alfalfa Bill" deliver a speech. The newspaper editor headlined the story "Alfalfa Bill on Alfalfa," and the name stuck.[32]

Murray also grew other crops on his rapidly expanding lands. In December, 1903, he purchased a claim to a farm in the Washita River bottoms and built a log house on the land. There he experi-

29 *Tishomingo News*, Nov. 23, 1904; Certificate of Commission, Nov. 19, 1904, Murray Coll., OHS Library; Chickasaw–Foreign Relations, claim filed by William H. Murray, Oct. 11, 1905, Indian Archives, 7245, OHS.

30 O. P. Sturm, "The Sage of Tishomingo," *Sturm's Oklahoma Magazine*, Vol. IX (September, 1909), 20.

31 Murray, *Memoirs*, I, 241–44.

32 *Ibid.*, I, 267–68; article reprinted in *New-State Tribune* (Muskogee), Apr. 17, 1906.

mented with corn and, according to his campaign biographer, developed a hybrid, "Murray's corn." While most of the planting, cultivating, and harvesting was done by tenants, Murray spent many hours on the farm. Adopting ideas from Luther Burbank's writings and agricultural journals, he concentrated on improving his crops and diversifying production.[33] By 1909 he owned 1,400 acres of rich bottom land, of which 400 acres were in cultivation.[34] The land along the Washita was heavily timbered and swampy, but eventually he obtained a conservation district for the area, and the resulting drainage system permitted more extensive farming.[35] In addition to this farm, Murray and his family, as enrolled members of the Chickasaw Nation, received several other allotments of land.[36]

The income from the farm and from his law practice provided Murray with leisure time. He spent the time studying law, to which he was now devoted. He read widely, took notes, and memorized lengthy passages.[37] Across the front of the log house was a large porch; this became his study. When he was not in Tishomingo practicing, he could often be found dressed in overalls, lying in a hammock strung between two pecan trees, reading a book of statutes or a constitution. On the porch stood a large roll-top desk with a multiplicity of pigeonholes and drawers filled with thousands of bits of paper upon which he had scrawled notes and ideas. More notes hung from wire hooks above the desk. Murray realized that in a few years the Indian Territory would become a state; the tide was moving inevitably in that direction. He determined to prepare himself as a constitutional lawyer so that he could take an active part in the formation of the new state government. To the same end he took a leading role in territorial politics and farm organizations.

The Chickasaw farmer-lawyer did not neglect his beloved Demo-

[33] Hines, *Alfalfa Bill*, 168; Murray, *Memoirs*, III, 91–100; Murray, *The Finished Scholar*, 14–15, 110.
[34] Sturm, "The Sage of Tishomingo," 27.
[35] Murray, *Memoirs*, I, 299–301.
[36] *Index to the Final Rolls of Citizens and Freedmen of the Five Civilized Tribes*, II, 186, 202, 206, 208, Indian Archives, OHS; E. Hastain, *Index to Choctaw-Chickasaw Deeds and Allottments* (Muskogee, E. Hastain, 1908), 966.
[37] Burbank Murray, interview of Feb. 10, 1966.

cratic party during these years. In 1900 he attended the Indian Territory Democratic convention at Ardmore. Delegates to the convention adopted a platform condemning trusts, imperialism, territorial expansion, and "carpetbaggers"—a reference to Republican officeholders in the territory. A rousing endorsement of William Jennings Bryan for President climaxed the meeting. Murray served on the credentials committee and presented further resolutions for the platform. The convention adopted his resolutions favoring the direct election of senators and opposing life-term appointments for federal officials. The latter resolution was aimed at the Republican judges in Indian Territory. At the meeting Murray became acquainted with delegates who would later join him as political leaders of Oklahoma. Among those he met were R. L. Williams of Durant, Reford Bond of Chickasha, and J. B. Thompson and Claude Weaver of Pauls Valley.[38]

Ever eager for positions of leadership, Murray remained the joiner and organizer. He belonged to the Farmers' Union and the Red Oak Camp of the Woodmen of the World. He was particularly active in the Farmers' Union. It had developed out of the Farmers' Alliance, as had the Populist party. The three organizations had similar programs and platforms. Founded in Texas in 1902, the Farmers' Union was organized by low-income farmers primarily to form co-operatives selling farm products and buying machinery and commodities. The union was concerned about tenant farmers and subsistence farming and has been considered the most "radical" of the major farm organizations. Initially a nonpolitical group, the union engaged primarily in social and educational activities during its early years. Always strongest in the Great Plains, the group attracted low-income farmers in Indian Territory in the early 1900's.[39] Murray formed local chapters around Tishomingo and lectured to them on diversification and improved farming methods.[40]

In 1904 a joint session of the Farmers' Union of the Twin Terri-

[38] *Daily Ardmoreite*, June 11, 12, 1900.
[39] Gideon, *Indian Territory*, 865; David B. Truman, *The Governmental Process* (New York, Alfred A. Knopf, 1963), 89–90; Theodore Saloutos, *Farmer Movements in the South, 1865–1933* (Berkeley, University of California Press, 1960), 184–212.
[40] Hines, *Alfalfa Bill*, 169.

tories led to the formation of the Indiahoma State Farmers' Educational and Cooperative Union of America. Murray claimed to have written the constitution of this body and to have led the fight against its "radical" element, thereby winning a strong personal following in the group.[41] The following year he arranged for the Farmers' Union convention to be held in Tishomingo. As chairman of the arrangements committee, he induced the railroads to lower passenger rates for the meeting and secured R. E. Smith, the "king of alfalfa," as a speaker. When the convention met on July 18, Alfalfa Bill presided as temporary chairman.[42]

He continued his activities for the Farmers' Union in the fall of 1905, when he spoke on the history of the group at the Madill, Oklahoma, anniversary celebration. Reporting the event, the local editor described Murray's forceful speech and his organizing efforts for the union.[43] The union re-enforced Murray's beliefs in agricultural education, abolition of commodity exchanges, and limits on corporate land holdings.

By contrast, his activities in the Indian Territory Democratic party were less harmonious and far less successful. The territory had been divided into recording districts to facilitate the work of the Dawes Commission, and these districts served as the basis of the Democratic party structure. When the Democratic convention of the Twenty-second Recording District met on May 16, 1904, Murray served as temporary chairman. Despite strong opposition, he held the chair, refusing to permit the permanent chairman to preside until the afternoon session.[44] Because of this attempt to control the meeting, his every utterance was hissed, and the special correspondent of the *Madill News* wrote a lengthy "political obituary." Murray and his allies in the fight "died ignoble deaths," according to the correspondent, and Murray was not selected to attend the territorial Democratic convention.[45] His arbitrary rulings and obviously illegal seizure of power caused him to lose his position in the party for a time.

[41] Murray, *Memoirs*, I, 296–97.
[42] *Tishomingo News*, Apr. 26, May 31, July 17, 1905.
[43] *Madill News*, Aug. 11, 1905.
[44] *Tishomingo News*, June 1, 1904.   [45] *Madill News*, May 27, June 3, 1904.

Now that Murray's political career had suffered a setback, he turned to his family for the security and affection he needed. He kept his family completely removed from his public life, a practice he continued throughout his career. The two Murray children were growing rapidly at Twelve Mile Prairie, and on July 25, 1905, they were joined by another brother, William Henry, named for her husband at Alice's insistence.

The family was a harmonious one. Rarely were there disagreements between Bill and Alice Murray, and when there were, the children never knew about them. Alice always called her husband "Mr. Murray," even to the children; to them, he was "Papa." She was a dutiful wife and shared with her husband a Victorian concept of the woman's role. He was the breadwinner and public servant; the home was her domain. The rigidity of this relationship was tempered by the tenderness and devotion with which they regarded each other. Alice would always be there with the family, providing her husband a refuge from the political storms.[46]

Although Murray had suffered political defeat in 1904, the events of 1905 gave him a platform of broader dimensions upon which to further his political ambitions. The Curtis Act provided that all tribal governments would be terminated on March 4, 1906. This meant that the Indian Territory must either reorganize along the lines of Oklahoma Territory or become a state. With regard to the latter proposal the Indians were deeply split on the question of single statehood for Indian Territory versus joint statehood with Oklahoma Territory. They feared that union would mean subjugation by whites and, even worse, possibly by Republicans. Indian Territory appeared to be strongly Democratic in its politics, while Oklahoma Territory appeared to be strongly Republican, for it had sent Republican territorial delegates to Congress in every election but one since 1889. A sense of pride in their own accomplishments inclined most Indians toward single statehood for Indian Territory. The Chickasaw Nation was an exception.[47] The Chickasaws had

---

[46] Johnston Murray, interview of Dec. 29, 1965; Burbank Murray, interview of Feb. 10, 1966.

[47] *Tishomingo News*, Aug. 2, 1905; *Muskogee Daily Phoenix*, Aug. 13, 1905.

36

refused to participate in a territorial constitutional meeting in 1870–71 and had reluctantly sent Murray to a conference on statehood at Eufaula in 1903. The Chickasaws were influenced by the editorials of Sidney Suggs, editor of the *Daily Ardmoreite*, who supported joint statehood, and by Chief Johnston, who believed that any move toward statehood was premature.

The meeting at Eufaula in 1903 had been called by Chief Green McCurtain of the Choctaw Nation, and delegates from the Five Civilized Tribes attended. Meeting from May 21 to May 23, the body proposed that a constitutional convention be held in February, 1904, to create a separate state. Although each tribe was to memorialize Congress to prevent annexation to Oklahoma Territory, only the Choctaws acted on the call, and the Eufaula meeting came to nothing.[48] However, it was not the last time the Five Tribes would confer on the problem of statehood.

The issue of separate or joint statehood also became a national political question. While both national-party platforms of 1900 endorsed statehood for the territories, congressional leaders could not agree about the number of states to be admitted or the date of admission. The future of the territories of New Mexico and Arizona also became part of the problem. In the main, Democrats favored four states, arguing that this would mean eight new Democratic senators. The Republicans favored only two states, fearing that the Democrats might be correct in their prognosis. Beginning with the first session of the Fifty-seventh Congress in December, 1901, a series of bills was introduced in an attempt to resolve the statehood question. Numbers of representatives and senators, and even President Theodore Roosevelt, toured the Twin Territories sampling opinions and then disregarded their findings.

Angered by these frustrating prospects, a Cherokee, James A. Norman, startled the people of Indian Territory on July 5, 1905, by calling for a constitutional convention to meet in Muskogee on August 21 to form a new state. Joined by Chief William C. Rogers of the Cherokees and Chief Green McCurtain of the Choctaws,

[48] Amos D. Maxwell, *The Sequoyah Constitutional Convention* (Boston, Meador Publishing Company, 1953), 35–36.

Norman asked that towns in each of the twenty-six recording districts elect delegates to the meeting. The call came just as a joint-statehood rally was being held in Oklahoma City.[49] These meetings divided the citizens of the territory into two camps.

William Murray stood with those advocating the separate-statehood convention at Muskogee. He hoped that this meeting would strengthen the position of the Indian Territory in the event of a joint-statehood convention, which he felt would ultimately decide the fate of the territories. In the fall of 1903, while attending a meeting at Tuskahoma, the Choctaw capital, he had given a speech on separate statehood at the request of Chief McCurtain.[50] Actually, Murray wanted to postpone the whole question of statehood until the Indian land problems had been settled.[51] Nevertheless, he became an active promoter of the Muskogee convention.

After Norman's convention call and the Oklahoma City single-statehood meeting, Charles N. Haskell, a Muskogee businessman and railroad promoter, went to Chief Pleasant Porter of the Creek Nation and proposed to amend Norman's call to include the chiefs of all Five Civilized Tribes. Porter agreed, and Haskell called a meeting for July 18 at the Turner Hotel in Muskogee. Porter, Rogers, Haskell, Norman, George W. Scott, representing Chief McCurtain, and Murray, representing Chief Johnston, assembled and issued an amended convention call. Chief John F. Brown of the Seminole Nation sent a letter endorsing the separate-statehood movement.[52] The chiefs were to appoint the presiding officers of the recording-district conventions, with seven delegates and seven alternates to be selected from each district.

Since the Chickasaws in general opposed the statehood movement, Murray worked almost alone to secure delegates from the Chickasaw Nation to the Muskogee meeting. On August 7 he organized the meeting at the Tishomingo Court House. Seven dele-

49 *Ibid.*, 48–49.

50 Murray, *Memoirs*, I, 313.

51 William H. Murray, tape-recorded interview of Nov. 20, 1952, by B. B. Chapman (Oklahoma City, Oklahoma Historical Society Library). Hereafter cited as Murray, tape-recorded interview of Nov. 20, 1952, OHS Library.

52 Maxwell, *The Sequoyah Constitutional Convention*, 50–51.

gates from the Twenty-second Recording District, including himself, were selected.[53] The *St. Louis Republic* correspondent for the Indian Territory reported that Murray urged all the Chickasaw recording districts to elect delegates. The reporter quoted him as saying, "I do not think that a constitution framed by that convention will be accepted by Congress, but it will be the beginning of an organization for the Indian Territory around which every citizen, both Indian and White, must rally in the future affairs of the Indian Territory." He believed that the convention would put the territory in a better position to cope with Oklahoma Territory in the event of a joint-statehood convention.[54] This possibility was to become a reality sooner than even Murray anticipated.

For a time Murray's recording district was the only district in the Chickasaw Nation that responded to the call for delegates. Urged to action by Haskell, who offered to pay his expenses, Murray traveled through the nation securing delegates. He visited Marietta, Ardmore, Ryan, Chickasha, Pauls Valley, and Ada, seeking out personal friends and reporting meetings to the press.[55] On August 18 he telegraphed Haskell that all the Chickasaw districts had elected strong delegations and that they would arrive in Muskogee for the opening session on August 21.[56]

Murray stepped off the train in Muskogee carrying copies of the constitutions of Switzerland, New Zealand, and Australia.[57] Between 1902 and 1905 he had obtained the constitutions of nearly every state and many foreign countries. He had studied them and selected those provisions he deemed most suitable. Out of the roll-top desk and off the wire hooks had come some of the scraps of paper noting provisions of other constitutions. Bill Murray had prepared himself for a major role in drafting the basic instrument of a new state.

The convention assembled at the Hinton Theater on August 21, 1905. Mayor F. B. Fite welcomed the delegates on behalf of the

---

[53] *Tishomingo News*, Aug. 9, 1905.
[54] *St. Louis Republic*, Aug. 15, 1905.
[55] Murray, *Memoirs*, I, 314.
[56] *Muskogee Democrat*, Aug. 19, 1905.
[57] Hines, *Alfalfa Bill*, 180.

city of Muskogee; Murray responded for the delegates in a lengthy speech. He said that Indian Territory would make a great state and that the convention proved it was not a land of savages. Comparing the territory with its northern neighbor, he said, "We raise everything they do in Kansas except hell and grasshoppers." Prolonged applause followed his remarks.[58]

Then the convention began the task of organizing to write a constitution for the new state. Shortly after the opening ceremony Murray moved that a committee on permanent organization, rules, and order of business be appointed. This motion passed, and at the afternoon session the committee presented a list of nominees for permanent officers. Chief Porter was elected chairman of the convention, and Haskell was elected vice-chairman. Murray later wrote that each tribe had a vice-chairman and that he represented the Chickasaws. While this informal arrangement may have existed, it was not indicated by the local press.[59] Nevertheless, Alfalfa Bill played an important role at the convention.

At the afternoon session on August 27 Murray moved that prominent speakers be invited to address the convention, and the motion carried. He agreed to a proposal that the convention adjourn for two weeks, leaving a constitution committee to draft the document.[60]

During the two weeks eleven subcommittees, meeting in offices scattered over Muskogee, formulated proposals, which were to be turned over to a redrafting committee composed of Murray, Haskell, John R. Thomas, A. Grant Evans, and Sol J. Holmer.[61] Murray remained in Muskogee during the entire period, the only representative of the Chickasaw Nation to do so.

In addition to membership on the redrafting committee, Murray was also a member of the subcommittee on county boundaries, and he and Haskell used the power of this subcommittee to build support for the constitution. Virtually every town wanted to be a

[58] *Muskogee Democrat*, Aug. 21, 1905.
[59] Murray, *Memoirs*, I, 314; Maxwell, *The Sequoyah Constitutional Convention*, 64; *Muskogee Daily Phoenix*, Aug. 24, 1905.
[60] *Muskogee Democrat*, Aug. 22, 1905.
[61] *Muskogee Daily Phoenix*, Sept. 1, 1905.

county seat, and each recording district wanted to become a county. Delegates who supported Murray-Haskell provisions found their home towns designated the county seats of large counties. Delegates who balked on a provision of the constitution were threatened with divided districts. The suggestion that a boundary might split a town in half or leave it isolated brought anger and anguish but usually resulted in eventual approval of a measure.[62]

After the subcommittees had filed their reports, the redrafting committee wrote the final draft. The result was the Sequoyah constitution, a remarkable document. The 35,000-word constitution contained eighteen articles that reflected the most advanced social and political thinking of what has been called the Progressive era. The first article was a lengthy bill of rights providing for freedom of religion, press, and speech; jury trial; and protection of property. The articles concerning the legislative, executive, and judicial branches were similar to those of other states. However, no member of the executive branch could run for re-election. Only men could vote, but there were provisions regulating the employment of women and children, as well as a system of mine inspection.

The longest article of the constitution dealt with corporations. It created a state corporation commission with broad powers to restrict business activities. The commission was to combine the powers of the Texas railroad commission with the still more restrictive controls being advocated by William Jennings Bryan. Murray actively promoted these restrictions on business and the adoption of the Texas railroad statute. A pure-foods section forbade the sale of adulterated or harmful foods and drugs. Homesteads to the value of $5,000 were exempted from property taxes, and the ownership of farm lands by aliens or corporations was forbidden.

A dual system of education for whites and Negroes was created, and Murray wrote into the education article a provision for teaching horticulture, agriculture, and the domestic sciences in the public schools. The sale, transportation, and manufacture of alcoholic beverages was prohibited, a measure heartily endorsed by Murray. The

62 Murray, *Memoirs*, I, 315–16.

41

Haskell-Murray recommendation to create forty-eight counties was accepted and incorporated into Article Twelve.[63]

In slightly over two weeks the delegates had written a sound instrument of government. Though some of the writers, such as Murray and Haskell, were white, many other active participants were of Indian extraction. An incomplete survey of the delegates at the first session revealed a racial mixture of forty Indians, fourteen whites, and one Negro and a political mixture of forty-two Democrats, nine Republicans, and four whose affiliation was unknown.[64]

The convention reassembled at the Hinton Theater on September 6 to review the work of the redrafting committee. The county-boundary controversy was the focal point of further angry debate, but on September 7 the entire constitution was accepted. A committee made up of Haskell, Murray, and the four men who had been nominated for Congress was appointed to bear the document to Congress after the ratification election, which was set for November 7.[65]

In the intervening time the convention campaign committee labored to win popular support for the Sequoyah constitution. Murray, Haskell, and John R. Thomas were in the forefront of this effort. The people of Indian Territory remained divided over the statehood proposal, as evidenced by the editorials in the press. Of the 105 newspapers in the territory, 78 opposed separate statehood, 16 were for it, and 11 remained neutral. Despite this sentiment, citizens approved the constitution by a vote of 56,279 to 9,073.[66] Tishomingo, Murray's home town, endorsed the document, 576 to 23.[67] The size of the victory margin was misleading, however; one-half of those qualified to vote failed to do so, and many of them opposed the constitution.[68]

[63] The Sequoyah constitution is reprinted in Seth K. Corden and W. B. Richards (comp.), *The Oklahoma Red Book* (Oklahoma City, Democrat Printing Co., 1912), I, 623–74.

[64] *Muskogee Daily Phoenix*, Aug. 23, 1905.

[65] Maxwell, *The Sequoyah Constitutional Convention*, 78–83.

[66] McReynolds, *Oklahoma*, 314.

[67] *Muskogee Daily Phoenix*, Nov. 16, 1905.

[68] Roy Gittinger, *The Formation of the State of Oklahoma, 1803–1906* (Norman, University of Oklahoma Press, 1939), 253.

The fruits of victory were spoiled less than two weeks later, when President Roosevelt announced that he favored single statehood for the Twin Territories.[69] After the Fifty-ninth Congress convened in December, several bills were introduced dealing with the future status of the territories. One bill proposed the admission of the state of Sequoyah, but it never gained support. On June 16, 1906, President Roosevelt signed the Enabling Act providing for the admission of Oklahoma and Indian territories as a single state.[70] Murray and Haskell, recognizing the futility of pursuing the Sequoyah proposal, joined forces to gain positions of strength in the formation of the state of Oklahoma.[71]

Despite the failure of the Sequoyah movement, it was a highly significant event in the history of Oklahoma and the career of William H. Murray. It marked the end of Indian opposition to union with Oklahoma Territory. Moreover, out of the convention came the nucleus of a power group that was to dominate Oklahoma politics for the next thirty years. The experiences of this convention produced a trained and organized leadership with a capacity for teamwork that would enable it to dominate the Oklahoma constitutional convention.

The Sequoyah constitution was to be a model for the Oklahoma constitution; some provisions were adopted word for word. The content of the Sequoyah constitution reflected the presence in the territory of two political philosophies. It has been described as "radically progressive in some of its provisions" and also as composed of "largely Populist doctrine."[72] Both statements are correct, as shown by many of the provisions of the constitution, among them the restrictions on corporations, the inclusion of statutory law, and the limitations on terms of office. The child-labor and pure-food provisions and the protection of laboring men and their rights reflected Populist and Progressive thought. The Oklahoma constitu-

---

[69] *Muskogee Daily Phoenix*, Nov. 16, 1905.

[70] Maxwell, *The Sequoyah Constitutional Convention*, 114.

[71] Murray, *Memoirs*, I, 318.

[72] Joseph B. Thoburn and Muriel Wright, *Oklahoma: A History of the State and Its People* (New York, Lewis Publishing Company, Inc., 1929), II, 629; Maxwell, *The Sequoyah Constitutional Convention*, 110.

tional convention, as will be seen, demonstrated more fully the sources and direction of the two philosophies.

Murray and Haskell had personally gained much from the Sequoyah meeting. Though neither would achieve the seat in the United States Senate he coveted, both would help to design and lead the government of the state of Oklahoma. When the frustrated Cherokee James Norman issued his call for the Sequoyah convention, few realized the impact this meeting would have on the future course of the Twin Territories. But Alfalfa Bill, recognizing the opportunity to become one of the leading figures of the new state, leaped at the chance to take part in forming the government of Oklahoma. At last he could realize his ambition to lead men and hear their applause. Murray had succeeded in injecting some elements of his agrarian program into the Sequoyah constitution—restrictions on land ownership, agricultural education, and limited taxation of homesteads—and he would be even more successful at the Oklahoma constitutional convention.

PRESIDENT OF THE
CONSTITUTIONAL CONVENTION

III

Five years before President Theodore Roosevelt signed the Enabling Act by which the Twin Territories were to become a single state, a writer in *Harper's Weekly* had described the political tenor of the territories in this way:

> The population is agrarian in its tendencies and should there ever be another tide of Populism, such as swept over the Middle West in 1896, it might be expected that Oklahoma would follow the trend of thought prevailing in that entire section of the United States. The Populist party, though now quiescent, has a strong following among the prairie farmers.[1]

Populism and progressivism were both to be found in Oklahoma; they were deeply ingrained in the settlers and were a profound influence on the political leaders of both territories. The only large organized pressure groups in the proposed state, the Farmers' Union, the railroad brotherhoods, the United Mine Workers, and the Anti-Saloon League, reflected the two philosophies. When Oklahoma entered the Union, both territories had achieved highly developed political systems, and both had four active political parties—Democratic, Republican, Populist, and Socialist—organized at the local level.[2] In Oklahoma Territory the Populist party had held the balance of power in the 1890's, and in 1896 J. Y. Callahan, the Democratic-Populist fusion candidate for territorial delegate, had beaten Republican Dennis Flynn.[3] People in both territories

[1] F. D. Whelpley, "The Forty-sixth State," *Harper's Weekly*, Vol. XLV (Apr. 20, 1901), 420.

[2] James Ralph Scales, "Political History of Oklahoma, 1907–1949" (Doctoral thesis, University of Oklahoma, 1949), 1–12.

[3] Elmer L. Fraker, "The Spread of Populism into Oklahoma Territory" (Master's thesis, University of Oklahoma, 1938), 39–59.

were discontented with their Republican-appointed, "carpetbag" territorial governments and were ready to mobilize for self-government.

Although the economy of the two territories was basically agricultural, there was also an industrial element. Coal deposits had been discovered in the Choctaw Nation before the Civil War, and in the 1890's large-scale mining operations had begun to flourish as thousands of Czechs, Italians, Slovenes, and Hungarians joined the work force in the mines. By 1906 Indian Territory was producing 2,500,000 tons of coal a year, and the coal miners had become a potent political force through their union, the United Mine Workers. The other large body of industrial laborers, the railroad workers, some of whom had belonged to Eugene Debs's American Railway Union, joined their respective railroad brotherhoods, which also became important political factors in both territories. In 1907 the state federation of labor had more than twenty thousand dues-paying members.

The people who moved into the territories came from two distinct heritages, southern and middle western. Their political and religious beliefs stemmed largely from their geographical backgrounds.[4] By 1900 this division had become apparent in Oklahoma Territory. The census of that year reported a population of 398,331, of which 35.1 per cent had been born in southern states—that is, in the eleven states of the Confederacy plus Kentucky—and 41.4 per cent had been born in the North.[5]

In 1907 a special statehood census enumerated 1,414,177 people in both territories. There were only five towns with populations of more than 10,000—Oklahoma City, Muskogee, Guthrie, Shawnee, and Enid—and only six more with populations greater than 5,000. There were, however, 200,000 farms, upon which three-fourths of the people lived. The census of 1910 indicated an increase in population to 1,657,155, but the most startling statistic concerned farm tenancy. From 1900 to 1910 the number of tenant farms grew from

[4] James D. Tarver, "The Regional Background of Oklahoma's People," *Proceedings of the Oklahoma Academy of Science,* Vol. XXXVII (1956), 95–99.

[5] Solon J. Buck, "The Settlement of Oklahoma," *Transactions of the Wisconsin Academy of Sciences, Arts, and Letters,* Vol. XV, Part II (1907), 373–74.

47,250 to 104,137, an increase of 120 per cent, while the total number of farms increased only 76 per cent.[6] An outgrowth of the 1907 depression and low prices for farm products, tenancy was a prime cause of rural discontent and was one of the bases of the Socialist party in the state.

The farmers and tenants who came to the two territories were looking for new homes and financial success. Many had met with failure in other parts of the country because of adverse conditions or a lack of those talents necessary for successful farming. Other groups of settlers, known throughout the Southwest as the "movers," had come west without real purpose; they had been stricken with "boom fever" and were never able to settle down.[7]

The passage of the Enabling Act offered hope to those who felt that statehood might resolve some of the problems of the territories. The act provided for a constitutional convention of 112 delegates. Each of the two territories was to elect 55 delegates, and the Osage Nation was to elect 2. All males over twenty-one who had been residents of either territory for six months could vote and run for election as delegates.[8] With the machinery thus established for elevation of the Twin Territories to statehood, the political parties began to mobilize.

The Democratic party quickly moved to elect a majority of the delegates to the convention. On July 10, 1906, the Democrats adopted a platform for their candidates. They advocated the "Bryan interpretation of democracy"; racial segregation on trains, in railroad stations, and in public schools; free textbooks for public schools, printed by a state printing plant; elected corporation and railroad commissioners; an eight-hour workday on public projects; initiative and referendum; antimonopoly and anti-injunction statutes; municipal ownership of utilities; state inspection of mines, factories, and railroads for the protection of the health and safety of workers; restricted use of child labor; and the election of all state

[6] U.S. Bureau of the Census, *Thirteenth Census of the United States, 1910: Abstract of the Census with Supplement for Oklahoma* (Washington, U.S. Government Printing Office, 1913), 595–632.

[7] Buck, "The Settlement of Oklahoma," 375–80.

[8] McReynolds, *Oklahoma*, 314–15.

officials.[9] This platform dispelled any doubts about the direction the Democratic party of the new state would take.[10] Meanwhile, the Republicans, generally opposed to statehood, decided to allow their candidates to run independently, without benefit of a platform, a decision that proved to be a fatal mistake.[11]

A further indication of the political beliefs and desires of the people of the territories was the joint convention of the Farmers' Union, the railroad brotherhoods, and the Twin Territories Federation of Labor, which met at Shawnee on August 20, 1906. This convention selected a committee to draw up "demands," or positions on which every candidate for convention delegate had to agree to be endorsed by these groups. The committee met at Shawnee on September 10 and issued its demands. Delegates had to support the Oregon forms of initiative, referendum, and recall; the blanket primary and the Australian ballot; authorization of the state to engage in any enterprise or industry; the eight-hour day in coal mines; a state railroad commission; compulsory education and free textbooks; an office of mine inspector; elected commissioners of labor and agriculture; a liberal exemption of homesteads from taxes; and a three-man corporate tax commission.[12] The Joint Legislative Board, as the committee was called, demanded further that the candidates oppose employment of children under sixteen years of age in mines, mills, or factories; use of the convict-lease system; restriction of the political activities of employees by employers; and the issuance of irrevocable utility franchises.[13] The largest organized groups in the territories thus made their positions known.

The joint committee signed the "Shawnee demands" and circulated them among their members, in the press, and among the candidates.[14] The committee was chaired by Pete Hanraty, president of the Twin Territories Federation of Labor, but it was Kate

[9] Albert H. Ellis, *A History of the Constitutional Convention of the State of Oklahoma* (Muskogee, Economy Printing Co., 1923), 41–45.

[10] Scales, "Political History of Oklahoma," 31.

[11] *Ibid.*

[12] *Shawnee Herald*, Sept. 11, 1906.

[13] Ellis, *A History of the Constitutional Convention*, 45–48.

[14] *Shawnee Herald*, Sept. 11, 1906.

Barnard, a young social worker from Oklahoma City and a member of both the Farmers' Union and the Federation of Labor, who exerted the greatest single influence on the formation of the demands. Though not a member of the committee, she drafted the measures for compulsory education, the restriction of child labor, and the elimination of the convict-lease system. The political significance of the farmer-labor platform was not lost on the Democratic candidates, seventy-one of whom endorsed the entire list. Many of the Republican candidates also accepted some of the demands, and in their district conventions approved many of the committee's "radical" proposals.[15]

Governor Douglas Johnston of the Chickasaws urged Alfalfa Bill to become a candidate for delegate to the constitutional convention. Murray needed little encouragement. Both he and Charles Haskell feared that Oklahoma Territory, with its better political organization, would dominate the convention.[16] Tishomingo was situated in Election District 104, and Murray entered the campaign with the endorsement of the local Democratic club.[17] In the primary he faced C. A. Skeen, whom he defeated by 678 votes after both conducted what the press called a "clean campaign."[18] In the general election Murray received 1,309 votes, Martin Cheadle, the Republican nominee, received 748, and the Socialist, James D. French, received 113 votes.[19] "The great body of Indians and whit[e] Republican farmers voted for 'Alfalfa Bill' Murray, the Democratic Moses," reported the *Muskogee Times-Democrat*. His was the third-largest majority in the Twin Territories.[20]

The contest in Murray's district was not unlike those in the other districts, and the results were generally the same. Of the 112 delegates, the Democrats elected 99 and the Republicans 12. One man, elected as an independent, actually joined the Democratic caucus.

[15] Scales, "Political History of Oklahoma," 32.
[16] Hines, *Alfalfa Bill*, 187.
[17] Murray, *Memoirs*, I, 322–23; *Tishomingo News*, Sept. 19, 1906.
[18] *Tishomingo News*, Oct. 3, 1906.
[19] *New-State Tribune*, Nov. 17, 1906.
[20] *Muskogee Times-Democrat*, Nov. 7, 12, 1906.

The voters spoke clearly, and the worst fears of the Republicans were realized. Most of the delegates were young men; the average age was forty-two. By origin, 75 of them had come from slave states, and 35 had been born in free states. By vocation, there were 33 farmers, 29 lawyers, 14 merchants, 7 teachers, 6 ministers, 5 stockmen, and 3 bankers.[21] As a group they were determined to put every instrument of government firmly in the hands of the people. One of their number wrote. ". . . it was a body of earnest, well informed men, met to write the progressive thought of the 20th century into the organic law of Oklahoma."[22]

After a quick study of the election returns Bill Murray realized that he was a leading contender for president of the convention. Thirty-four delegates were former Sequoyah convention members, thirty from Oklahoma Territory belonged to the Farmers' Union, and he had been an active member of both bodies. Since railroad interests ruled Haskell out of the contest, he worked to get Murray elected president. Two influential men stood in the way. One was Thomas Pryor Gore, Murray's old Populist adversary from Corsicana, Texas. Though not a delegate, Gore had powerful connections in Guthrie, where he had served in the Oklahoma territorial legislature. An even more serious threat to Murray's ambitions came from an Indian Territory delegate, Robert L. Williams, who as Democratic national committeeman from Indian Territory could strongly influence his fellow delegates.[23] He considered Murray a political rival and prepared to oppose his election as convention president.

Haskell proved to be a worthy ally for Murray. In the editorial columns of his new paper, the *New-State Tribune*, Haskell alternately sent up and shot down trial balloons for the various contenders, always keeping Murray's name in the foreground. This campaign gave Murray's candidacy the appearance of a bandwagon. Then, when Murray and Williams remained mutually distrustful, Haskell became a mediator. He brought the protagonists

[21] Lewis E. Solomon, "The Personnel of the Oklahoma Constitutional Convention of 1906–1907" (Master's thesis, University of Oklahoma, 1924), 30–31.

[22] Ellis, *A History of the Constitutional Convention*, 129.

[23] Hines, *Alfalfa Bill*, 189–90; Murray, *Memoirs*, I, 320–21.

together, and the result was a triumvirate that was to have lasting influence upon the convention.[24]

Murray arrived in Guthrie a week before the opening session and began to buttonhole the delegates in a search for votes. With almost unanimous backing from the Indian Territory delegates, Murray issued a statement designed to gain him support among Oklahoma Territory representatives. He said:

> The people have placed superior confidence in the democratic party to settle rightly the corporation and race questions finally and forever. The democrats were thoroughly sound in their platform principles and pledges and elected men honest and competent. The party must do right else factions will arise and other parties spring up to be fused with republicans and give us trouble again.[25]

He assured the delegates that he had made no promises to any group, but desired only to unite the two territories. He promised that, if elected president, he would grant no special favors to delegates from Indian Territory. In the time-honored tradition of politicians, he claimed that he did not desire to be elevated to this position but was being drafted by friends.[26] As Murray's strength grew, candidate W. C. Hughes, a labor leader, recognized the futility of his efforts and withdrew. The labor-union delegates then united behind John Buchanan of Norman, but he also withdrew.[27]

In fact, Murray's endorsement by Williams and other Democratic leaders doomed any opposition. Robert L. Owen of Muskogee favored Murray and was a potent force in holding the Indian Territory delegates for him. Ignoring the workings of the triumvirate, Owen issued a statement saying that "Mr. Murray is a strong man and has no entangling alliances."[28] Murray's campaign among the Oklahoma Territory delegates was greatly advanced when Henry S. Johnston of Perry, Charles Moore of Enid, and D. S. Rose of

---

[24] Hines, *Alfalfa Bill*, 191–93; Murray, *Memoirs*, II, 7–9; *New-State Tribune*, Nov. 22, 1906; Edward Everett Dale and James D. Morrison, *Pioneer Judge: The Life of Robert L. Williams* (Cedar Rapids, The Torch Press, 1958), 163.

[25] *Oklahoma State Capital* (Guthrie), Nov. 18, 1906.

[26] *Guthrie Daily Leader*, Nov. 19, 1906.

[27] *Oklahoma State Capital*, Nov. 20, 1906.

[28] *Kansas City Journal*, Nov. 19, 1906.

Blackwell joined his cause. When the Democratic caucus met on November 19, Williams nominated Murray, and seconding speeches by Haskell, W. N. Littlejohn of Brushy, C. H. Pittman of Enid, and Neal Gardner of Stigler demonstrated the broad base of support for Murray.[29] The "Sage of Tishomingo," as he was called by his friends and neighbors, received the votes of fifty-nine of the eighty-five Democrats present. Pete Hanraty received twenty-six; the labor-union men stubbornly voted for one of their own rather than the farmers' candidate. But Murray won their good will, if not their votes, by casting his own ballot for Hanraty. After his nomination, in a move designed to win the support of the labor bloc, Murray persuaded the caucus to nominate Hanraty for first vice-president. Then he addressed the caucus, stressing his opposition to corporate greed and his support of segregated schools and railroad accommodations.[30] Approving the nominee's forthright stand, the Democrats closed ranks behind him and moved to organize the convention.

Charles H. Filson, secretary of state for Oklahoma Territory, called the constitutional convention to order on the afternoon of November 20, 1906, in the Guthrie City Hall. Filson then relinquished the chair to Henry S. Johnston, Democratic caucus chairman. After a short address by F. F. King, the temporary president, Williams nominated Murray for permanent president. The Republican minority nominated P. B. Hopkins of Muskogee, who received 11 votes to Murray's 97; four of the delegates were absent. "With cries of 'Alfalfa Bill' from all sections of the house, Murray was called to the platform and delivered an address defining his position and what he would stand for during the convention."[31]

Escorted to the chair by Williams, Haskell, J. H. Maxey, and Hopkins, Murray stated that he had made no pledges or promises to any man or group and that his only commitment was to a young boy who wanted to be a convention page.[32] He asked the delegates to submit to him the platforms upon which they had been elected,

[29] *New-State Tribune*, Nov. 22, 1906.   [30] *Kansas City Journal*, Nov. 20, 1906.
[31] *Ibid.*, Nov. 21, 1906.
[32] Proceedings of the Oklahoma Constitutional Convention, Nov. 20, 1906, typescript, Bureau of Government Research Collection (Norman, University of Oklahoma Library, Division of Manuscripts). Hereafter cited as Bur. Govt. Res. Coll., Univ. of Okla. Library.

so that he could study them before deciding on the membership of the various committees. All points of view should be represented on every committee, he said, and this he would try to ensure in making his selections. The constitution must be nonpartisan and without prejudice to any group of citizens.

Murray then discussed the agrarian proposals he wanted included in the constitution. They were the same proposals he had supported over the years. He opposed the ownership of land by aliens or corporations. As an example of the evils of alien ownership he described the problems in his native state of Texas, where one British subject owned five million acres of land. Recalling the troubles Governor Hogg had faced with only statutory prohibition, Murray called for a constitutional prohibition on such landholdings. He also asked for a provision restricting corporation ownership of lands to those holdings indispensable to the corporation's main commercial activity, a position earlier adopted by the Farmers' Alliance and by the Populist party. Common carriers should not engage in farming or any business other than transportation, he maintained, and he urged the adoption of the Texas statute of 1893 dealing with this question.

There were also positive planks in Murray's agrarian program. His main goal was to promote ownership of land by men who would make their homes on it.[33] He proposed to do this by a graduated land tax. He argued that the power to tax, when properly exercised, could eliminate large landholdings without recourse to socialism. On holdings of more than 3,000 acres he advocated a 2 per cent surtax. The rate would increase so that anyone owning 30,000 acres or more would pay an annual land tax equal to the total value of the property. Murray made his aim clear when he added, "The owner will sell some of it, don't you think he will? And don't you think this tendency to divide the great bodies of real estate would destroy the evils of landlordism and promote home-owning in the State of Oklahoma?"[34]

[33] "President of the Constitutional Convention," *Sturm's Oklahoma Magazine*, Vol. III (January, 1907), 3.
[34] Proceedings of the Oklahoma Constitutional Convention, Nov. 20, 1906.

Although the convention would refuse to adopt this virtually confiscatory measure, Murray remained convinced that the inequitable distribution of land was the cause of the plight of the farmers. His position was shared by a scholar of the period, Joseph B. Ross, who wrote, "The fundamental problem in American economics always has been that of the distribution of land."[35]

To safeguard the titles of the small farmers to their lands, Murray advised the delegates to adopt the Torrens system. Land-title verification was difficult in both territories, and Murray's solution was this simplified method of recording titles and deeds. Developed in Australia by Sir Robert Richard Torrens, the system employed a simple one-page register of title, much like a stock certificate. It had been adopted in Australia in 1857, and a number of American states were permitting its use.[36] The abstractors and bar associations were appalled by this proposal, which would deny them an important source of income, and opposed Murray vigorously when he made the adoption of the Torrens system a lifelong crusade.

Realizing that he needed to win labor support, the farm leader devoted part of his speech to objectives in that field. He urged constitutional provisions to provide for safety and health inspections of coal mines, the eight-hour working day on railroads and public works, and the prohibition of the fellow-servant clause, a labor-contract provision which stated that employers were not liable in industrial accidents caused when one employee injured another.

That he was no friend of the corporations can be seen in his proposals for control of business, particularly of the railroads. He favored fixed maximum rates for common carriers, prohibition of ownership of coal lands by transportation companies, fair property evaluation of railroads for tax purposes, and state control of railroad stock-and-bond issues. He advocated a gross-receipts tax of 1 per cent on coal and oil producers, as well as on railroads and transportation companies.

[35] Joseph B. Ross, "Agrarian Changes in the Middle West," *Political Science Quarterly*, Vol. XXV (December, 1910), 625.
[36] Edward Lawrence McKenna, "State Insurance of Land Titles in the United States (the Torrens System)" (Doctoral thesis, University of Pennsylvania, 1925).

Many of his proposals were designed to give the voters maximum direct control over state and local governments. As in the Sequoyah convention, Murray pleaded for the adoption of initiative and referendum provisions similar to those of Oregon. However, he was not in favor of the recall provision, stating that he had never understood its use and that it would be conducive to anarchy. To protect the common people, he favored limits on the taxing power of cities and counties. Taxes should be kept low, and municipal-bond issues should be limited to prevent scandals in city government like those recently experienced in St. Louis. Utility franchises should be granted only by voters, he argued, and should not be irrevocable.

The educational system of the new state should be as liberal as possible and should be designed to provide a child with nonprofessional training. Murray preferred a practical education. He said, "As we look about us and see the achievements of the great horticulturalist Luther Burbank, we can only say there is but one Luther Burbank, while there should be a thousand where there is but one." Despite his earnest efforts to supplement his own inadequate education, the product of one-room Texas schools and College Hill Institute called for a vocationally oriented school system.

The constitution should be made equitable to all men. He proclaimed, "Would to God that we could say to Great Britain, 'Hands off Ireland,' to Russia, 'Hands off the Jew,' to Hitchcock and other grafters, 'Hands off the Indian and his property.' " However, this plea for tolerance did not mean equality for the Negro. According to Murray, the Negro was a failure as a soldier, doctor, and lawyer. Not yet equal to the white man, he belonged in separate schools, railroad coaches, and depot waiting rooms. Murray claimed to know the Negro well and said, "I appreciate the old time ex-slave, the old darkey, (and they are the salt of the race), who come to me talking softly in that humble spirit which should characterize their actions and dealings with the white man, and when they thus come they can get any favor from me." The delegates warmly applauded this exposition of the prevailing national racial attitudes. Murray also asked for an antimiscegenation law, for the worst Negroes, he said, were those in the Creek Nation who had been partially assimilated. He maintained that Negro educational facilities should share equally with those of the whites with respect to appropriations of funds, for the Negro should be taught agriculture, mechanics, and industrial jobs—the things he could do best. To his credit, Murray would later strongly oppose the delegates who sought to deprive the Negro of his right to vote.

In closing, Murray denounced the radicals of the day: "Let us avoid the extremes of radical socialism on the one side and extreme conservatism on the other; the extremes of no one owning anything on the one hand, the existence of a few men owning everything on the other." This straightforward statement summed up his views and gave direction to the course of the convention and the constitution which that body produced.

His address elicited favorable response from Vice-President Hanraty, his former opponent. Following Murray to the chair, he said, "I heartily endorse all that has been said by our President and see little room for expansion upon his suggestions." The opinions expressed by Murray encompassed the attitudes of the Sequoyah men, the Farmers' Union members, and the labor-union representatives, who constituted the majority of the delegates.[37]

As convention president, Murray appointed all the members of the forty-five committees and named himself chairman of the committee on rules and an ex officio member of all committees. According to the rules, the president was allowed to place another delegate in the chair so that he could step down and speak from the floor, and Murray was to exercise this privilege often. The large number of committees allowed him to use the chairmanships to build political support. Williams became chairman of the committee on corporations, Johnston chaired the committee on the executive branch, and Haskell presided over the primary-elections committee. Other Murray friends also received chairmanships: Milas Lasater was named chairman of the committee on revisions, style, and ar-

[37] Proceedings of the Oklahoma Constitutional Convention, Nov. 20, 1906; *Dallas Morning News*, Nov. 22, 1906.

rangement; Hanraty, on labor; A. H. Ellis, on public health; George Henshaw, on suffrage; and C. H. Pittman, on legislative apportionment.[38] Murray's appointments were received favorably by the delegates and the local Democratic press.[39]

Though the committees drafted their assigned portions of the constitution, the major policy decisions were made in the Democratic caucus. The twelve Republican delegates, known as the "Twelve Apostles," served on committees but were without great influence. The huge Democratic majority obviously planned to ignore the minority party, although they sometimes asked national Republican leaders for advice.

As in the Sequoyah convention, Murray urged that letters be sent to national political leaders inviting them to address the convention. The invitation list was indicative of the thinking of the convention. Among those invited were President Roosevelt, Senator Robert LaFollette of Wisconsin, Henry Watterson of the *Louisville Courier-Journal*, Senator John Sharpe Williams of Mississippi, Texas railroad commission member O. B. Colquitt, and William Jennings Bryan. Of these men only Colquitt accepted, but nearly all of them sent suggestions for provisions to be incorporated into the constitution.

The most profound influence on the convention from outside the Twin Territories was William Jennings Bryan, the "prairie orator," Democratic Presidential nominee, and hero of the Oklahoma Democrats. Bryan had toured Oklahoma Territory in 1895, winning broad popular support, and the delegates from the territory had voted for him at the 1896 Democratic convention. He had made further speaking tours of the territories in 1897, 1902, and 1903. In his speeches Bryan had advocated free homesteads and immediate statehood for the territories. Both issues were close to the hearts of most residents, and many Oklahoma Democrats urged him to move to the future state. Bryan appeared in the territories again in 1906 and 1907 on the Chautauqua circuit. In September, 1906,

[38] Murray, *Memoirs*, II, 15–17, 38–39.
[39] *Guthrie Daily Leader*, Nov. 27, 1906.

he campaigned for the Democratic candidates to the constitutional convention.[40] While Senator Ben Tillman of South Carolina and Governor Jeff Davis of Arkansas also campaigned for the delegates, Oklahoma Democrats continued to look to Bryan for guidance.

On December 11, 1906, Murray entered a letter from Bryan into the convention proceedings. In the letter, which was a precursor to the Democratic national platform of 1908, Bryan apologized for being unable to attend the convention but sent a lengthy list of suggestions and urged the delegates to select the best provisions of other state constitutions. He advised them to protect the industrial liberties of workers and to provide for jury trials in equity cases and for arbitration in labor disputes. All party nominees should be selected in direct primaries rather than by conventions, and he advocated initiative, referendum, and recall. To control corporations, he suggested an elected board of corporations, which would limit the issuance of stocks and bonds and prevent interlocking directorates and monopolies. Cities should be permitted to own and operate utilities, and utility franchises should be awarded by popular vote.[41] Ultimately all the Bryan proposals except recall were included in the constitution.

The constitutional convention met in three sessions. The first met from November 20, 1906, to March 15, 1907; the second convened on April 16, 1907, for six days, and the third met for six days, beginning July 10, 1907. Most of the work was accomplished during the first session. Murray, Haskell, Williams, Hughes, and Hanraty shared the leadership of the convention, but on many issues it was Murray's influence that was most discernible.

A typical "Murray measure" provided for the direct popular nomination of candidates for United States Senate. Murray introduced this proposal and made a long speech supporting it.[42] The delegates incorporated the provision into the constitution, leaving the details to be worked out by the first legislature.

The convention also enacted many of the agrarian proposals

[40] Norbert R. Mahnken, "William Jennings Bryan in Oklahoma," *Nebraska History*, Vol. XXXI (December, 1950), 253–62.

[41] Proceedings of the Oklahoma Constitutional Convention, Dec. 11, 1906.

[42] *Ibid.*, Dec. 5, 1906; *Guthrie Daily Leader*, Dec. 12, 1906.

Murray had urged in his opening remarks. One historian has described the situation in this manner:

> After the turn of the century, the hostility to alien landownership persisted primarily in those areas where frontier conditions continued to exist. When Oklahoma became a state in 1907, for example, its constitution, framed under the influence of the farmers' leader, William H. Murray, included limitations on the rights of aliens to own land, and these provisions were amplified by legislation in 1908.[43]

The convention duly incorporated into the constitution Article XXII, which Murray wrote, forbidding land ownership by aliens.[44] Although the convention rejected his graduated land tax, Murray fought for exemption of homesteads from foreclosure. He urged the convention to adopt Article XII, which exempted from foreclosure 160-acre homesteads valued at less than $5,000. There was no need to exempt a larger holding, he declared; 160 acres was plenty of land for one family.[45] While Article XXII included restrictions on corporate landholding, particularly by railroads, it did allow banks to foreclose on farm properties provided the banks divest themselves of the land within seven years. No corporation could buy, sell, or speculate in land as its sole endeavor. Two of Murray's agrarian proposals were rejected: the Torrens system and the sale of almost two million acres of state school lands. The future state was to receive from the federal government vast acreage to aid the public-school system. Murray wanted the lands divided into 160-acre tracts and sold to halt the growing tide of tenancy, but the convention refused to accept this proposal.[46]

These setbacks did not deter Murray from pushing for his agricultural-education program, which had been adopted by the Sequoyah convention. The delegates at Guthrie also approved

[43] Roger V. Clements, "British Investment and American Legislative Restrictions in the Trans-Mississippi West, 1880–1900," *Mississippi Valley Historical Review*, Vol. XLII (September, 1955), 223.

[44] Robert L. Williams to J. K. Armstrong, Mar. 28, 1908, Robert L. Williams Collection (Oklahoma City, Oklahoma Historical Society Library). Hereafter cited as Williams Coll., OHS Library.

[45] Proceedings of the Oklahoma Constitutional Convention, Feb. 11, 1907.

[46] *Ibid.*, Feb. 14, 20, 1907.

Murray's plan to provide courses in agriculture and the domestic sciences in the public schools. In *Sturm's Oklahoma Magazine* he explained why he supported this measure:

> The elements of agriculture and horticulture and domestic sciences shall be provided in every common school to the end that the boys and girls may be taught to protect themselves in a vocation rather than to burden them with a false education which leads exclusively to professions and office holdings, the breeder of the vagabonds of society. In this way, an intelligent system of farm life may be taught to the children, and thus lead them back to the farm, and encourage and promote farm life as an intelligent, respectful vocation, insuring a higher development of agriculture, and thereby commerce, benefiting the whole population by reason of happy, prosperous homes and home life.[47]

Through his efforts the state of Oklahoma was to develop an extensive system of agricultural schools at the secondary and junior-college levels.

Murray also took part in the heated controversy over the place of demon rum in the new state. The Enabling Act stipulated that the constitution must prohibit the sale of intoxicants in the Indian Territory and the Osage Nation for twenty-one years after its ratification. There was no prohibition against the sale of liquor in the rest of the state. Because Murray had favored prohibition at the Sequoyah convention, the Anti-Saloon League had supported his candidacy for president of the Oklahoma convention.[48] He claimed to have had no feelings on the liquor question until he realized that the saloonkeepers and the whisky interests were opposing the work of the constitutional convention. Rather than prohibition Murray preferred a state-owned liquor-dispensary system, such as the one that "Pitchfork" Ben Tillman had created in South Carolina. During a protracted speech on the liquor problem Murray read the South Carolina statute to the delegates.[49] When the delegates re-

[47] William H. Murray, "The Constitution of Oklahoma," *Sturm's Oklahoma Magazine*, Vol. LV (March–April, 1907), 8–9.
[48] Hines, *Alfalfa Bill*, 211; Murray, tape-recorded interview of Nov. 20, 1952, OHS Library.
[49] Proceedings of the Oklahoma Constitutional Convention, Feb. 1, 1907.

jected this plan, Murray, fearing that the liquor question might defeat the constitution at the polls, devised a stratagem to circumvent the problem and at the same time exert pressure on President Roosevelt to approve the constitution when it was finished. His plan called for the prohibition question to be proposed to the voters as a constitutional amendment and placed on a separate ballot at the ratification election. This compromise was adopted by the delegates. He also secured the help of the Anti-Saloon League, the Women's Christian Temperance Union, and local church leaders in petitioning President Roosevelt to accept the constitution after it and the prohibition amendment had been ratified by the voters.[50]

Murray continued to oppose Farmers' Union and labor demands for recall, mandatory referendum, and woman suffrage. He argued that in a representative government recall was unnecessary, as was a referendum on every law passed by the legislature.[51] Largely owing to the opposition of Murray, Haskell, and Williams, woman suffrage was narrowly defeated.[52] Like many other delegates, Alfalfa Bill also opposed granting suffrage to members of the army; the legend of thousands of federal troops voting in the southern states during Reconstruction was vivid in the minds of these men.[53]

By and large, Murray and the other delegates supported the Populist fetish for direct legislation. While mandatory referendum was not adopted, referendums were possible on measures that did not contain an emergency clause. A petition signed by 5 per cent of the registered voters or the legislature itself could authorize a referendum. To be placed on a ballot, an initiated statute required the signatures of only 8 per cent of the voters, while a constitutional amendment required 15 per cent. Both provisions were similar to those previously adopted in Oregon.[54]

Several factors influenced Murray and the other delegates in arriving at provisions for election of state and county officials. Re-

---

[50] Murray, *Memoirs*, I, 331–36.
[51] Proceedings of the Oklahoma Constitutional Convention, Mar. 2, 1907.
[52] *Oklahoma State Capital*, Feb. 7, 1907.
[53] Proceedings of the Oklahoma Constitutional Convention, Feb. 7, 1907.
[54] Charles A. Beard, "The Constitution of Oklahoma," *Political Science Quarterly*, Vol. XXIV (March, 1909), 99–100.

sentful of years of rule by Republican appointees, they made every state office elective, including such positions as that of the chief mine inspector, the state examiner and inspector, the superintendent of public instruction, the commissioner of charities and corrections, and the clerk of the supreme court. The result would be a bed sheet-size ballot. Murray opposed the election of some lower officials, but he favored the popular election of all judges.[55] Long a plank in Populist platforms, it was this provision of the Oklahoma constitution that was to receive the brunt of President Roosevelt's criticism. Popular democracy also ran rampant at the county level; all the county officials were to be elected, including the surveyor and the weigher. The convention made sure that the governor would exercise only supervisory power over the executive branch of the state government, and almost total decentralization was achieved. In the 1930's Bill Murray would regret this diffusion of power.

Murray and the other Democratic delegates intended that corporations should be subject to restrictions even more severe than those adopted by the Sequoyah convention. Article Nine of the Oklahoma constitution, the second-longest in the document, was devoted almost entirely to corporations and the elected three-member state corporation commission. This article was written by Williams, who borrowed extensively from the Sequoyah provision on corporations.[56] On Bryan's suggestion the three-member commission was to be elected for staggered six-year terms, and their decisions could be appealed only to the state supreme court. The article gave the corporation commission power to control railroad rates, stock-and-bond issues, and utility charges and to levy fines for violations of commission rules. Further, the commission had the right of unrestricted search through company records, books, and files at any time. As one observer commented, "The spirit of fierce opposition to monopolies and that jealousy of large business enterprises which have filled the statute books of western states with

[55] Proceedings of the Oklahoma Constitutional Convention, Feb. 7, 1907.
[56] Murray, tape-recorded interview of Nov. 20, 1952, OHS Library.

drastic measures, appear in almost every article of the Oklahoma Constitution."[57]

Labor received extensive benefits in the constitution. Hanraty, Hughes, and the other labor delegates, with the assistance of Murray, Haskell, and Williams, secured a provision for the eight-hour day on public works and the prohibition of convict labor, the use of the injunction in a strike, and the fellow-servant doctrine. A department of labor headed by an elected commissioner was to enforce these provisions, supplemented by a board of arbitration to work with the commissioner in resolving labor disputes. Boys under sixteen, women, and girls were forbidden to work in the coal mines, and the eight-hour day was made standard for miners. Despite the fact that most of the delegates were primarily interested in agriculture, the convention alliance of farmers and labor-union men wrote into the constitution the most advanced labor provisions of the day.

One unsavory aspect of the Progressive era in the South influenced the delegates with regard to the rights of Negroes and Negro suffrage. Observers had noted that in the campaigns for election as delegates to the convention Democratic candidates had promised to place Jim Crow laws in the constitution.[58] After the election L. J. Abbott, professor of history at Central State Normal School at Edmond, had concluded: "The recent election for constitutional delegates chiefly hinged on the question of separate schools, separate railway coaches, and separate waiting rooms for blacks. Hardly a candidate for delegate, be he Kansas Republican or Texas Democrat, who did not base his campaign on these 'three issues.' "[59] Abbott said that the Democrats won because they promised the more rigid restrictions on the Negro. The convention wrote into the first draft of the constitution Jim Crow regulations for schools and railroads as well as a provision forbidding whites to marry Negroes.[60]

---

[57] Beard, "The Constitution of Oklahoma," 104.

[58] Grant Foreman, "Statehood for Oklahoma?" *Independent*, Vol. LXIII (Aug. 8, 1907), 331–35; L. J. Abbott, "The Race Question in the Forty-sixth State," *Independent*, Vol. LXIII (July 25, 1907), 206–11.

[59] Abbott, "The Race Question," 209.

[60] Murray, *Memoirs*, II, 78.

Murray and Haskell, while sympathetic to the Jim Crow laws, feared that their inclusion in the constitution would result in its rejection by President Roosevelt. On January 28 Murray announced in a hotel lobby that the debate over the Jim Crow provisions was causing a deep split among the Democrats and that these restrictions must be removed from the proposed constitution.[61] Oklahoma Territory Governor Frank Frantz also announced that Roosevelt would not approve the document with discriminatory clauses against the Negro.[62] After further debate the restrictions were removed, but provisions were made in the constitution for the first state legislature to enact the laws, and resolutions were passed urging the legislature to do so.[63]

Murray precipitated a controversy with Oklahoma Negroes during the convention. His views on the racial question had been spelled out in his opening remarks, and another incident further illustrated his feelings toward the Negro. At the sixth meeting of the convention the president of the Negro Agricultural and Mechanical Normal University and Industrial School at Langston addressed the assembly and presented Murray a desk and gavel made by students at the school. In reply Murray said, "We desire to assure him and his race that as far as they are concerned there will be equality before the courts of this country; that the juries will be made under the law in such a way as will give him and his race their rights, their property and their liberty." Then he said that the Negro should prepare for those tasks for which they were best suited, agriculture and mechanics. He continued, "The false notion that the colored man can attain the same place in other lines is an absurdity, because he must take his place in society as the great God intended, and be given an oppurtunity [sic] starting alone as he will, to rise or fall."[64] This statement was denounced by the Negro Press Association as "impolite and sarcastic and indecent."[65] Yet Murray's position was more moderate than that held by some of the delegates, who favored

61 *Beaver Journal*, Jan. 31, 1907.
62 *New-State Tribune*, Feb. 23, 1907.
63 "Oklahoma and Statehood," *Outlook*, Vol. LXXXV (Mar. 30, 1907), 728.
64 Ellis, *A History of the Constitutional Convention*, 90–91.
65 *Muskogee Times-Democrat*, Nov. 28, 1906.

retaining the Jim Crow provisions in the constitution and complete disfranchisement of the Negro.

Murray's role in the convention drew much press comment. The *Oklahoma State Capital*, the leading Guthrie paper, attacked him from the opening session.[66] The editor, Frank Greer, was an extremely partisan Republican who opposed both the constitution and statehood. From April to June, 1907, Greer ran front-page cartoons savagely attacking Murray and Haskell. In the cartoons Murray was labeled "Cockleburr Bill," an epithet used by Murray's enemies. The name had originated during a flood on the Washita River in 1906, which destroyed Murray's crops and deposited a layer of cockleburs on his lands.

The *Guthrie Daily Leader*, the local Democratic organ, defended Murray and the convention.[67] It reported that the Republican Press Bureau stories on Murray, Haskell, and Williams were being reprinted as objective news items by Greer and other Republican editors. The views of the Oklahoma City newspapers reflected the political affiliations of their editors, who were generally Republican. However, the residents of Tishomingo approved the actions of their adopted son and gave Murray a banquet and a courthouse reception on New Year's Day, 1907. He received a gold watch and chain and responded with an hour-long speech reviewing the work of the convention to that time.[68]

One of the chief sources of Murray's power in the convention was his influence over the determination of county boundaries and county seats. The delegates often expressed great concern about this matter. One member, E. F. Messenger of Holdenville, later said that, while he wanted initiative, referendum, regulation of corporations, and prohibition, his major concern was to assure his home town a courthouse and a large county. Delegate Messenger succeeded in his task.[69]

Murray tried to keep the number of counties to a minimum, but

[66] *Oklahoma State Capital*, Dec. 22, 1906.
[67] *Guthrie Daily Leader*, Jan. 14, 1907.
[68] *Ibid.*, Jan. 2, 1907.
[69] Abbreviated Memoir and Reminiscences of E. F. Messenger, E. F. Messenger Collection (Norman, University of Oklahoma Library, Division of Manuscripts).

their number increased as he found it necessary to obtain favorable votes on contested proposals.[70] R. J. Allen, chairman of the committee on boundaries, was thoroughly exhausted by the clamor. Fearing a disaster when the boundary committee's report was presented, Murray persuaded one of the committee members to resign and named Haskell in his stead. Haskell presented a report calling for seventy-five counties, which was adopted.[71] Once again Murray and Haskell had used the effective system of rewards and punishments to broaden their power. The delegates named several counties after fellow members—Murray, Haskell, Ellis, and Rogers— and a number for Democratic heroes, such as Andrew Jackson, Thomas Jefferson, Ben Tillman, Roger Q. Mills, Henry Grady, and Grover Cleveland.

As the work of the convention dragged on, Bill Murray deeply missed Alice and the three boys. He made arrangements for them to come to Guthrie on short visits, providing Alice with detailed instructions for the train trip from Tishomingo. His letters expressed concern for Massena, "Jonty," and "Billy," and when a smallpox epidemic swept Guthrie, he told Alice how glad he was that the boys were safe at home. By February, 1907, he was longing to get home to the family and wrote that he had dreamed of "little Billy" the night before.[72] But it would be many months before the family would be reunited for a long period; after the convention Alfalfa Bill would lead the campaign for ratification of the constitution and run for office in the 1907 campaigns.

On March 15, 1907, the work of the convention was completed, and the president adjourned the body. He spent the next four weeks traveling through the territories making speeches for the constitution. On April 10 he spoke to 2,000 people in Altus, and the townspeople presented him with a gold-headed cane in appreciation of his efforts. When he addressed a large audience in Fairview on

[70] Murray, *Memoirs*, II, 33.

[71] Two more counties were formed between 1907 and 1910, one from the southwestern part of Greer County, and one from the southern part of Comanche County, making a total of seventy-seven counties.

[72] Murray to Alice Murray, Nov. 29, 1906, Feb. 12, 1907, Murray Coll., Univ. of Okla. Library.

April 5, the German population of the area expressed pleasure with the provision for agriculture courses in the common schools.[73] It was clear that most of the people were favorable to the proposed state charter.

Murray reconvened the assembly on April 16 to approve the engrossed document and make a few minor changes. On April 19 the convention voted to adopt the constitution. Murray gave the pen used to sign it to Pete Hanraty, to be sent to Samuel Gompers, president of the American Federation of Labor. Only one of the Republican delegates was present, and, of the eighty-five delegates at the meeting, twenty-seven refused to vote.[74] Ultimately all but two of the Democratic delegates signed the constitution.[75] The convention again adjourned, agreeing to reconvene on August 5.

President Theodore Roosevelt and certain members of his cabinet, particularly Attorney General Charles J. Bonaparte, voiced great displeasure with the proposed Oklahoma constitution. They felt that its length, 50,000 words, was excessive and that too much statutory law was included. Particularly repugnant to Roosevelt was the definition of "colored race" as anyone of African descent. He advised the territorial Republican committee to oppose the adoption of the constitution. On hearing about this, Alfalfa Bill sent a copy of the constitution to the President and asked him to list his objections. Roosevelt sent a reply to Murray, who called the delegates together on July 10 and read them the President's letter. As a consequence, a few minor changes were made in the document. The convention then adjourned again, to be reconvened September 16, or sooner, if called by the president.[76]

The money appropriated for the convention had been exhausted before the July 10 session, and Murray had to issue a public appeal for funds. A total of $2,067.15 was received, almost one-half of which was donated by the delegates themselves.[77] Murray's receipt

[73] *Guthrie Daily Leader*, May 4, 1907; *Muskogee Times-Democrat,* Apr. 10, 1907.
[74] *St. Louis Republic*, Apr. 20, 1907.
[75] Marginal note on manuscript copy of the Oklahoma Constitution, OHS Library.
[76] *Proceedings of the Constitutional Convention of the Proposed State of Oklahoma* (Muskogee, Muskogee Printing Company, n.d.), 454–56, 347, 384.
[77] *Ibid.,* 458.

book indicates many contributions of $1.00 from private citizens but few large donations.[78] Alfalfa Bill later claimed that he spent $4,000 of his own money on convention expenses. The state never reimbursed him.

Another crisis had arisen over the disposition of the engrossed copy of the constitution. Murray had sent a copy of the document to Charles Filson, secretary of state of Oklahoma Territory, but he had kept the original and placed it in a tin lockbox, which he kept with him all the time. Governor Frantz refused to call the ratification election until Murray sent the engrossed copy to the secretary. Murray argued that it was his duty to keep the document until President Roosevelt had signed the proclamation making Oklahoma a state.[79] When Frantz steadfastly refused to call the election, Murray took it upon himself to do so.

On June 3, claiming to have the authorization of the convention, Murray issued an election ordinance for August 6. In an "Appeal to the People" he stated that he had been forced to act by Frantz and that, if necessary, he would defy the territorial courts to call the election.[80] He denounced Frantz's demand for the parchment copy, calling it a Republican plot to destroy the work of the convention and circumvent the will of the people.[81] In the election proclamation Murray told the story of a disputed Texas election in which one faction had ousted another with the help of a body called the "Squirrel Rifles." Walter Ferguson, a Republican newspaper editor friendly to Murray, suggested forming a similar group to defend him and the constitution. Thus was created the Chickasaw Squirrel Rifles, with Alfalfa Bill as commander-in-chief, and more than five thousand commissions of membership were issued.

Now editor Frank Greer had a real topic for his cartoonist. Day after day the front page of the *Oklahoma State Capital* featured cartoons of Murray, his face hidden behind a huge mustache, running about the state with his tin lockbox, guarded by the Chickasaw

[78] Ledger of "Accounts and Contributions to and with the Oklahoma Constitutional Convention, 1907," OHS Library.

[79] *Proceedings of the Constitutional Convention*, 447–51.

[80] *Ibid.*, 397–400.

[81] *Ibid.*, 447–51.

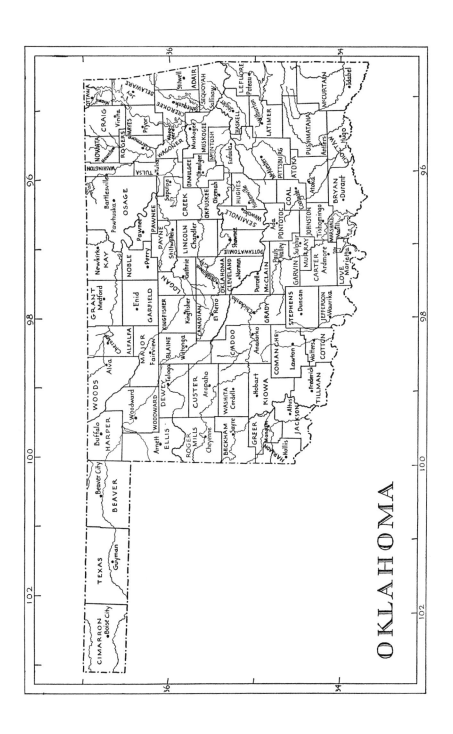

OKLAHOMA

Squirrel Rifles. Finally, after some of the changes suggested by Roosevelt had been made, Frantz agreed to issue a call for the election if Murray would withdraw his proclamation. Murray did so, and on July 24 Frantz called the election for September 17.

The ratification campaign was the first of the lusty, brawling, vindictive election-year spectacles that Oklahomans came to know.[82] Murray, Haskell, Williams, Gore, Owen, and other Democrats led the battle for ratification. To oppose it the Republicans sent in their largest speaker, in every sense of the word. On August 24 the corpulent Secretary of War, William H. Taft, spoke in Oklahoma City and denounced the document as a "code of laws." "The question which you are going to solve next month," he warned, "is whether you are going to permit bourbonism and despotism flavored by socialism to hamper your feet as you go on."[83] He criticized the cost of the convention, the apportionment of the legislature, and the direct-legislation provisions. Taft later described the authors of the constitution as a "zoological garden of cranks."[84]

The Democrats also brought in their most effective spokesman, William Jennings Bryan. Bryan addressed the state Democratic convention on June 18, 1907, and gave the constitution a ringing tribute: "I tell you that you have the best constitution of any state in the union, and a better constitution than the constitution of the United States." During a Chautauqua tour the first week of September, Bryan made several speeches for the constitution and was given the welcome of a conquering hero.[85] Murray, Haskell, and Williams had made Oklahoma a living experiment in Bryan democracy, and the "Peerless Leader" gave them his enthusiastic endorsement.

Murray wrote an article on the constitution which summed up the opinion of many Democratic leaders about its opponents:

> The three C's—corporations, "carpetbaggers" and "coons"—we are aware, will fight the ratification of the Constitution; but will not

[82] The election campaign of 1907 will be discussed in the next chapter.
[83] *Kansas City Star*, Aug. 25, 1907.
[84] L. J. Abbott, "The 'Zoological Garden of Cranks,' " *Independent*, Vol. LXIX (Oct. 20, 1910), 870.
[85] Mahnken, "William Jennings Bryan in Oklahoma," 268.

all patriotic citizens, irrespective of party affiliations, vote for this Constitution and bring the blessing of statehood and self-government.[86]

The citizens did approve the constitution, by a vote of 180,333 to 73,059. The prohibition amendment carried by a smaller margin, 130,361 to 112,258.[87] On November 16, 1907, President Roosevelt proclaimed Oklahoma the forty-sixth state. The battle was over.

The national press and journals greeted the new state and its constitution with mixed reactions. The *Washington Post* stated that Oklahoma had the most radical of all constitutions. The *St. Louis Post-Dispatch* commented that the more objectionable features had been removed.[88] The editor of the *New York Daily Tribune* felt the voters had no other choice than to approve the document, adding, "The new commonwealth is, however, more Populist than Democratic."[89] The *Nation* commented, "As a matter of fact, it undoubtedly comes nearer than any other document in existence to expressing the ideas and aspirations of the day."[90] From the *Arena*, long a supporter of the Populist cause, came this praise: "No people in the great Republic have of late so conspicuously evidenced the splendid spirit of 1776 as have the citizens of Oklahoma . . . ."[91]

The constitution represented an amalgamation of the Populist and Progressive ideologies. Indeed, the two philosophies became so intermeshed in the document that it is impossible to determine which was the more important influence. The control of railroads and corporations, the initiative and referendum provisions, and the election of state and local officials illustrate the strength of both traditions. The social thought of the Progressive era was reflected in the child-labor provision, in the protection of laboring men and their unions, and in the prohibition amendment. The Oklahoma constitution was a living testimonial to the continuation of Populist

[86] Murray, "The Constitution of Oklahoma," 13.

[87] McReynolds, *Oklahoma*, 317.

[88] *Washington Post*, Nov. 17, 1907; *St. Louis Post-Dispatch*, Sept. 18, 1907.

[89] *New York Daily Tribune*, Sept. 19, 1907.

[90] "A New State's Ideas," *Nation*, Vol. LXXXIV (Apr. 4, 1907), 304.

[91] "The Victory for Popular Government in Oklahoma and Its Political Significance," *Arena*, Vol. XXXVIII (November, 1907), 543.

ideology after 1896 and the blending of this philosophy with progressivism.

Alfalfa Bill Murray, the man in whom many elements of these philosophies were fused, had manipulated, coerced, and dictated to the delegates and had strongly flavored the constitution with his own agrarianism. In securing provisions against land ownership by aliens and corporations and provisions for agricultural courses in the public schools, protection of homesteads from foreclosures, and a state board of agriculture, he had won many of his battles for the yeoman farmer. Moreover, the convention had provided him with the leadership role he had sought so long. Though many men had taken part in the convention, one man above all had provided direction and leadership. Even his severest critics were forced to answer "Yes" when William H. Murray asked, "May I not claim to be the Author of the 'Blueprint' of the Constitution?"[92]

[92] Murray, *Memoirs*, II, 43.

SPEAKER OF THE HOUSE AND
CANDIDATE FOR GOVERNOR

IV

Wнen тне voтers ratified the Oklahoma constitution on September 17, 1907, they also gave the Democratic party almost total political control of the new state. The years of Republican rule in both territories had served only to alienate the people; opposition to the popular constitution and a negative platform failed to gain support for the Republicans. The voters' choices were also a reflection of the demographic divisions of the territories. Most of the Republican votes came from the northern third of the state; the central portion voted Democratic by moderate majorities, and the southern third gave the Democratic party large margins of victory. The divisions were products of the pattern of settlement and the lines of transportation that ran from north to south in both territories. When the territories were opened to settlement, most of the former Kansans and other middle westerners moved into northern Oklahoma, while the former Texans usually settled in southern Oklahoma. When the settlers went to the polls, they voted similarly to the voters of their previous homes. These political divisions were to remain almost constant for the next fifty years.

When the constitutional convention adjourned for the first time in the spring of 1907, the Democrats organized to gain both approval of the document and political offices for their party. Bill Murray and the other leaders of the Democratic party made the constitution a partisan issue; the labels they bestowed on its opponents were not conducive to winning the respect of the average Oklahoman.

The members of the convention triumvirate had political aspirations of their own. Charles N. Haskell wanted to be the first governor of the state, Robert L. Williams wanted to be the first chief justice of the state supreme court, and Alfalfa Bill coveted a seat in the United States Senate.[1] As early as December, 1906, the *Oklahoma State Capital* reported that Murray was a candidate for the office.[2] The Democrats had agreed to nominate their senatorial candidates in a primary, with the understanding that a man from each territory would be nominated for the two United States Senate seats. As the date of the primary election drew near, it became apparent that Robert L. Owen, who had strong support in the populous Cherokee and Creek nations, would probably win the seat from Indian Territory. Murray decided to withdraw from the race.

In the meantime, friends of Murray in Tishomingo, believing that he was needed in the first state legislature, had filed his name for state representative. In spite of charges by his opponent in the primary that he was part of a clique, Murray won the race with ease and went on to win the general election.[3]

Haskell's campaign for the gubernatorial nomination was a hard-fought contest. Lee Cruce, an Ardmore banker, gave him strong competition. But Murray actively campaigned for Haskell and rallied the farmers to his cause, and he won the nomination. Williams also won his race for the supreme-court nomination,[4] and Robert Owen and Thomas Gore were nominated for the Senate.[5]

Murray's brother John Shade, now a schoolteacher at Nida, Oklahoma, in Johnston County, had filed for the office of commissioner of labor. The labor unions favored one of their own leaders, Charles Daugherty. Alfalfa Bill persuaded his brother to withdraw from the contest, realizing that John Shade's candidacy had angered the unions and jeopardized Haskell's chances for the governorship. Despite his withdrawal and the absence of his name from the ballot in some counties, John Shade won the nomination. When the state

[1] Hines, *Alfalfa Bill*, 220; Dale and Morrison, *Pioneer Judge*, 175.

[2] *Oklahoma State Capital*, Dec. 22, 1906.

[3] *Tishomingo Weekly News*, June 7, 1907.

[4] *Guthrie Daily Leader*, Apr. 15, May 4, 1907; *New-State Tribune*, Apr. 11, 1907; Murray to William Utterback, May 14, 1907, Williams Coll., OHS Library.

[5] Robert Furman actually ran second to Owen, but since both men were from Indian Territory, Furman withdrew, and Gore became the other nominee. After the general election of 1907 Haskell appointed Furman to the state court of criminal appeals.

Democratic convention met on June 18, 1907, Bill Murray, at the insistence of the party leaders, announced John Shade's withdrawal. The state central committee, of which Alfalfa Bill was chairman, then put Daugherty on the ballot as the Democratic nominee. Murray placed the union men under obligation to him by getting his brother to withdraw,[6] but John Shade's primary victory demonstrated the power of the Murray name.

In the general election the Democrats received an unqualified mandate. Haskell won, as did the entire slate of state executive and judicial officers, and the party elected all but one of the congressmen. Both houses of the state legislature had overwhelming Democratic majorities: thirty-nine Democrats and five Republicans went to the senate, and ninety-three Democrats and sixteen Republicans went to the house. However, the Socialist party had polled just under 10,000 votes, a sign that portended danger to the two major parties.[7]

The composition of the first legislature paralleled that of the constitutional convention. Of the ninety-three house Democrats, fifty-one had been born in the states of the Confederacy and Kentucky; in the senate twenty-three of the thirty-nine Democrats were of southern birth.[8]

A week after the Democratic victory W. A. Durant, a representative-elect from Bryan and Atoka counties, urged that Murray be elected speaker of the first house. The Sage of Tishomingo wrote to Durant saying that he would accept the nomination and adding that the first legislature would have to work hard to overcome the pressures of the metropolitan press and other lobbyists.[9] The opportunity to chair the Oklahoma house would, to some degree, compensate for his failure to achieve a seat in the United States Senate.

6 Scales, "Political History of Oklahoma," 59; Murray, *Memoirs*, II, 91–92; *New-State Tribune*, June 20, 1907.

7 Leo Winters (comp.), *Directory of the State of Oklahoma* (Oklahoma City, State Election Board, 1959), 118.

8 Scales, "Political History of Oklahoma," 70–71.

9 *Muskogee Times-Democrat*, Sept. 24, Nov. 20, 1907; *Shawnee Daily Herald*, Nov. 21, 1907.

Murray's battles in the constitutional convention, the ratification campaign, and the general election left him in financial trouble and physically exhausted. He wrote to Haskell that he would be forced to remain in Tishomingo until the inauguration to settle his personal affairs. Haskell suggested that the legislature convene on December 2, and Murray agreed that the "anniversary of Napoleon's Sun of Austerlitz" was a fitting date.[10] Murray arrived in Guthrie on the fifteenth of November, and the triumvirate took control of the state government.

"At high noon," reported the local press, "with hundreds of voices singing anthems of praise to the Lord of Hosts, the first legislature of Oklahoma was born."[11] Meeting on the second floor of the courthouse, in the same room used by the constitutional convention, the members of the house elected their officers. Davis Turner of Murray County nominated Alfalfa Bill for speaker, the Republicans passed, and by a vote of 97 to 0 Murray was elected. Only ten of the members present refused to join in the vote, and Murray received a bipartisan endorsement when Republican Representative Abel Sand moved that his election be made unanimous. Cries for "Murray!" filled the room, and when he reached the rostrum, the Republican members presented him with a bouquet of flowers.[12]

He expressed his deep appreciation for the honor extended to him and said, "After the ridicule, slander and abuse of the recent campaign and then to receive the unanimous vote of the caucus of my party for this position—when I think of these things it makes this the happiest moment of my life." He paused, his voice quavered, and he wiped away a tear. Then, regaining his composure, he outlined his proposals for the first legislature. He urged the members to create a good school system, a highway program,

[10] Murray to Charles N. Haskell, Oct. 19, 30, 1907; Charles N. Haskell Collection (Norman, University of Oklahoma Library, Division of Manuscripts). Hereafter cited as Haskell Coll., Univ. of Okla. Library.

[11] *Guthrie Daily Leader*, Dec. 2, 1907.

[12] *Oklahoma State Capital*, Dec. 3, 1907; *New-State Tribune*, Dec. 5, 1907; *Journal of the House of Representatives of the Regular Session of the First Legislature of Oklahoma* (Guthrie, Leader Printing and Manufacturing House, 1908), 5.

76

and a strong judiciary. He advocated the sale of state school lands, the purchase of Indian-owned coal lands, a new capital for the state, and the Torrens system. Murray closed his speech by saying that he held ill feelings toward none and in this light revealed his first appointments: two Civil War veterans, one a Rebel and the other a Yankee, as house doorkeepers, and Jim Noble, a Negro, as janitor.[13]

As speaker, Murray found himself in a significant position. As just another member of the legislature, he had been relegated to the fourteenth carriage in the inaugural parade. Now he could give direction to the legislative program. The triumvirate held sway over all three branches of the state government: Haskell as governor, Williams as chief justice, and Murray as house speaker. There were, however, differences of opinion among the three leaders, and the alliance was under constant stress. Although Murray supported most of Haskell's proposals and the Governor often appointed Murray's friends to office in preference to the men proposed by Williams, a degree of animosity developed. Regardless of the tenuousness of the alliance, the hold the three men maintained on the state government was very real.

The first legislature met from December 2, 1907, to May 26, 1908, and during that brief time a comprehensive program was enacted. Murray threatened, cajoled, punished, and herded the house members, using the rules adopted by "Czar" Thomas Reed in the United States House of Representatives. In the first three weeks the Oklahoma legislators passed eighteen laws, including the Jim Crow and bank-guaranty laws, and transferred $5,000,000 of federal funds to the State School Land Commission. At the end of six months the members had passed laws to enforce the prohibition amendment, determined the locations for a number of state institutions, and set the state government in order.[14]

That the first bills introduced were the segregation proposals

13 *Guthrie Daily Leader*, Dec. 2, 1907; *Journal of the First House of Representatives*, 5–9; *Oklahoma State Capital*, Dec. 3, 1907.

14 Robert L. Williams to B. L. Dennison, Nov. 25, 1907; Williams to E. C. Patton, Nov. 22, 1907; Williams Coll., OHS Library.

came as no surprise. The senate voted overwhelmingly for their passage, and Murray joined the majority voting for the bills in the house.[15] With this piece of bigotry accomplished, the legislature proceeded to enact the laws the new state really needed.

The legislature had to enforce prohibition, as provided for by the first constitutional amendment. Murray again advocated the state-dispensary system of South Carolina. Unlike that system, however, liquor would be sold only for medicinal purposes.[16] Representative Fred Branson led the fight against Murray's proposal, and the speaker was soon convinced that Branson's opposition was directed at him personally. He left the chair to attack Branson's conduct, which he labeled ungentlemanly.[17] As a consequence the two men became bitter political enemies, and their feud continued through the elections of 1910 and 1912. Unable to get the state-dispensary system passed by the legislature, Murray had the measure placed on the general-election ballot of 1908 in the form of a referendum.

Haskell and Murray together led the fight for the bank-guaranty law. This precursor of the Federal Deposit Insurance Corporation created a fund to be used to prevent runs on banks and to protect individual depositors in the event of bank failure. A banking board supervised the fund, to which each bank contributed 1 per cent of the average daily balance. The law was suggested by William Jennings Bryan when he spoke to the state legislature on December 21, 1907. The law became an issue in the 1908 Presidential campaign, when Bryan cited Oklahoma's experiment as a basis for a national bank-guaranty law.[18]

Murray continued to battle for his agrarian proposals that had been rejected by the constitutional convention. The state had received from the federal government sections of land in the former Oklahoma Territory for financing schools, as well as $5,000,000 in

[15] *Journal of the First House of Representatives*, 14.

[16] Murray, *Memoirs*, II, 127–28.

[17] *Muskogee Times-Democrat*, Jan. 16, 1908.

[18] Dale and Wardell, *History of Oklahoma*, 322; William Jennings Bryan, *Guaranteed Banks* (speech delivered at Topeka, Kansas, Aug. 27, 1908), (Chicago, M. A. Donohue & Company, 1908).

lieu of lands in Indian Territory. Murray voted with the majority for a bill that established the State School Land Commission to manage the school properties and then attempted to gain passage of a bill to sell the lands. Murray reasoned that the lands might be leased by commission members to political friends and also that continued state ownership of the lands would perpetuate tenancy. Despite his efforts the bill was defeated.[19] A Murray-sponsored initiative petition for the sale of the lands in 160-acre tracts would be presented to the voters in the general election of November, 1908.

Another agrarian scheme of Murray's, the Torrens system, became the focal point of heated legislative controversy. The system, defeated at the constitutional convention, was still bitterly opposed by abstractors.[20] A joint resolution proposing a constitutional amendment for this proposal was filed by Murray and placed on the November ballot.[21]

Not content with the constitutional provision for teaching agriculture in the common schools, Murray advocated a state system of two-year agricultural colleges. He secured passage of a law authorizing district agricultural colleges, to be situated at Lawton, Goodwell, Helena, Broken Arrow, and Tishomingo. The names given to the schools were indicative of Murray's influence: the school at Helena was named for J. H. Connell, an agriculturist and a friend of Murray's; the school at Broken Arrow was named for Haskell; and the school at Tishomingo became Murray State School of Agriculture. The schools at Helena and Broken Arrow were closed during the administration of Robert L. Williams, but the others continued operation as agricultural and mechanical colleges.[22]

Murray favored the creation of the office of state printer to publish official state documents and, more importantly, to print free school textbooks. His bill provided for the election of the state printer, but when he refused to agree to restrict candidates to men with printing experience, the Oklahoma Typographers Union bit-

[19] *Journal of the First House of Representatives*, 62, 595–96.
[20] Murray, *Memoirs*, III, 356–60.
[21] *Journal of the First House of Representatives*, 559–60.
[22] McReynolds, *Oklahoma*, 320; Dale and Wardell, *History of Oklahoma*, 488.

terly attacked him. Though the elective position was later established, it existed only from 1911 to 1915.[23]

Probably as a result of the poor public accommodations Murray had found during his travels about the state, he urged the legislature to pass a law providing for the inspection of hotels. During the session the Murray-Whitehead bill was passed, providing for state hotel inspection and requiring nine-foot-long bedsheets on hotel beds. The latter provision made Murray a laughingstock among newspaper editors and political enemies, but to the average citizen the idea of a long sheet to protect him from the blankets of small-town hotels was not so funny.[24]

To its credit, the first legislature also passed a significant number of labor laws. The legislature used every means at its disposal to protect the workingman, and the resulting laws formed a virtual bill of rights for labor. They represented a remarkable achievement in a basically agricultural state.[25] Among the measures were a safety code for miners, a system of factory inspectors, a health code for factories, and an employer's liability law. Employers were forbidden to advertise for strikebreakers or to use black lists, the sale of convict-made goods was prohibited, and railroads had to establish safe procedures for repair of locomotive fireboxes.

The laws protecting the coal miners reflected the strength of their union. Pete Hanraty, president of the miners' union, wrote the mining laws, and Murray said that while he knew nothing of mining he trusted Hanraty's judgment and would vote for them.

Murray also voted for final passage of most of the other labor statutes, though he opposed some of them in early stages and proposed amendments for others. He opposed a locomotive-headlight measure, arguing that strong lights on switch engines were dangerous. The railroad men persuaded the legislature otherwise, and the bill passed.[26] Because of this and other objections, Murray came

---

[23] *Oklahoma State Capital*, Dec. 10, 1907.

[24] *Journal of the First House of Representatives*, 178; *Shawnee Daily Herald*, May 6, 1908.

[25] Frederick L. Ryan, *A History of Labor Legislation in Oklahoma* (Norman, University of Oklahoma Press, 1932), 15, 30.

[26] *Journal of the First House of Representatives*, 239–40, 312.

under attack by the labor leaders and by Kate Barnard, who had been elected the first commissioner of charities and corrections.

Kate Barnard first roused Murray's ire when she used the house floor to lobby for an increased appropriation for her office. Speaker Murray ordered her out of the chamber and attempted to cut the appropriation, a move that he later regretted. He also refused to support a stringent child-labor bill proposed by her.[27] A strong believer in the Victorian concept of womanhood, Murray opposed woman suffrage, and to his thinking a woman officeholder was an abomination.

Though small of stature, the lady carried a large political stick. A member of the State Federation of Labor, she brought down the wrath of that organization on the speaker. At the fifth annual convention of the federation in July, 1908, she delivered an address praising the work of the legislature in passing the labor statutes but labeling the Sage of Tishomingo an enemy of labor. After giving three cheers for her speech, the convention adopted the following resolution:

Whereas, Speaker Wm. H. Murray of the First House of Representatives of Oklahoma, has by his own action proved himself to be a representative of class interests instead of the interest of the masses. His duplicity in connection with the graduated land tax bill, the usury bill, the 8-hour bill, the full crew bill, the bills known as 81a and 81b, and his opposition, as well as his underhanded work, to practically all legislation proposed in behalf of the agricultural and laboring masses, shows conclusively, that he was a representative of corporations. His gag rule as speaker of the House and disrespect shown to ladies has proved him to be a man destitute of honor and void of principle; therefore be it Resolved, that the Oklahoma State Federation of Labor, does hereby pronounce Wm. H. Murray as unfair to all members everywhere and we urge and pledge our efforts and ballots to the end that he shall be defeated for every political office he may aspire to, and we shall regard any official or party that continues to boost Wm. H. Murray as an enemy to the masses of Oklahoma.[28]

27 *Daily Ardmoreite*, July 29, 30, 1908; Murray, *Memoirs*, II, 122.
28 *Alva Review-Courier*, Aug. 6, 1908; *Proceedings of the Fifth Annual Conven-*

There was some truth to the charges about Murray's gag rule of the house and his disrespect for Kate, but to call Alfalfa Bill a representative of the corporations was ridiculous. Nevertheless, the *Oklahoma Labor Unit*, a newspaper published by the federation, proclaimed that Murray's name had become a synonym for double-dealing and rascality.[29]

In reply Murray called the delegates to the Ardmore convention a "bunch of grafters." He denounced them as a small coterie who no longer represented the workingman but were agitators who wanted Socialists elected to state office. On the subject of the labor bills the speaker pointed out that he had opposed provisions that seemed unfair or irrelevant, such as the one forbidding the employment of men as miners without two years' experience. He reminded union members that he had ultimately voted for all thirteen measures. In the child-labor bill he had opposed the provision that no one under sixteen years of age could hold a job unless he could read and write, but he wanted a child-labor law forbidding the employment of children in coal mines and factories and all dangerous employment. The child-labor bill that had been proposed by Kate Barnard was too severe, Murray claimed, and Governor Haskell's veto proved it. The commissioner of charities and corrections was not a substitute for a child's parents, and some children under sixteen had to work, he said, citing his own experience as an example. In summary, Murray argued that he was not anti-labor but that he did oppose the extreme laws advocated by some labor leaders.[30] He favored labor legislation within certain limits, but when the unions demanded a law providing for the eight-hour day for all workers, he refused to go along. Some of the labor leaders were Socialists, and their opposition to him intensified in the campaigns of the next eight years.

Murray made no attempt to deny his arbitrary rule of the house.

---

tion of the Oklahoma State Federation of Labor, July 27–29, 1908, Oklahoma State Federation of Labor Collection (Norman, University of Oklahoma Library, Division of Manuscripts), 27–28. Hereafter cited as Oklahoma Federation of Labor Coll., Univ. of Okla. Library.

[29] *Oklahoma Labor Unit*, Aug. 15, 1908.

[30] *Shawnee Daily Herald*, Aug. 18, 1908.

He often left the chair during debates to argue for passage or defeat of proposals, though a group of insurgents tried unsuccessfully to limit this procedure. He was very strict with house employees, having their names called each day and docking the absentees. When the house reconvened in January, 1908, after the Christmas recess, the speaker made a new rule that no member or employee of the house who was absent for more than three consecutive days would be paid for the time he was absent.[31] In making committee appointments, he gave the best assignments to rural-county and small-town representatives, especially Farmers' Union members. After delivering a speech against nepotism, he did not protest when the house suspended the rules so that a half brother, W. C. Murray, could be named journal clerk of the house.[32]

Nevertheless, despite arbitrary rulings, favoritism, and the personal attacks which they often suffered, the house members recognized Murray as their leader, as did Governor Haskell. Near the end of the session the legislators held a banquet in his honor at the Ione Hotel in Guthrie and delivered a series of speeches praising his labors in the house.[33]

Governor Haskell lauded the speaker's efforts to provide for courses in agriculture and the domestic sciences in the public schools and sent him the pen used to sign the bill, which Murray had authored.[34] When Haskell spoke to the house before adjournment, he told the members, "My friends, from among your membership you selected a Speaker—it is not a misrepresentation, he is a Speaker." The reference to Murray's propensity for oratory provoked uproarious laughter. Haskell went on to comment that Murray had been fair, that everyone always knew where he stood on issues, and that he always looked out for his fellow man.[35] With these comments from his comrade-in-arms and political ally, Mur-

---

[31] *Muskogee Daily Phoenix*, Dec. 7, 1907; *New-State Tribune*, Jan. 9, 1908.

[32] *Muskogee Times-Democrat*, Apr. 1, 1908; *Chickasaw Capital* (Tishomingo), Feb. 12, 1908; *Guthrie Daily Leader*, Dec. 4, 1907; *Oklahoma State Capital*, Dec. 5, 1907.

[33] Banquet program, May 23, 1908; Murray Coll., Univ. of Okla. Library.

[34] *Journal of the First House of Representatives*, 681.

[35] Charles N. Haskell, "Three Years with Bill Murray," manuscript of speech, May 24, 1908, Indian Archives, OHS.

ray's stint as speaker ended. On the whole, the work of the first legislature had been progressive and of lasting benefit to the state, and Murray could claim a major share of the credit for these constructive efforts.

At this point in his political career Murray's partisans and detractors had become clearly identifiable. His appeal was to the rural and small-town voters. He was never able to win the urban middle and upper classes to his cause. The well-educated, the wealthy, the urban editors, and the educators—the "best people"—would not accept as a political leader a man of crude appearance, unsophisticated manners, and purple prose. One of his detractors, the editor of the *Ada Democrat,* wrote:

> Jerusalem had its Judas Iscariot, the Continental Congress its Benedict Arnold, Arkansas had its Jeff Davis, Balaam had his Jackass, but Oklahoma has the whole shooting match from Dan to Beersheba when it comes to misfortune, plagues, and incompetent braying machines in the person of Cockleburr Bill.[36]

A friendly editor saw him in a far more favorable light:

> "Alfalfa Bill" occupies the unique position of being altogether a self-made man. He is not a spellbinder, and when the people see him there is no beauty that they should desire him, for the sage of Tishomingo is not handsome. But a man without these advantages, who "munches" popcorn while presiding over the legislature; who invades a public dining room coatless; wearing old fashioned "duck" shirts, who "swills" his coffee until he disturbs the peace of his fellow boarders; who persists in eating his pie with a knife, and still holds the commanding position of a foremost statesman of a state like Oklahoma is to be reckoned with when it comes to a fight.[37]

Murray had engaged in such a fight with Governor Haskell early in 1908. The issue was the Oklahoma delegation to the national Democratic convention in Denver. There was little doubt that Oklahoma would send a delegation committed to William Jennings

---

[36] *Ada Democrat,* June 17, 1908.

[37] Newspaper clipping, Henry S. Johnston Collection (Norman, University of Oklahoma Library, Division of Manuscripts). Hereafter cited as Johnston Coll., Univ. of Okla. Library.

Bryan; the question was who would control the delegation. On January 20, 1908, Alfalfa Bill announced his candidacy for delegate-at-large and asked the county Democratic conventions to instruct their delegations to vote for him at the state convention.[38] The state convention would prove to be a test of strength between the speaker and the Governor.

The convention met on February 21, and the contest began. Murray supporters favored electing four delegates-at-large, to include Murray, Haskell, and two others. Haskell preferred eight delegates, each with one-half vote. During the first session of the convention, Murray and his cohorts, some of whom were delegates, held out against Haskell, but at the second session they were soundly defeated. When Alfalfa Bill tried to speak in support of his plan, he was shouted down. Then he attacked the press as the major source of opposition, but three times the delegates howled him into silence and then voted 1,082 to 294 against his proposal. In an extremely conciliatory mood, the Governor appeared before the convention and defended Murray's right to disagree. He placed Murray's name on the list of delegates-at-large, but the speaker peevishly asked for it to be withdrawn. Haskell would probably have done so if Alfalfa Bill had not been endorsed by fifty county conventions and if he had not known that he would need Murray's support in a future Senate contest. The delegation remained as Haskell proposed, and the affair ended with a wound-healing political-harmony session.[39]

Haskell, Murray, Williams, and Thomas H. Owen went to Lincoln, Nebraska, early in July to confer with Bryan about the Democratic platform. They felt that they could make a sizable contribution to the platform, since Oklahoma had put many of Bryan's ideas into effect. As Haskell said, "Oklahoma was built on Bryanism and its popular form of government is Bryanism in operation."[40] Bryan responded favorably to their ideas, and the

[38] Press release, Jan. 20, 1908, Murray Coll., Univ. of Okla. Library.

[39] *Oklahoma State Capital*, Feb. 22, 23, 25, 1908; *Muskogee Daily Phoenix*, Feb. 23, 1908.

[40] "A State Built on Bryanism," manuscript of speech, May 11, 1908, Haskell Coll., Univ. of Okla. Library.

Oklahomans were filled with pride when he told the press: "Politically, I suppose I am nearer kin to Oklahoma than to any other state in the union, and I can say that without hurting the feelings of anyone in Nebraska."[41] With this pronouncement, the four Oklahomans left for Denver to inject Bryanism into the platform and, they hoped, into the federal government.

On their arrival in Denver they proceeded to the Brown Palace Hotel, where Murray immediately began speaking to a crowd gathered in the lobby.[42] It was the first of many impromptu speeches he was to give during the next five days. His verbosity annoyed some of the delegates and at least two reporters. With tongue in cheek one correspondent reported:

> At 7 o'clock tonight "Alfalfa Bill" Murray starts on his three hundred and thirty-third speech in the lobby of the Brown Palace Hotel. "Alfalfa Bill's" mission is to explain the constitution of Oklahoma, a comprehensive document that contains all legislation needed for setting up a new state, from the classification of the voters to the length of sheets that shall be used on hotel beds. "Alfalfa Bill" has a liberal interpretation for each paragraph, and if he talks steadily, as he probably will, it is expected he will be through next Sunday afternoon at 2 o'clock. He is accompanied by two hundred other orators from Oklahoma, each with an explanation of the constitution. The result has been that the day has been a noisy one, and that Oklahoma has furnished most of the noise.[43]

In an article headlined "Alfalfa Bill Heads Band of Oklahoma Spellbinders," reporter C. E. Van Loan wrote that Murray had made eighteen speeches, one on the trusts and seventeen on the price of the rooms at the Brown Palace. As the "longest, strongest singer of them all," he held overflow meetings on the hotel stairs, setting forth his views.[44]

The Oklahoma orators and their "radical" ideas proved a source of embarrassment to Bryan. Bryan's strategy to win the nomina-

41 *Oklahoma State Capital,* July 5, 1908.
42 *Muskogee Times-Democrat,* July 6, 7, 1908.
43 *Denver Post,* July 7, 1908.
44 *Ibid.*

tion required support from the conservative eastern delegations, those most disturbed by the Oklahomans' proposals. The *Denver Post* reported, "That long-haired outfit from Oklahoma is likely to queer Mr. Bryan's conservative play before 'Alfalfa Bill' gets through." To alleviate the situation, Murray drew up a resolution praising former President Grover Cleveland, hero of the conservative easterners.[45]

Though the resolutions committee viewed the proposals of the Sooner State delegation with trepidation, the platform that was finally adopted was a combination of the Oklahoma constitution, the Nebraska Democratic platform, and the program of the American Federation of Labor. Murray had been responsible for a plank favoring the extension of agricultural, mechanical, and industrial education through district agricultural experiment stations and secondary agricultural and mechanical colleges. Though some Oklahoma proposals were defeated, the *Denver Post* commented, "The Oklahomans, fresh from adopting a constitution that is the most radical constitution of any state in the Union, practically controlled the convention."[46] While this was an overstatement, the Oklahomans returned home satisfied with their work and hopeful of Bryan's election.

During the summer of 1908 Murray spent considerable time and energy campaigning for Bryan and for the five propositions on the general-election ballot. These proposals included the state-dispensary system, the Torrens system, the sale of the state school lands, and the relocation of the state capital and the securing of a site for the new capitol building. The school-land proposal had been placed on the ballot through initiative petition, and Murray and ten others had served on the committee that circulated the petitions. During the long, hard campaign, Murray traveled the state until he became seriously ill and had to curtail his efforts.[47] All but one of the measures were defeated, and one observer felt

[45] *Ibid.*, July 5, 9, 1908.

[46] *Official Report of the Proceedings of the Democratic National Convention* (Chicago, Western Newspaper Union, 1908), 170; *Denver Post*, July 10, 1908.

[47] *Muskogee Times-Democrat*, June 18, Aug. 10, 1908; *Guthrie Daily Leader*, July 9, 1908.

that they would all have been approved if Murray had not been ill during the latter part of the campaign.[48]

For the rest of the year Murray remained in Tishomingo, ill and at the brink of financial ruin. In 1905 he had owned several farms, 250 head of cattle, 300 hogs, and a house and lot in Tishomingo. By 1908 he was $6,000 in debt and had sold all but 2 cows, as well as the house and lot.[49] Moreover, his family was growing. On September 30, 1908, Alice gave birth to a daughter, whom they named Jean. Bill Murray's pride in his Scottish ancestry was reflected in the name chosen for her.[50]

Good health was slow to return. In the fall Murray wrote to Haskell that he was only slightly improved.[51] Robert L. Williams tried to help him out of his financial difficulties by cosigning a note for $300, a favor for which Murray expressed deep gratitude. Williams apparently thought highly of him, though he felt that Murray created controversies in the Democratic party by his accusations and personal attacks on his opponents.[52]

Williams also probably became irritated by the number of Murray's relatives whom Haskell had placed on the state payroll. One of Murray's brothers-in-law was appointed to the State Medical Board, and Murray also tried to get his brother John Shade a job in the proposed dispensary system. John Shade rejected this post, as well as a position with the State Highway Commission, and wrote to Williams that he had not been offered a job by Haskell as he had been promised when he withdrew from the labor commissioner's race.[53] Another brother-in-law, W. H. Skeen, received Murray's support for the state senate, but labor opposition defeated him. The

---

[48] L. J. Abbott, "Initiative and Referendum in Oklahoma," *The Independent*, Vol. LXVI (Feb. 25, 1909), 422.

[49] Murray to T. Holmes Mills, Mar. 21, 1910, Murray Coll., OHS Library.

[50] Johnston Murray, interview of Dec. 29, 1965; Burbank Murray, interview of Feb. 10, 1966.

[51] Murray to Haskell, Oct. 24, 1908; Haskell to Murray, Nov. 19, 1908; Haskell Coll., Univ. of Okla. Library.

[52] Williams to Durant National Bank, Dec. 1, 1908; Murray to Williams, Dec. 3, 1908; Williams to J. R. McCalla, Nov. 21, 1908; Williams Coll., OHS Library.

[53] Williams to W. M. Turner, Sept. 28, 1908; J. S. Murray to Williams, Nov. 17, 1908; Williams Coll., OHS Library; Murray to Haskell, Sept. 12, 1908; Haskell to Murray, Nov. 19, 1908; Haskell Coll., Univ. of Okla. Library.

desire to help his relatives and friends by getting them patronage jobs was one of Bill Murray's most serious problems. He used his position as speaker of the house and later as congressman and governor to load the state and federal payrolls with those to whom he had great loyalty. Too often, his relatives and friends were sources of embarrassment and became political issues.

While Murray spent most of 1909 in semiretirement, rebuilding his physical and financial resources, he was also organizing his first gubernatorial campaign. In 1907 a Murray-for-second-governor club had been organized in Canadian County, and at the banquet given for Murray by the members and employees of the house in January, 1908, some of the speakers had urged him to run.[54] These men represented one faction in the Murray organization that managed his gubernatorial campaigns.

Murray used his personal friendships to put together an organization of men with strong followings in various counties over the state. A tactic used again and again was to stage a "reunion" of these friends. The first of these had been held at Sulphur in August, 1908, with members of the Sequoyah constitutional convention, the Oklahoma constitutional convention, the first house of representatives, and the Chickasaw Squirrel Rifles. These bodies were recognized as "Murray groups," and they remained faithful to him for thirty years. He reached many of his supporters by appearances at the state capitol and speeches before the legislature. A second reunion of constitutional-convention delegates at Sulphur on September 17 and 18, 1909, signified Murray's return to state politics.[55]

His spirits soared as he prepared his strategy for the gubernatorial primary. Referring to himself as "Your progressively advancing plebian [sic] friend," he wrote to associates and allies, listing the names of his presumed friends and foes in the contest: Kate Barnard, Charles Daugherty, and all but one member of the supreme court would oppose him, but he felt that Pete Hanraty would support him.[56] Murray wrote to his campaign managers, H.

54 *Muskogee Times-Democrat*, Dec. 16, 1907; *Chickasaw Capital*, Jan. 23, 1908.
55 *Daily Ardmoreite*, Aug. 2, 1908; *Chickasaw Capital*, Jan. 14, Sept. 9, 1909.
56 Murray to John F. Easley, Sept. 11, 1909; Murray to O. G. Harper, Nov. 3, 1909; Murray Coll., OHS Library.

L. Muldrow, B. R. Brundage, and G. W. Dudley, that he agreed to their plan to raise a campaign fund through small subscriptions. No money was to be accepted from corporations, he warned, no large contributions were to be accepted, and a record would be kept of the names and addresses of contributors and the amount of their donations.[57]

The extent of Murray's hopes can be seen in a letter to a Texas boyhood friend, Tom Gilbert. He wrote:

> Well, I will invite you to the inaugural. Of course, I wouldn't dare write such stuff as this to anybody in Oklahoma as I haven't so much as announced for any office, but I have got them skinned two city blocks. Although the great bankers, oil interests, especially representing Standard Oil, railroads, other ins and outs are fighting me to a stand still and have been all the while when there was no talk of me for governor.[58]

In the same letter Murray expressed deep satisfaction in news that Tom Watson, the Populist champion in Georgia and former candidate for the presidency, planned to publish an article about him in *Watson's Jeffersonian Magazine*. "Tom Watson you know is an old time populist but thinks, judging from my work here in Oklahoma, that I am a bully boy."

Watson did think that Murray was a "bully boy," for the article praised him and his efforts in Oklahoma. A full-page picture and four pages of text and smaller pictures reported the exploits of Alfalfa Bill at the Sequoyah and Oklahoma constitutional conventions. The foundation of the Oklahoma constitution was attributed to him, a self-educated and self-made man, who had retired to the seclusion of life on the farm. The article concluded, "Indeed, Mr. Murray is one man among many, an exception to the rule."[59] Such praise elated Murray as he entered the contest for the gubernatorial nomination.

His chief opponent in 1910 was Lee Cruce, an Ardmore banker

[57] Murray to H. L. Muldrow *et. al.*, Nov. 29, 1909, Murray Coll., OHS Library.
[58] Murray to Tom Gilbert, Nov. 3, 1909, Murray Coll., OHS Library.
[59] J. D. Watson, "Hon. W. H. Murray, State Builder," *Watson's Jeffersonian Magazine*, Vol. IV (January, 1910), 22.

and Democratic politician. Cruce did not belong to the inner group from the two constitutional conventions, but he had attended the Denver convention in 1908 and had been Haskell's leading opponent in the gubernatorial primary of 1907. Cruce's home-town paper, the *Daily Ardmoreite*, accused Murray of plans to run on a slate with A. H. Ellis for lieutenant governor, Ben Harrison for secretary of state, Bill Cross for auditor, Milas Lasater for insurance commissioner, and J. C. Graham for corporation commissioner. The editor speculated that the Murray slate would not include candidates running against Kate Barnard or Charles Daugherty, since Alfalfa Bill desired not to alienate the labor bloc further.[60] This analysis appears to have had merit, for on January 29, 1910, Murray wrote to Samuel Gompers, president of the American Federation of Labor, asking for help in the gubernatorial race. He told Gompers that some Oklahoma labor leaders, many of whom were Socialists, opposed him. Murray asked for a favorable statement from Gompers, who wrote Pete Hanraty that Murray should be elected by an "overwhelming majority."[61]

While the *Chickasaw Capital* of Tishomingo was reporting that Murray was being "urged" to run for governor, the candidate himself was preparing for the campaign. On February 3 Murray announced for governor. Taking a swing at his banker opponent, he said that, as a farmer, he had no financial interests that might be furthered by his election. Harking back twenty years, he added, "In many respects it will be such a campaign as characterized the race of the immortal Jim Hogg."[62] Murray often referred to his Texas hero on this and other occasions throughout his life.

Alfalfa Bill knew the sources of his political strength and shaped his campaign to garner this vote. The editor of the *Daily Ardmoreite*, the leading Cruce organ, admitted that Murray would get the Farmers' Union vote.[63] There was no doubt about the attitude

[60] *Daily Ardmoreite*, Jan. 19, 1910.
[61] Murray to Samuel Gompers, Jan. 29, 1910, Murray Coll., OHS Library; Samuel Gompers to Peter Hanraty, Apr. 4, 1910, Peter Hanraty Collection, Indian Archives, OHS Library.
[62] *Chickasaw Capital*, Jan. 13, 20, Feb. 3, 1910.
[63] *Daily Ardmoreite*, Feb. 13, 1910.

of the rural voters. As one farmer put it, "I want to say that the boys from the forks of the creek are for Murray." John Flenner, the Washington correspondent for a number of Oklahoma newspapers, reported that the Oklahoma congressional delegation felt that Murray was very strong in the rural areas and was gaining in the smaller towns.[64] Alfalfa Bill did not neglect his rural friends and opened his campaign among them.

The "Oklahoma Commoner," so labeled by Flenner, opened his campaign on April 19 in the southwestern Oklahoma town of Altus. Petitions had been circulated in Jackson, Tillman, Harmon, and Greer counties urging him to open his campaign in Altus, as he had in the 1907 ratification campaign. Five thousand people, mostly farmers, turned out for the event. Special trains brought hundreds to view the parade of bands and floats and to hear Murray speak from a platform decorated with alfalfa. During the lengthy oration he advocated better state highways and bridges and the use of convict labor on the roads. In the field of education he endorsed a free-textbook program for the first three grades, the improvement of rural high schools, and better management of the state school lands. He reiterated his position in favor of the labor laws and the bank-guaranty law passed by the first legislature and urged that they be strengthened. The farmers were pleased to hear his attack on usury and monopolies and his advocacy of limits on interest rates.[65] This broad program, reflecting Murray's agrarian philosophy, was wildly cheered by the audience.

An incident during the parade proved to be extremely embarrassing for Murray. As the parade formed, he noticed a Confederate flag displayed, but not the United States flag. He held up the procession until the latter was added to his buggy. His opponents twisted the story and reported throughout the southern part of the state that Murray had insulted the Confederate flag.[66] The Cruce campaign was geared to force Murray to defend his position on this

[64] *Chickasaw Capital*, Feb. 10, Mar. 24, 1910.
[65] *Ibid.*, Mar. 31, Apr. 21, 1910; manuscript of Altus speech, Apr. 19, 1910, Murray Coll., Univ. of Okla. Library.
[66] Murray, *Memoirs*, II, 151–52; *Wagoner Record*, July 21, 1910.

charge as well as on the Jim Crow laws and the proposed grandfather clause, to be voted on in the coming primary election. According to this proposal, only persons who had voted before 1866 or whose ancestors had voted before 1866 would be exempted from the required literacy test. The clause was a common device in southern states determined to deprive the Negro of his right to vote. By raising these issues, managers of the Cruce campaign hoped to cut Murray's strength among those Democratic voters who could be aroused by the race issue.

The Murray organization operated from two headquarters, one in Oklahoma City and the other in Tishomingo. He had specified that the Oklahoma City headquarters were to be located in either the Treadgill Hotel or the Stewart Hotel rather than in the Lee Hotel, which he said housed his enemies and was full of "politicians."[67] The Tishomingo headquarters was operated by Muldrow, and Press Lester of McAlester acted as general campaign manager. The finance committee of Muldrow, Brundage, and Dudley solicited contributions for the campaign, but Murray depended less upon these men than upon his friends in the counties who got out the people for his campaign appearances. In Sequoyah County, for example, W. N. Littlejohn, a former constitutional-convention delegate, led the Murray forces and made arrangements for his speeches.

Murray found himself opposed by both the "left" and the "right" during the campaign. The Socialist party of Oklahoma attacked him for opposing mandatory referendums and recall.[68] The *Oklahoma Labor Unit*, voice of the State Federation of Labor, savagely denounced Murray's "antilabor" record, and the executive board of the federation passed the Ardmore resolution of 1908 a second time on July 17, 1910.[69] In a move to exploit the race issue, Cruce campaigned for a "white man's government" in Oklahoma and the end of alleged Negro domination of the state government. Cruce's

[67] Murray to Judge M. Fulton, Feb. 18, 1910, Murray Coll., OHS Library.
[68] *Oklahoma Pioneer*, Feb. 23, 1910.
[69] *Oklahoma Labor Unit*, July 23, 1910.

negative platform opposed sale of the state school lands, the Torrens system, and any use of convict labor.[70]

Cruce's campaign leaders were more direct than their candidate in their comments about Murray. In what became the classic vilification of the campaign, Judge Stillwell Russell of Ardmore addressed a Cruce rally at the Overholser Opera House in Oklahoma City on July 22, 1910. Russell charged that Murray was a former drunkard, a dope fiend, a blackguard, and an election thief. Russell accused Murray of lying so often that he was afraid to let a stenographer take down his speeches. He repeated the story that Murray tried to have the Confederate flag removed during the Altus parade and reported that "Cockleburr Bill" had threatened to have Kate Barnard rotten-egged if she appeared in Tishomingo.[71] As the campaign progressed, speeches of this type became more frequent.

The Murray strategy consisted of appeals to the rural voter and attacks on Cruce as a national banker and a friend of big business. Murray charged Cruce with dodging the issues and being insincere about the bank-guaranty law, which as a banker Cruce had opposed. He also criticized Cruce's stand in favor of woman suffrage.[72] While stating that he would beat Cruce by 20,000 votes, even if he lost the "electric-light towns" by a four-to-one margin, he eagerly campaigned in Enid, Muskogee, Guthrie, Shawnee, and other small cities. Local Murray clubs made arrangements for him to speak in theaters, courthouses, town squares, and parks. The large, enthusiastic crowds at the Murray appearances caused even Republican editors to suggest that he had the Democratic nomination "grabbed."[73]

The issues that gave Murray the most concern were the Jim Crow laws and the grandfather clause. That any voter could doubt that

[70] Political broadside, C. L. Daugherty Collection (Norman, University of Oklahoma Library, Division of Manuscripts) ; hereafter cited as Daugherty Coll., Univ. of Okla. Library; *Daily Ardmoreite*, June 30, 1910.

[71] *Oklahoma City Times*, July 22, 1910.

[72] Murray to T. P. Gore, Mar. 19, 1910; campaign card and political broadside; Murray Coll., OHS Library.

[73] *Muskogee Times-Democrat*, Apr. 14, May 3, 1910; *Enid Morning News*, May 25, 1910; *Johnston County Capital-Democrat*, May 26, 1910.

he favored the Jim Crow laws is difficult to understand, considering their swift passage by a legislature presided over by him and his close friend Henry S. Johnston. At the constitutional convention he had argued for leaving the proposals out of the constitution only because he feared Theodore Roosevelt would not approve the document if they were included. However, the grandfather clause was altogether a different situation, for Murray contended that this was not a real issue. At a time when Negro voting had become the political issue in the South and men like Cole Blease in South Carolina and James K. Vardaman in Mississippi were making careers out of Negro baiting, Murray declined to exploit racial passions in Oklahoma. In a speech at Enid on June 2, Murray said he was for the Jim Crow laws but refused to endorse the grandfather clause, saying he did not believe in making "the poor old darky part of the platform." In a statement to the press after the speech Murray also expressed fear that the proposed voting restriction would be used against white voters.[74] Since the proposed amendment specifically exempted even those voters who had lived in a foreign country and had voted for any government, his statement appeared to be an attempt to avoid the issue. The Cruce partisans continued to charge that Murray opposed all restrictions on Negroes, a charge he was forced to deny repeatedly. Fearing that he had taken an untenable stand, Alfalfa Bill changed positions in the middle of the campaign and endorsed the grandfather clause.[75] If, in switching his position, Murray was morally wrong, he was politically right, for the voters adopted the grandfather clause by a vote of 135,443 to 106,222.[76]

Murray sensed indifference among the voters during the campaign, and, confident of his abilities as an orator, he proposed a series of joint debates among the Democratic gubernatorial candidates. In an open letter he challenged Cruce, J. B. A. Robertson, and Leslie Ross to a series of joint appearances. Robertson later withdrew from the race, and Brant Kirk became the fourth par-

[74] *Enid Morning News,* June 2, 9, 1910.
[75] *Johnston County Capital-Democrat,* June 16, 1910; *Daily Ardmoreite,* July 3, 1910.
[76] Winters, *Directory of the State of Oklahoma,* 175.

95

ticipant. Debates were scheduled at Anadarko, Enid, Oklahoma City, Ada, and Durant during the first week of July. The meetings were to begin at 10:30 in the morning, and each candidate would be allowed to speak for one and one-half hours.[77] The political managers who made the arrangements must have had great faith in the voters to ask them to endure six hours of political speeches on a dry, hot, windy day in the middle of an Oklahoma summer. The poor attendance seems to indicate they had too much faith.

The first debate, forced upon the people of Anadarko, resulted in a Cruce victory before a sparse crowd of two hundred. Cruce used a Horatio Alger rags-to-riches theme to offset Murray's warnings against elevating bankers to political office. Kirk spoke only about enforcing the law forbidding the manufacture and sale of alcoholic beverages, while Ross attacked prohibition and the Haskell administration. Murray presented a résumé of his platform, and the campaigners moved on to their next appearance.[78]

The results of the other debates were similar to those of the first. At Enid no arrangements had been made and attendance was poor. None of the speakers engaged in personal attacks, though Murray accused Cruce of opposing the bank-guaranty law. Cruce struck out against the Torrens system and free textbooks for schools. The debate in Oklahoma City lasted just four hours, only five hundred people attended, and the only innovation was a vitriolic attack on Murray by Kirk. The final meetings were echoes of the first three. The debates were failures; they were well reported in the press but created little popular interest. The Murray forces vainly announced a series of victories, but it was obvious that their candidate had not gained from the exercise and may have actually lost ground.[79]

Murray's personal attacks on Cruce began to cause alarm among his supporters. He accused Cruce of charging exorbitant interest rates at his bank and called him "40% Cruce." The former banker labeled the charge a lie and offered to permit an examination of his

[77] *Review* (Muskogee), May 28, 1910; *Johnston County Capital-Democrat*, June 9, 1910.

[78] *Muskogee Times-Democrat*, July 6, 1910; *Daily Ardmoreite*, July 6, 1910.

[79] *Enid Morning News*, July 6, 7, 1910; *Daily Ardmoreite*, July 8, 1910; *Johnston County Capital-Democrat*, July 14, 1910.

bank's books. This accusation and others antagonized some newspaper editors, and the metropolitan press became even more hostile. Some of the small-town weeklies stayed with Murray because of his advocacy of agricultural and educational programs.[80] Murray, Cruce, and Kirk were all prohibitionists, but Murray received the endorsement of his old ally, the Anti-Saloon League, a strong organization in the state.[81] In the closing week of the campaign Murray sent out the former convention delegates and legislative members to defend his position on the grandfather clause and to organize the voters.[82] Newspaper advertisements described Murray as an "exponent and leader of the militant progressive democracy of Oklahoma," and a newspaper favoring him characterized the contestants as a "Rich man versus a Poor man."[83]

The voters made their choice on August 2, and Cruce won the nomination. The final returns showed that Cruce received 54,262 votes; Murray, 40,166; Ross, 26,792; and Kirk, 2,514.[84] The Murray "slate" did not fare well. Ellis ran next to last in the race for lieutenant governor; Graham, second for attorney general; and Lasater, third for insurance commissioner. Cross and Harrison won their races for auditor and secretary of state, but each had strong personal followings and organizations. Murray's main areas of support were Cimarron, Beaver, Alfalfa, Ellis, Garfield, Major, Noble, Payne, Logan, Lincoln, and Pawnee counties in the northern part of the state. He ran poorly in the entire southern third of the state, except for Haskell County and his home county, Johnston. The Cruce charges about the Jim Crow laws, the grandfather clause, and the Confederate-flag episode sharply reduced Murray's vote in the area. The counties where he ran best were settled mainly by farmers from Kansas, Nebraska, Iowa, and Missouri. His appeal was apparently greater among the middle western Bryan Demo-

[80] *Purcell Register*, July 29, 1910; *Muskogee Times-Democrat*, July 16, 1910; *Daily Ardmoreite*, July 20, 1910; *Pawhuska Journal*, July 21, 1910; *Davidson Record*, July 22, 1910.
[81] *Pauls Valley Democrat*, July 21, 1910.
[82] *Enid Morning News*, July 31, 1910.
[83] *Johnston County Capital-Democrat*, July 28, 1910.
[84] Winters, *Directory of the State of Oklahoma*, 114.

crats than among the southern Democrats seduced by Cruce's racist platform. In a letter of thanks to his supporters after the election, Murray claimed that he had been defeated by fraudulent returns, but this charge is highly improbable.

A bitter campaign, a stunning defeat, and accusations of fraud did not mean that Alfalfa Bill was discouraged or intended to bolt the party. To the 1910 Democratic state convention he declared, "Born in a November storm, cradled in the lap of adversity, chastened by hardships and poverty, I have neither been over-elated by success nor unduly depressed by defeat."[85] The Democratic state campaign committee recognized the need for his oratorical talents in the election campaign, for Cruce was locked in a bitter fight with Republican J. W. McNeal and Socialist J. T. Cumbie. Between October 14 and November 1 Murray made many speeches for Cruce, mainly in eastern Oklahoma.[86] In the general election the Democrats defeated the Republicans by a larger margin than that of 1907, but the Socialist vote increased to over 24,000 and Cruce won by only a plurality. Socialist strength was rising in the dry marginal farm areas of western Oklahoma and in the tenant-farm counties of southern Oklahoma.

Murray's first campaign for the governorship established a pattern that would be repeated in future years. The issues, organizations, campaign managers, and tactics would vary only slightly from the 1910 race. The defeat did not discourage Alfalfa Bill. Still a young man of forty-one, he looked ahead to the Presidential-election year of 1912 and contemplated a return to the state and national political arenas. His insatiable appetite for political leadership and recognition had only been whetted by his service in the constitutional conventions and in the legislature. Defeat did not cause him to falter in his quest for acclaim and acceptance. In fact, he now looked to the nation's capital as the place to enact and enlarge his agrarian program.

[85] Hines, *Alfalfa Bill*, 228.
[86] *Muskogee Times-Democrat*, Oct. 19, 1910.

✪

ALFALFA BILL GOES TO CONGRESS

V

Defeat in the gubernatorial primary of 1910 served only to fuel the fires of ambition which drove Bill Murray. Throughout his life he never allowed reversals of fortune to dampen his spirits, and the resiliency of his personality withstood the vagaries of the voters. After the unsuccessful race for the governorship, he retired to the farm in the bottom lands of Johnston County to rebuild his physical strength and financial position. Some political prognosticators suggested that Murray had been permanently retired from politics, but these men did not know the intense forces which drove Alfalfa Bill.

He continued to fight for his agrarian program, which was becoming a personal crusade. During the heat of the campaign for governor he had left the state to speak before the National Farmers' Union convention to proclaim the virtues of rural America and his plans to preserve the sanctity of the family farm.[1] His absolute devotion to his agrarian schemes brought him back to the political arena in 1912, to become a candidate for Congress and a vociferous supporter of Woodrow Wilson for President.

Alfalfa Bill had championed William Jennings Bryan because of the "Great Commoner's" concern for agriculture and the farmer. The reasons for his support of Woodrow Wilson in 1912 are less apparent. During his years at Princeton University, Wilson displayed little interest in farm problems. Yet Murray became one of his leading supporters in Oklahoma. In December, 1911, Alfalfa Bill endorsed Wilson as a "progressive, clean, able, and scholarly," and stated that he was the only candidate who could get the independent vote necessary to win the Presidency.[2] He would spend the

[1] *Chickasaw Capital*, May 12, 1910.
[2] *Shawnee Daily Herald*, July 6, 1912.

year 1912 working for Wilson's nomination and election, and for a seat in Congress for himself.

Murray joined a large number of southern agricultural leaders who supported Wilson, and the New Jersey Governor largely owed his nomination to them.[3] Alfalfa Bill and Senator Gore served as the Wilson leaders in Oklahoma. The triumvirate of Murray, Haskell, and Williams now divided sharply, for Haskell and Williams favored Speaker of the House Champ Clark of Missouri for President.[4] Senator Robert L. Owen and Representative Scott Ferris also supported Clark. Both sides tried to persuade the county Democratic conventions to endorse their candidate and send delegations to the state convention pledged to him.

Wilson-for-President clubs were organized in many of the cities and small towns to marshal support among the rank and file. The success of the campaign was demonstrated in a state-wide straw vote on February 14, which gave Wilson 13,103 votes, Bryan 7,569, Clark 4,881, and Judson Harmon 425.[5] When the county conventions met, Wilson was endorsed by thirty-three counties, Clark by only twenty.[6] Murray's home county, Johnston, favored Wilson and selected Alfalfa Bill as a delegate to the state convention.[7] Wilson showed surprising strength over the entire state, while the Clark supporters were centered primarily along the Missouri border. The opposing factions prepared to resolve the conflict at the state convention.

Gore and Ferris tried to prevent a floor fight at the convention in Oklahoma City by suggesting that the delegation be divided equally between Wilson and Clark, but this conciliatory effort failed. Murray led the Wilson forces on the convention floor and attempted to gain control of the convention committees.[8] He kept the Wilson men united during the proceedings, in which both sides claimed a

[3] The story of the Wilson preconvention campaign in the South is related in Arthur S. Link, "The South and the Democratic Campaign of 1912" (Doctoral thesis, University of North Carolina, 1945).

[4] *Daily Ardmoreite*, Feb. 16, 1912.

[5] *Daily Oklahoman* (Oklahoma City), Feb. 14, 1912.

[6] *Ibid.*, Feb. 12, 1912.

[7] *Johnston County Capital-Democrat*, Feb. 22, 1912.

[8] *Daily Ardmoreite*, Feb. 23, 1912.

majority. Fearing that further strife would lead to defeat in the general election, both groups finally agreed to a divided delegation, with each candidate to have 10 of the 20 votes.[9] Should either Wilson or Clark withdraw, the remaining candidate would receive all the votes. On the surface the wounds seemed to have healed, but Oklahoma Democrats remained severely divided. The primary election in August would reveal the depth of the scars from the state convention fight.

Alfalfa Bill received as much attention from the press at the national Democratic convention in Baltimore in 1912 as he had at Denver in 1908. In the lobby of the Emerson Hotel, wearing three day's growth of beard and puffing on a corncob pipe, he taught the bellboys to sing Wilson's campaign songs.[10] He tried to gain control of the delegation, but the presence of Williams, Ferris, Gore, Owen, Fred Branson, and Roy Hoffman among its members prevented anyone from dominating the group. He also wanted to serve on the resolutions committee, but was not selected.[11] Murray did become a member of the "general staff" of Wilson managers that met to map convention strategy.[12] However, it was on the convention floor that he rendered his greatest aid to the Wilson cause.

During the deliberations of the convention Murray became a conspicuous figure. He forced the Oklahoma delegation to be polled on the selection of the temporary chairman, and, although the Wilson candidate, William Jennings Bryan, was awarded all the Oklahoma votes, Bryan lost to Alton B. Parker.[13] The division within the Sooner delegation was made apparent when Gore seconded the nomination of Wilson and Ferris gave a speech for Clark. On the first nine ballots Oklahoma cast ten votes each for Wilson and Clark. The split in the Oklahoma delegation reflected the plight of the entire convention.

[9] *Johnston County Capital-Democrat*, Mar. 7, 1912; *Daily Oklahoman*, Feb. 24, 1912.

[10] *Muskogee Times-Democrat*, June 24, 25, 1912.

[11] Urey Woodson (comp.), *Democratic National Convention Proceedings, 1912* (Chicago, Peterson Linotyping Co., 1912), 112; *Muskogee Times-Democrat*, June 25, 1912.

[12] Link, "The South and the Democratic Campaign of 1912," 413.

[13] Woodson, *Democratic National Convention Proceedings, 1912*, 15–16.

The delegates were deadlocked between Clark and Wilson, and on the tenth ballot, when it appeared that the Missouri congressman was about to move ahead of the New Jersey Governor, Murray saved the day. On that ballot Charles Murphy, the political boss of New York, cast the state's ninety votes for Clark. This gave Clark over half of the convention votes and seemed to signal the beginning of a bandwagon drive for the nomination. As the states following New York were polled, each side watched for a break to Clark, but it never came. When the Sooner State was called, a delegate asked for a poll of the twenty men, as he had instructions to vote for Wilson first and Clark second and now it appeared that the convention was shifting to Clark. Murray immediately got the floor and electrified the delegates. Collarless, and wiping his face with a red bandanna, Alfalfa Bill bellowed and roared that he did not mind the delegation being polled, but "we do insist that we shall not join Tammany in making the nomination."[14] This reference to New York and its switch to Clark and the refusal of the Oklahomans to join the bandwagon brought on a Wilson demonstration that lasted for fifty-five minutes. When the uproar subsided, the Oklahoma delegation stood firm with ten votes for each of the major contenders. Murray and Gore held their men together through 146 ballots, when Alabama's Oscar Underwood switched his support to Wilson and gave him the two-thirds majority necessary to win the nomination.

Following Wilson's victory, Murray seconded the nomination of Governor John Burke of North Dakota for the vice-presidency. He praised Burke as a man capable of balancing the ticket for a "progressive Democracy."[15] Wilson, however, preferred Thomas Marshall, and he was nominated.

Murray's demonstration-provoking speech on the tenth ballot was credited by Wilson's secretary, Joseph Tumulty, with keeping Clark from getting the full benefit of the New York shift. According to Tumulty, Murray's statement stemmed the tide to Clark and

14 *Ibid.*, 219–20.
15 *Ibid.*, 378–79.

changed the whole complexion of the convention.[16] Ray Stannard
Baker, Wilson's biographer, praised Murray's effort to stop the
move to Clark and wrote, "Alfalfa Bill struck the keynote of the
hour."[17] The *Baltimore Sun*, in a feature article on Alfalfa Bill,
gave him credit for part of Wilson's success.[18] The Oklahoma
agrarian returned home believing that he had played a major role
in Wilson's nomination and was not unappreciative of the publicity
it had given him in his race for congressman.

The census of 1910 revealed that Oklahoma had a population
increase of such magnitude as to give the state three additional
congressmen. The legislature failed to redistrict in 1911, which
meant that the new congressmen would be elected at large in 1912.
The Democrats engaged in a free-for-all primary, with twenty-
eight candidates running for the three posts. Among the candidates
were Fred Branson, running as a Georgian and a defender of the
grandfather clause; Leslie G. Niblack, editor of the *Guthrie Daily
Leader*; J. B. A. Robertson, a Lincoln County politician; Leslie P.
Ross, a Murray opponent in 1910; Joe B. Thompson; and Claude
Weaver. Against this large field Murray made a strange campaign:
he did not give a single speech.

On May 9, 1912, he issued a statement in Tishomingo announcing his candidacy. He had neither time nor money to conduct a
major primary campaign, he said, and was running on his 1910
platform. In addition he advocated tariff reform, the direct election
of senators, and an extensive federal program of irrigation. He
asked his friends first to search out his name among the list of candidates and then to vote for two others. The Democrats would need
a strong ticket that fall, and Murray urged voters to consider this
factor when selecting congressional nominees.[19]

16 Joseph P. Tumulty, *Woodrow Wilson as I Knew Him* (Garden City, Double-
day, Page & Company, 1921), 119–20.

17 Ray Stannard Baker, *Woodrow Wilson Life and Letters, Governor 1910–1913*
(New York, Charles Scribner's Sons, 1931), 349.

18 *Sun* (Baltimore), June 30, 1912.

19 *Johnston County Capital-Democrat*, May 16, 1912; *Muskogee Times-Democrat*, May 11, 1912.

During the summer he wrote letters and mailed campaign cards but made no personal appearances other than at Medford, where he conferred with William Jennings Bryan, who was on a speaking tour.[20] Campaign letters, accompanied by sample ballots emphasizing the location of Murray's name, called him a "progressive candidate" whose nomination had been conceded by his opponents. The letter announced that he would spend fifteen to twenty days campaigning for Wilson in the fall but that he would not campaign before the primary.[21]

The results of the August 6 primary indicate that this campaign by mail was very effective. Murray led the field of candidates with 39,140 votes. J. B. Thompson was second with 31,887, and Claude Weaver was third with 26,923.[22] Murray's name was undoubtedly the best known, and the large field drastically divided the vote. He issued a letter thanking the voters for their support and stated that he had won "without making a canvass and without making a single speech for which I am profoundly grateful to the people."[23]

The split among the state Democratic leadership, evident in the spring, became more pronounced during the primary. Former Governor Haskell challenged Robert L. Owen for the Senate and was soundly beaten. Murray worked to defeat Haskell, blaming him for the loss of the gubernatorial nomination in 1910. The Murray-Haskell-Williams alliance had ended, though the three men continued to exert great individual influence within the party and the state government.

Murray's strong primary race returned him to the forefront of the party leadership. *Harlow's Weekly*, a political review published in Oklahoma City, contended that he would be a candidate for the governorship in 1914. At the state Democratic convention after the primary, the party organization, aware of his political appeal, urged him to campaign throughout the state to combat the rising strength of the Socialist party. It was apparent that the Sage of

[20] *Johnston County Capital-Democrat*, June 13, July 18, 1912.

[21] *Ibid.*, Aug. 1, 1912; Murray to Charles L. Daugherty, July 18, 1912, Daugherty Coll., Univ. of Okla. Library.

[22] Winters, *Directory of the State of Oklahoma*, 111.

[23] *Daily Ardmoreite*, Aug. 8, 1912.

Tishomingo depended on his personal political strength rather than on the party.[24] Always the loner in politics, he nevertheless answered the call.

From early September until the November election he campaigned for the Democratic nominees. He spoke in Socialist strongholds throughout the state, carrying the message of Wilson's "New Freedom." He wrote to Alice that it was one of the most extensive campaigns of his career. Toward the end of October he toured southern Oklahoma in an attempt to cut the Socialist vote.[25]

The division in the Republican party between the Bull Moose Progressives, led by Theodore Roosevelt, and the regular Republicans, led by President William Howard Taft, guaranteed Wilson's election. Oklahoma gave its electoral votes to the New Jersey Governor, and the Democratic party again swept the state. The Republicans were able to elect only two congressmen and a small minority in the state legislature. Murray led his two friends in the race for congressman-at-large, receiving 121,202 votes. The leading Republican in the race received only 87,409 votes, while each of the three Socialist candidates polled over 41,000 votes.[26] Indeed, the Socialists of Oklahoma polled a higher percentage of the vote than their counterparts in any other state. Though the Oklahoma Democrats were concerned about the six Socialists elected to the state legislature, they were also jubilant, for they had helped to elect the first Democratic President in twenty years.

Immediately after the election Murray rushed back to Tishomingo to be with his family. While out on the hustings he wrote to Alice expressing his hopes that the older boys were studying hard. He also asked about Jean and the baby, Watson Burbank, who had been born on May 15, 1911.[27] Like the other boys, the most recent addition had been named for heroes of his father's. The Watson probably reflected Murray's brief friendship with the Populist Tom Watson; after Murray and Watson took opposing views on

---

[24] *Harlow's Weekly*, Aug. 17, 31, 1912.

[25] *Ibid.*, Sept. 28, 1912; *Daily Ardmoreite*, Oct. 10, 1912; Murray to Alice Murray, Oct. 22, 1912, Murray Coll., Univ. of Okla. Library.

[26] Winters, *Directory of the State of Oklahoma*, 110.

[27] Murray to Alice Murray, Oct. 22, 1912, Murray Coll., Univ. of Okla. Library.

American entry into World War I, the name was dropped. There can be no doubt about the origin of Burbank, for until his death Alfalfa Bill was to praise the work of the California horticulturist. For almost three months, Murray stayed at Tishomingo, resting and preparing for his departure for the national Capital.

Like other newly elected Democrats, Murray was plagued by office seekers. On November 19 the congressman-elect issued an open letter concerning patronage. He stated that he would not attempt to interfere with senatorial or congressional patronage but would oppose appointments made only for political reasons. He asked his friends interested in positions to withhold requests until after March 4, 1913, for he had urgent personal business and could do nothing official until he was sworn into office. He felt that conflicts over federal jobs would be few and told those sending endorsements to indicate only that the applicants had good character, were competent, and came from upright families.[28] This idealistic approach to patronage problems came to an end rather quickly when Murray found he had few jobs to give, many applicants, and a large number of irritated constituents.

Before leaving for Washington, he could not resist the temptation to lecture Governor Lee Cruce and the legislature on their responsibilities. On January 6, 1913, he issued a statement to the press advising the legislature about the laws it should enact during the approaching session. Assuming the function of a governor, he called for thirteen new laws, including rotating district judgeships, increased funds for public schools, and blue-sky provisions. The legislature reacted adversely to these suggestions, and the Governor was extremely displeased by Murray's arrogance.[29]

In February he arrived in Washington to witness a scene of transformation as the Republican occupants, from those in the White House to the clerks in the departments, prepared to depart. There was little for a new congressman-elect to do, and Alfalfa Bill spent much of his time at the motion pictures. He stayed at the

[28] *Weekly Chieftain* (Vinita), Nov. 22, 1912; *Harlow's Weekly*, Nov. 23, 1912.
[29] *Johnston County Capital-Democrat*, Jan. 9, 1913; *Muskogee Times-Democrat*, Jan. 7, 1913.

New Fredonia Hotel with his wife's uncle, Chickasaw Governor Douglas Johnston.[30] On March 4 the new administration was sworn in, and he assumed office.

The first few months as a congressman were frustrating for Alfalfa Bill. He had imagined that as a new member of the Administration he would be warmly received and quickly assume a leading role. He was soon disappointed. Writing to Alice and the children, he complained about the weather, which was foggy and frigid, and about a nagging cold. What was worse, he was being ignored: "This is the hardest place to get anything done. I start out to see all of the Department heads. If I get to see one in a day I'm doing well."[31] Like the other new members of Congress, he and his staff were forced to spend most of their time on patronage matters. Hordes of office seekers came to see him, and his two stenographers were unable to carry on the business of his office. Part of the patronage problem was his own fault. He wrote to Alice that he was trying to get his brother John Shade a position at the Chilocco Indian school and brother George a job as a registrar in the land office.[32]

The congressman had enacted much of his agrarian program through the Oklahoma constitution and in the first legislature. Now he was determined to put agrarianism into the federal statutes. In the field of domestic legislation Murray, like most progressive Bryan Democrats, wanted laws providing a lower tariff, an income tax, a federal banking system, and regulation of the trusts. But he wanted these laws written so that their major purpose would be the preservation and extension of the family farm. Reduction of the tariff would lower the cost of goods farmers purchased. Federal control of banking could mean low-interest land loans to tenants who desired to purchase farms. An income tax would fall on wealthy urbanites and help equalize the heavy property taxes paid by farmers. The regulation of trusts could result in lower farm-machinery prices and the abolition of commodity exchanges. Murray sought to amend each piece of Wilson's New Freedom legislation to make

[30] Murray to Alice Murray, Feb. 25, 28, 1913, Murray Coll., Univ. of Okla. Library.
[31] Murray to Alice Murray, Mar. 17, 1913, Murray Coll., Univ. of Okla. Library.
[32] Murray to Alice Murray, July 6, 16, 1913, Murray Coll., Univ. of Okla. Library.

it part of his agrarian schemes. The test used by the Oklahoman was, "Is it good for the farmer?"

Alfalfa Bill, though a freshman congressman, refused to accept the role of a neophyte. When the House Democratic caucus convened, he spoke as though he were a veteran member.[33] He joined a distinguished group of young southerners in the House of Representatives. Among his colleagues were Sam Rayburn and Martin Dies of Texas, Cordell Hull of Tennessee, Carter Glass of Virginia, James Byrnes of South Carolina, Oscar Underwood of Alabama, and Alben Barkley of Kentucky. Barkley later wrote that Murray was a forceful, well-informed speaker who "usually received the close attention of the members of the House."[34] His fellow congressmen did not have to wait long to hear him, for he took the floor the first day of the first session.

Most freshmen congressmen wait for several months before they speak, but not Murray. As the House began to debate the adoption of the rules, he argued for the assignment of permanent seats and participated in a discussion of an intricate question of parliamentary procedure.[35] Although the House members were not assigned seats, by listening for a moment they could always discover the whereabouts of Oklahoma's mustached congressman-at-large. He became a member of three House committees: coinage, weights, and measures; pensions; and Indian affairs.[36] While he participated in the work of the Indian-affairs committee during the next few years, he would not contribute much to the other committees; he preferred to use the House floor as a forum.

Murray shared Wilson's desire to lower the tariff and heartily agreed with the President when he made tariff reduction the first important issue before Congress. The President appeared before a joint session on April 8 to ask for tariff revision and an income tax, and the proposal was presented to the House by Oscar Underwood.

[33] *St. Louis Globe-Democrat*, Mar. 16, 1913.
[34] Alben W. Barkley to David Clinton Ralph, Aug. 7, 1952, quoted in David Clinton Ralph, "The Public Speaking of William H. 'Alfalfa Bill' Murray" (Doctoral thesis, Northwestern University, 1953), 282.
[35] *Congressional Record*, 63 Cong., 1 sess., 1913, L, Pt. 1, 69, 72, 74.
[36] *Ibid.*, Pt. 2, 1871–72.

Murray wanted the tariff reduced on manufactured goods but favored a high tariff on agricultural products.[37] Many of those demanding protection for manufactured items argued that a lower tariff would force down American wages to compete with cheap foreign labor. During the debate Murray replied to this argument, contending that wages had little to do with the tariff but were based on "the cost of keep," or the cost of living. Wages were high in this country because of the labor unions, he said, and that was as it should be. He wanted protection for the farmer, not for the manufacturer.[38]

The Underwood Tariff Bill included an income-tax provision which Alfalfa Bill favored. During the debate on the income tax he voiced opposition to an amendment lowering the base income from $4,000 to $1,000 per year. He demanded a tax on surplus wealth, which, he claimed, had gone untaxed for fifty years. Men who were making only a decent wage should not pay this tax, which was a means of redistributing surplus wealth.[39] When the Underwood Tariff Bill came to a vote, he joined 280 other members in support of it.[40] Senate amendments were accepted by the House, and on October 3, 1913, President Wilson signed the act into law. Bill Murray, who had spent hours in the Democratic caucus arguing for tax relief for the farmers, was well pleased.

The President and the Oklahoma congressman were also in agreement on the need for a more centralized banking system and an elastic currency. The next phase of the New Freedom called for a federally controlled system of national banks. The President was not committed to either the centralized control advocated by his new Secretary of State, William Jennings Bryan, or the loose regulation advocated by Congressman Carter Glass.[41] Murray preferred the compromise secured by Senator Robert L. Owen, which became the Glass-Owen Bill. This measure created the Federal Reserve

[37] Murray, *Memoirs*, II, 185.
[38] *Congressional Record*, 63 Cong., 1 sess., 1913, L, Pt. 1, 795.
[39] *Ibid.*, Pt. 2, 1252.
[40] *Ibid.*, 1386–87.
[41] Arthur S. Link, *Wilson: The New Freedom* (Princeton, Princeton University Press, 1956), 199–240.

System with currency-issuing branches governed by a board appointed by the President. Murray felt that this bill needed amending, however, to protect the farmers and to give them the benefit of more currency and credit.

He became a member of a bloc of southern and western congressmen who opposed portions of the Federal Reserve Bill. Led by Texas Representative Robert L. Henry, they maintained the Populist hatred of "Wall Street" and, as followers of Bryan, railed against the "money trust." Murray took a leading role in the bloc's fight against appointment of bankers to the board and requirements for a fixed money supply. The bloc also wanted a provision prohibiting interlocking directorates among member banks. Murray felt that in its present form the proposal would concentrate the "money power" in the hands of a few financiers, and he adamantly opposed the appointment of bankers to the Federal Reserve Board. He attributed the whole concept to "Morgan men" in the Cabinet, Secretary of Treasury William McAdoo in particular.

Murray favored a decentralized Scotch-bank system which would be authorized to issue currency based not on gold or silver but on the products of the soil. The 10 per cent federal tax on state bank notes was the chief obstacle to his inflationary scheme, and he advocated repeal of this tax as he had in the 1890's.[42] The Scotch-bank system, based on agricultural banking developed in Scotland, smacked of the earlier Populist subtreasury plan which Murray had opposed. However, on September 16, 1913, he told the House that he would vote for the Glass-Owen Bill, but only because he was bound by the Democratic caucus. The bill, he declared, was better for agriculturists than it was when it was first presented because of a number of amendments which congressmen from Oklahoma, Texas, Georgia, Arkansas, Kansas, Mississippi, and Missouri had forced Glass to accept. The President had been given absolute control of the banking system, claimed Murray, and now banks would enter the realm of Presidential politics to influence appointments to the Federal Reserve Board. He wanted all fifteen reserve districts represented on the board, and his amendment to limit the appoint-

[42] Murray, *Memoirs*, II, 186–200; Hines, *Alfalfa Bill*, 234–41.

ment of only one member from each district had been accepted by the caucus. His principal objections to the bill were the absence of any provision for agricultural credit, and guaranteed bank deposits along the lines of the Oklahoma bank-guaranty law. He closed his lengthy speech with a quotation from poet Thomas Moore:

> I feel like one
> Who treads alone
> Some banquet-hall deserted,
> Whose lights are fled,
> Whose garlands dead,
> And all but he departed![43]

After apologizing to Wilson for opposing the Glass-Owen Bill, Murray voted to recommit the measure. When this move failed, he joined the majority and voted for passage.[44]

Murray was given a second chance to amend the Federal Reserve Bill when it was returned to the House by the Senate with several amendments. One of the Senate amendments provided for limited rural credits for the farmers, and he took the lead in an attempt to gain House approval of the change. Carter Glass vigorously fought the amendment, which was defeated by urban legislators. Murray failed to win House approval for an amendment forbidding congressmen, senators, or federal bank directors from serving on the Reserve Board. He finally agreed to the conference report on the bill, and cast his vote for the Federal Reserve Act.[45] This initial defeat did not end his attempts to provide the farmers with low-interest federal loans, an integral part of his agrarian program.

Legislative matters relating to Oklahoma also received his attention. The only major committee work in which he participated was on the Indian-affairs commitee. He sought to obtain the release of tribal funds held by the Department of the Interior for the Chickasaws and Choctaws. He expressed his views on the Indian problem in a speech at the Lake Mohonk Indian Conference in October, 1913. The speech concerned restrictions placed on the Indians with

[43] *Congressional Record*, 63 Cong., 1 sess., 1913, L, Pt. 5, 5020–23.
[44] *Ibid.*, 5128–29.
[45] *Ibid.*, 2 sess., 1913, LI, Pt. 2, 1307, 1314, 1464.

regard to the disposition of their properties. The government restricted the sale of lands by some Indians but not by others, fearing
that the less well educated Indian would be cheated. Murray proposed that all restrictions on adults of less than three-fourths Indian
blood be removed, that the sale of estates of Indian minors should
be forbidden, and that all remaining tribal property should be sold.
His proposals were intended to end graft in the management and
sale of Indian property.[46] The sale of these lands would also make
additional farm properties available to Oklahoma tenant farmers.

He approved of some progressive social reforms, although his
views were shaped by his rural background. He presented his ideas
in a speech entitled "The Trinity of Evils," delivered at the national
convention of the Anti-Saloon League in 1913. In the same way
that slavery had been an evil and had to be eradicated by national
action, liquor was also an evil, according to Murray, and he urged
a national prohibition amendment. The three basic evils in his
"trinity" were intemperance, gambling, and sexual debauchery.
In his opinion, the stock exchange represented gambling at its
worst and should be eliminated. He felt that immigrants were un-
justly blamed for the mounting crime rate and concluded: "The
foreigner in general among us does not constitute the evil. It is that
class coming by the 'contract system,' which having in view nothing
but cheap labor and in order to secure this cheap labor, makes contracts through agencies scattered all over continental Europe . . . ."[47]
Eventually, however, he came to advocate restrictions on immigration.

The question of patronage continued to haunt the Oklahoma
congressman. After March 4, 1913, he received a deluge of requests
for offices, postmasterships, and political favors. A congressman-at-
large was in the peculiar situation of having not a district but a
whole state, and yet he received nothing like the patronage available to a senator. Some rural newspapers bitterly criticized him for
failing to obtain federal appointments. The editor of the *Mangum
Weekly Star* denounced the congressman for having said that he

[46] *Ibid.*, 1 sess., 1913, L, Pt. 7, 424–25.
[47] *Ibid.*, 467–69.

would not handle post-office patronage, and added sarcastically that the Post Office Department was probably better off. According to that paper, Murray's admission that he had no patronage meant a black future for him politically.[48] F. W. Cameron, editor of the *Review* of Chandler, wrote to Secretary of State Bryan asking him to try to end the patronage squabble in Oklahoma.[49]

Although the Secretary of State could do little for Alfalfa Bill, President Wilson attempted to aid him by writing members of the Cabinet on his behalf. Wilson informed Attorney General James C. McReynolds that he had consulted with Senator Owen and Murray concerning the position of United States marshal in Oklahoma and that it would be a grave political mistake not to appoint their choice.[50] Wilson wrote Postmaster General Albert S. Burleson:

> Representative Murray of Oklahoma was in to see me yesterday. I like this man very much. He was a faithful and militant friend of mine, and very effective besides, in the pre-nomination contest in Oklahoma, and we have so far, apparently, not taken his advice in anything. I feel it all the more my duty therefore, to hand on to you what he said to me yesterday.[51]

Murray, wrote Wilson, asked only to be allowed to name the postmaster for Stillwater. Wilson's letters eased the patronage problem for the Oklahoman and strengthened his hand in future dealings with the Postmaster General. During the next three years Murray continued to try to find employment in the federal government for his friends and relatives.

In the summer of 1913, Congressman Murray entered into a field in which he had very little knowledge but many intemperate opinions—foreign affairs. The most serious foreign-relations problem faced by the Wilson administration at this time was the internal

---

[48] *Mangum Weekly Star*, June 26, July 3, 17, 1913.

[49] F. W. Cameron to William Jennings Bryan, June 23, 1913, William Jennings Bryan Collection (Washington, D.C., Library of Congress). Hereafter cited as Bryan Coll., Library of Congress.

[50] Wilson to James C. McReynolds, June 4, 1913, Woodrow Wilson Collection, Series VI, Box 301, Oklahoma (Washington, D.C., Library of Congress). Hereafter cited as Wilson Coll., Library of Congress.

[51] Wilson to Albert S. Burleson, Sept. 26, 1913, Wilson Coll., Library of Congress, Series VI, Box 301, Oklahoma.

chaos in Mexico. Wilson and Secretary of State Bryan wanted to see the military dictatorship of Victoriano Huerta replaced by a constitutional government. When civil war broke out in Mexico, Wilson and Bryan decided to declare an arms embargo, hoping that the Huerta government would fall. Alfalfa Bill created an embarrassing problem for Wilson and Bryan when, on July 22, 1913, he introduced in the House a concurrent resolution calling for the protection of American citizens in Mexico and authorizing the President to interfere in Mexican affairs for that purpose.[52] The resolution to subdue Mexico, by force if necessary, included lengthy "whereas" clauses telling of deplorable conditions in that country. Later Senator Albert Fall of New Mexico and Murray introduced almost identical resolutions authorizing the President to send the Army across the Rio Grande. Murray strongly denounced the Huerta regime at a time when Wilson and Bryan were trying to avoid debate on Mexico.[53]

Wilson's policy of "watchful waiting" received another jolt when Murray again precipitated discussions of Mexican affairs. When a bill to provide relief to destitute Americans in Mexico came before the House, the Oklahoman took the floor to demand that the United States protect American lives and property. He had no financial interests in Mexico, he said, but the United States was obligated to protect its citizens. While he did not want war, the historical position of the United States dictated a strong move, he claimed, and quoted party-platform statements from 1832 to 1912 to support his view. The arms embargo on Mexico aided Huerta, said Murray, and, while he agreed with Wilson that the dictator must be removed, the embargo policy was wrong.[54] The embargo was, in fact, helping Huerta, but Wilson had no other choice. The House approved the relief appropriation, but the Administration's policy had received a thorough flailing.[55]

Continued civil war in Mexico and the inactivity of the United

[52] *Congressional Record*, 63 Cong. 1 sess., 1913, L, Pt. 3, 2627.
[53] *Mangum Weekly Star*, Aug. 7, 1913.
[54] *Congressional Record*, 63 Cong., 1 sess., 1913, L, Pt. 5, 4257–60, 4280–81.
[55] *New York Times*, Sept. 5, 1913.

States government prompted Murray to issue another statement on the protection of Americans. He proposed an active and "constructive" Mexican policy. The United States should seize all Mexican customs houses on the border and the Navy should take over the major ports. This action would cut off arms and money to both Huerta and the Constitutionalists, led by Venustiano Carranza. The congressman's agrarianism led him to argue that the United States should forbid Mexico to give large land grants to non-Mexicans and should insist on the partition and sale of large estates to anyone except Negroes and orientals. This suggestion revealed his boundless faith in the small, landowning farmer. In an imperialistic tirade he added that if the Mexican people were permitted to vote on the question of annexation perhaps the United States could expand to Panama. The speech ended in a burst of Fourth of July oratory: "O! Flag of our Country, wave on, wave ever!"[56]

Murray's proposals were predicated on the misconceptions that a small army could conquer Mexico and that Japan was the real menace in that country. He had no training, firsthand knowledge, or any other preparation to engage in debate on Mexico. All that he said was based upon rural jingoism, as old in American history as that of the war hawks of the War of 1812.

Murray's opposition to portions of the New Freedom program apparently did not alienate Wilson, the Administration leaders, or his colleagues in the House. Alfalfa Bill visited the Bryans at their home and was asked to dinner by the Champ Clarks, though he waited to accept the latter invitation until Alice arrived from Tishomingo during the second session. Wilson also sent several personal invitations to the Murrays to call at the White House in the spring of 1914.[57] His colleagues in the House occasionally enjoyed a laugh at Murray's expense. During a discussion of agricultural products a congressman asked Representative Charles Carter of Oklahoma if his district did not produce alfalfa and corn. Carter replied, "Yes;

[56] *Ibid.*, Nov. 8, 1913; *Congressional Record*, 63 Cong., 1 sess., 1913, L, Pt. 7, 432–41.
[57] Murray to Alice Murray, Apr. 9, June 22, 1913; White House invitations, Murray Coll., Univ. of Okla. Library.

we do. And we raise not only alfalfa, but we also raise alfalfa statesmen." The obvious reference to Murray broke up the decorum of the chamber.[58]

Despite all of his furious and ofttimes misdirected activity, the congressman expressed great loneliness and missed his family. He wrote them long letters telling of the people he had met and the places he had been. His devotion to the children and their love for him were expressed in the trinkets, post cards, and clothes he sent them and in their printed thank-you notes enclosed in Alice's letters. He sent the older boys watches, Jean some toy ducks, and Burbank a top. He instructed Alice in detail about the care and feeding of the children; he prescribed the hours they were to read at night, and when the children became ill with whooping cough, he admonished her to use the best home remedies. Fearful that they might neglect their lessons, he cautioned Alice to "keep the boys 'keyed' up to their studies." One of the older boys wrote him that "Mama is getting fat," an unlikely statement since she had several hundred acres of land to oversee and five small children to care for.

Alice constantly pleaded with her husband to come home soon, for she was also lonely. There was no extra money to spend, and Murray urged her to keep the expenses down. He was short of funds throughout 1913, often borrowing from Governor Johnston. When it appeared that Congress might adjourn in July, Alfalfa Bill asked Alice if she would like to go to Panama on a congressional junket. Apparently he wanted to take his father, too, but decided not to do so because of his antagonism toward his stepmother. He wrote Alice: "I'm writing to Pa. I would not suggest his coming as that old huzzy will be down too and it will be a bit of trouble to get rid of her and it would raise talk if we made her go." The session did not end, and the trip was canceled.[59] Finally, in August, he returned briefly to Oklahoma to be with his family and to mend fences.

Murray returned to Washington before the adjournment of the

[58] *Congressional Record*, 63 Cong., 1 sess., 1913, L, Pt. 5, 4511.
[59] Murray to Alice Murray, Alice Murray to Murray, letters of February–July, 1913, Murray Coll., Univ. of Okla. Library.

extraordinary session, which ended only two days before the regular session opened on December 1. The second meeting of the Sixty-third Congress failed to produce the same avalanche of progressive legislation passed by the first session. Only the debates over the Federal Trade Commission and the Clayton Antitrust bills were of major significance. The Wilson New Freedom program was beginning to lose momentum amid a recession at home and war abroad.

Only ten days after the session opened, Murray delivered a speech on agricultural education, a subject in which he had long been interested. He spoke during debate on the Smith-Lever Bill for agricultural-extension education. He called for expansion of agricultural and mechanical education. Using Biblical stories and analogies, he stated that the white race knew less about agriculture than any other race. He contended that there were two basic kinds of education, classical and industrial, and it was the latter that needed federal aid. He edified the members of the House by relating his efforts for agricultural education at the Sequoyah and Oklahoma constitutional conventions. Vocational agriculture was a means to increase production, lower the cost of living, create better farmers, and improve marketing methods, he said, but too often the farmers themselves had opposed agricultural education. He planned to vote for the Smith-Lever Bill, but wanted to add an amendment to provide for district junior agricultural schools such as he had established in Oklahoma. Using the University of Oklahoma as an example, he said that state universities opposed agriculture and that graduates of agricultural and mechanical colleges often refused to return to the farm. Therefore, he believed that the only answer was a federal system of two-year vocational colleges. He concluded, "I have learned that men will take a cold, a cussing, or a rail off your fence; indeed, anything, except your good advice." The American farmer, complained Murray, knew more about every other man's business than he did about his own. The entire speech extolled agriculture, but one phrase, repeated throughout his life, gives the key to his thinking: "Civilization begins and ends with the plow."[60] Although his speech received praise from men in and

[60] *Congressional Record*, 63 Cong., 2 sess., 1913, LI, Pt. 1, 713–29.

out of Congress, his amendment was not accepted. Neither his animosity toward the University of Oklahoma nor his desire for agricultural education would diminish in the future.

In his declining years Murray would come to believe that the most important speeches he delivered in Congress were those concerned with Mexico.[61] He argued throughout 1913 and 1914 that Wilson's Mexican policy was wrong, and he generally followed Senator Albert Fall of New Mexico on foreign affairs, for he thought Fall was the best mind on the subject. He wrote in his memoirs that Senator Fall took the blame for the whole Cabinet in the Teapot Dome scandal of the 1920's. He knew Fall as an able senator who had made him welcome in the Fall home when he arrived in Washington. Fall, a gregarious rancher, was Murray's close friend for four years, and the congressman remembered him as honest, patriotic, learned, and courageous, a man who would have made an ideal Secretary of State.[62] Fall's connections with major oil companies which had concessions in Mexico probably prompted his views, which Murray echoed before the House. The Senator's outgoing manner and bellicose speeches on Mexico attracted Murray, who perhaps envied Fall's position in the Senate. Echoing Fall's position, Alfalfa Bill gave a speech on "Mexico and [the] Asiatic Menace." He resurrected his resolution of July 22, 1913, calling for American intervention in Mexico, saying that subsequent events had proved its validity. He claimed that the greatest danger in Mexico was from the Japanese, and he wanted the United States to give the Philippines to Japan and then acquire Mexico. The return to constitutional government in the latter country ultimately silenced jingoists like Murray.[63] He had not contributed to the solution of the Mexican problem and had managed to irritate the President and Bryan. Again the congressman had entered into an issue without doing his homework.

Another phase of American foreign affairs into which Murray entered, uninvited and uninformed, was the Panama Canal tolls

[61] Murray, *Memoirs*, II, 172.
[62] *Ibid.*, 214, 218–21.
[63] *Congressional Record*, 63 Cong., 2 sess., 1914, LI, Pt. 17, 263–66.

controversy. Wilson had proposed repeal of the law exempting United States coastwise ships from paying canal tolls. Great Britain was perturbed by the law, and the President made repeal a matter of personal prestige. Murray joined Speaker Clark and other Democratic representatives who opposed the Administration on this issue. The Oklahoman spoke at length on the question, returning to his position of 1891, which maintained that part of the American tradition was freedom of the sea, which meant free passage through the canal. Further, he claimed that the law strengthened the merchant marine, aided southern ports, and kept down railroad rates.[64] When Wilson began to pressure the rebellion leaders, Alfalfa Bill took the floor and declared that the President should not use the issue to attack members of his own party, for many good Democrats opposed the bill. The Republicans loudly applauded his attack on the measure, but it was passed.[65]

Murray continued his independent position on other issues. His concern for personal liberties and constitutional guarantees prompted him to take part in the drafting of the Jones Bill, an organic act for the Philippine Islands. Congressman William A. Jones of Virginia presented a bill providing for an all-Filipino government and eventual independence for the islands. Jones accepted Murray's amendments forbidding primogeniture and guaranteeing that private property could not be taken for public use without just compensation. The most important amendment Murray offered forbade any religious test for the exercise of political and civil rights or the use of public money for sectarian institutions. The Oklahoman feared that the Filipinos would be limited in the exercise of civil liberties because of the strength of the Roman Catholic church in the islands. The House approved the amendment and passed the entire measure.[66]

Murray and the President parted company on the issue of restricting immigration. Congress passed a bill limiting the flow of aliens by the use of a literacy test, but Wilson, like Presidents Taft

[64] *Ibid.*, 266–70.
[65] *New York Times*, Mar. 28, 1914.
[66] *Congressional Record*, 63 Cong., 2 sess., 1914, LI, Pt. 16, 16089–90, 16127–231.

and Cleveland before him, vetoed the bill. In January, 1914, the House debated the measure, and Murray offered an amendment to liberalize the bill by allowing immigration officials to admit immigrants who were suffering from religious persecution or discrimination without requiring them to take the literacy test. He argued that the United States must provide an asylum for religious groups of all creeds. For example, Jewish immigration had contributed to American commerce and prosperity, said Murray, and their religion was based upon the betterment of mankind. Therefore, he proclaimed, "I am for the Jew as an immigrant to this country." His statement was applauded, but his amendment was rejected by a vote of 73 to 89, and Murray voted for the measure which passed the House.[67] Later in his life he would oppose all immigration and come to view the Jewish people as part of an "international Communist conspiracy."

Murray's positions on domestic legislation were always designed to aid the farmer. During the second session a bill providing for rural post roads was debated, and the farmer from Twelve Mile Prairie advocated federal aid to the states for road building. He did not want money for interstate highways; a man who never owned a car, he believed such highways were unnecessary. Federal grants were necessary for mail and farm-to-market roads, but it would be a waste to build "peacock boulevards" for automobile tourists.[68]

As a member of the Indian-affairs committee, he spent untold hours working on behalf of the Oklahoma Indians. In the committee and on the floor of the House he called for equality for the Indians and the protection of their property. Some of his speeches concentrated on Indian achievements and were for home consumption, but others summarized the historical aspects of Indian claims to funds held by the Department of the Interior. He prepared committee reports calling for federal aid to improve Indian lands by the construction of drainage ditches. Many tribes were attempting to have the commissioner of Indian affairs distribute to their members the funds held in trust by the department of the Interior, and

[67] *Ibid.*, Pt. 3, 2660–715.
[68] *Ibid.*, 3089–90.

he introduced bills and reports to further these claims. He advocated giving all tribal funds to the members to end the entire question of grants, claims, and rolls.[69] No doubt he was strongly influenced by Governor Johnston on these issues.

One of the important facets of the New Freedom yet to be enacted was Wilson's proposal to restore competition in business. Alfalfa Bill had never had a good word for big business and throughout his career had attacked the trusts. He jumped gleefully into the debates on the Clayton Antitrust Bill and the Federal Trade Commission Bill. The Wilson administration was divided about whether the trusts should be regulated or destroyed or whether both policies should be pursued. Wilson favored Louis Brandeis' plan for a new antitrust bill to define the meaning of "restraint of trade." Representative Henry Clayton presented a bill to the House embodying Wilson's beliefs. While the Clayton Bill listed unfair trade practices and established rules for business, a second measure was introduced which provided for the creation of a trade commission to investigate and regulate business. The House began a long harangue over these proposals.

Murray took an active interest in the Clayton Bill and presented a series of amendments which he hoped would aid farmers and laborers. One of the points of the debate concerned the removal of labor unions from the antitrust provisions, which Murray favored, and he led the fight to exempt farm co-operatives as well. His amendment to exclude co-operatives was defeated, as was his proposal to lower from $2,500,000 to $1,000,000 the amount of capital stock which placed a business under the interlocking-directorate portion of the bill.[70] A speech he delivered the same day revealed the depth of disagreement among Democrats over the Clayton Bill. He said that in the coming congressional election his opponents might charge him with "getting off the Bryan bandwagon, quitting the Tumulty train, and [walking] out of the President's patronage pantry," but he favored excluding labor unions and farm co-

[69] *Ibid.*, Pt. 4, 3301–304; Pt. 17, 202–204, 374–91; U.S. Congress, House Committee on Indian Affairs, *Drainage for Indian Allotments*, 63 Cong., 2 sess., H.R. No. 294 (Feb. 20, 1914) ; *Congressional Record*, 63 Cong., 2 sess., 1914, LI, Pt. 17, 705–707.
[70] *Ibid.*, Pt. 10, 9481–84.

operatives from the bill. Parts of the measure were vicious, he claimed, such as the provision forbidding co-operatives from withholding products from market.[71] Through his efforts and those of other representatives, the House later approved amendments to the Clayton Bill which removed labor unions and farm co-operatives from many of its sections. Once again Murray had parted company with the Administration, though he would vote for passage of the measure.

The Oklahoma congressman supported the Trade Commission Bill, but he wanted to give the commission greater powers. He offered an amendment to authorize the commission to send all information gathered on the railroads to the Interstate Commerce Commission and the state railroad commissions. The idea was to make the Federal Trade Commission a clearinghouse of factual data. The amendment was rejected. Another Murray amendment provided that all business reports to the commission must be made under oath, corporations must submit lists of the names and addresses of all stock or bond owners, and corporate books and records must be opened to the commission. He argued that this information must be made available to aid in the prosecution of trusts and monopolies, for the only way to stop the growth of socialism was to get control of the corporations. He claimed that the lower federal courts could not be depended upon to work with the commission and, in fact, would probably hinder its work. Of these courts Murray said, "I have the utmost faith in the Supreme Court, but I have no more faith in many of the inferior Federal courts than I have in a common 'nigger,' and I want to say to you the only way to stop this howl against the courts is to take away that jurisdiction on corporations and give it to the Supreme Court, where the Constitution intended it to be."[72] The Murray proposals were rejected, but when the Trade Commission Bill came up for final passage, he voted for it.

None of the New Freedom measures presented by Wilson were specifically directed toward solving the needs of the farmers of the

[71] *Ibid.*, Pt. 17, 543–45.
[72] *Ibid.*, Pt. 9, 8973–94.

country. The farm problem became acute in the fall of 1914, when the prices of cotton and tobacco dropped drastically. Southern congressmen worked valiantly to get federal aid for agriculture as the prices of some crops fell below the cost of production. One proposed remedy was a program of guaranteed farm loans, or rural credit. When this proposal came before the House Democratic caucus in July, Murray urged postponement of a vote until a more propitious time, but the worsening of the price decline made it necessary to enact the proposal that fall.[73] Representatives of the cotton and tobacco states met on October 9 to formulate a program, and Murray was elected chairman of a resolutions committee. [74]

The strategy committee for the cotton-tobacco bloc prepared an agricultural-relief bill. This measure authorized the Secretary of the Treasury to issue $250,000,000 in bonds or to sell the same amount of Panama Canal bonds. The money derived from the sale of the securities would be deposited in the banks of the cotton and tobacco states, and the banks would then lend the money to farmers at a rate of 4 per cent or less. Murray served on the committee which formulated the bill.[75]

He delivered a lengthy address to the House on October 19, entitled "Cotton Crisis—Its Remedy, Both Temporary and Permanent." He said that the crisis was a product of the European war and that the Farmers' Union had demanded federal action on the problem when its representatives discussed the matter with the cotton-tobacco bloc. He had worked with Representatives Carl Hayden of Arizona, Kenneth McKeller of Tennessee, Alben Barkley of Kentucky, Tom Heflin of Alabama, and others to write the $250,000,000 bond-issue bill, and this was the answer to the need for credit in the rural South. Farm tenancy was a by-product of the existing credit system, and he argued that if the federal government aided other areas of the economy, why not the southern farmer?

73 Carter Glass to D. C. Pryor, July 9, 1914, Claude Weaver Collection (Norman, University of Oklahoma Library, Division of Manuscripts). Hereafter cited as Weaver Coll., Univ. of Okla. Library.

74 *Tishomingo Leader*, Oct. 16, 1914.

75 Arthur S. Link, *Wilson: The Struggle for Neutrality* (Princeton, Princeton University Press, 1960), 93–104.

He wanted to ensure a maximum interest rate of 4 per cent on the money to be made available.[76] President Wilson opposed all these emergency measures, and the bill was defeated. Murray's efforts for the inflationary scheme were partly influenced by the rising tide of protest in Oklahoma in the election year of 1914.

Alfalfa Bill did not have the same advantage in the 1914 election that he had had in 1912, for the state legislature had redistricted the state, eliminating the at-large congressional seats. A new plan of eight districts had been adopted, and his home county, Johnston, together with Pontotoc, Coal, Hughes, Seminole, Pottawatomie, Lincoln, Okfuskee, and Creek counties formed the new Fourth Congressional District. In late 1913 a concerted effort had been made to organize opposition to him, and Senator Reuben Roddie of Ada and Charles Barrett and H. H. Smith of Shawnee were among his opponents in the primary election.[77] Despite personal financial difficulties in the spring Murray decided to run for re-election in the Fourth District. A hot primary campaign ensued.[78]

From March to July his opponents campaigned strenuously in the district, while he was forced to remain in Washington. Murray had able opponents in Roddie, a member of the legislature, and Barrett, a former state senator and secretary of the State Board of Agriculture. Both men staged active campaigns and criticized him for failing to support President Wilson, especially on the Panama-tolls question. Roddie attacked Murray as a "squaw man" working in Congress to save the salary of his wife's uncle, Governor Johnston. By the end of July Roddie had delivered seventy-two speeches, most of them attacking Murray for his "anti-Administration record." He charged that the congressman had opposed the Federal Reserve and rural-credits bills and wanted war with Mexico.[79] As the session continued into the summer, Murray was forced to an-

[76] *Congressional Record*, 63 Cong., 2 sess., 1914, LI, Pt. 17, 1189–96; Pt. 16, 16867–92.

[77] *Harlow's Weekly*, Nov. 15, 1913.

[78] Murray to Kirk Gilstrap, Mar. 10, 1914, Murray Coll., OHS Library.

[79] *Harlow's Weekly*, Apr. 4, 1914; *Ada Weekly News*, Apr. 7, July 23, 1914; *Chandler Tribune*, May 14, June 11, 1914; *Tishomingo Leader*, June 19, 1914; *Shawnee Daily News-Herald*, June 30, 1914; *Bristow Record*, July 3, 1914.

swer these charges from Washington. He used the *Congressional Record* to respond to his opponents. He rose on a point of personal privilege on April 8, to defend himself against charges printed in the *Dallas Morning News*. According to that paper, he had been condemned at a mass meeting in Okmulgee for opposing Wilson on repeal of the Panama tolls, and the *Ada Weekly News* had called him an ally of the "shipping trust" on the same issue. Murray declared that he would not be the "rubber stamp" of any president and that, while he had opposed Wilson on interlocking directorates in the Federal Reserve, rural credits, bank-deposit guaranties, and certain tariff schedules, his opposition was a matter of personal integrity.[80]

One thing Alfalfa Bill learned in Washington was how to make the most of press releases and how to reverse charges made by his opposition. When his opponents accused him of mixing Negro and white tenants on his land and cheating both, he issued a pamphlet signed by his tenants, all of whom were white. The tenants praised their landlord for the new corncribs and barns he had built and for helping them build a local school. Murray also distributed a number of press releases on "the congressional game" and his role in Congress. A supporter, C. C. Galloway, secured a statement from Speaker Clark in which he said that not only was Murray regarded as one of the most able of the new members but also he was capable, industrious, and faithful to his duties. The statement found its way to the press for public consumption.[81]

A family story about the Murrays came out of Washington, where Alice and the children had joined the congressman. Murray told some fellow members in the House cloakroom that he had his sons selling newspapers to give them work experience. In fact, he said, one son earned fifty-nine cents in a single evening. When one of the listeners asked him if the boy put the money in a bank, he replied, "Hell, no, he spent thirty cents of it for ice cream and I

[80] *Congressional Record*, 63 Cong., 2 sess., 1914, LI, Pt. 7, 6401–402.
[81] "Murray's Tenants Defend Him," pamphlet, Murray Coll., Univ. of Okla. Library; *Shawnee Daily News-Herald*, June 9, 1914; Champ Clark to C. C. Galloway, June 19, 1914, Murray Coll., OHS Library; *Tishomingo Leader*, June 27, 1914.

borrowed the balance."[82] It was homely stories like this that helped him establish empathy with his constituents.

Traveling by car, Murray toured his district in the July Oklahoma heat, going from town to town, speaking in parks and at courthouses. He played up his activities in Washington and "imminent" legislation to explain his long absence from the district. Large crowds turned out for his two-hour speeches, in which he explained his votes on the tariff, the Federal Reserve, Mexico, and rural credits. He claimed that he and Representative Sam Rayburn of Texas were the only new men in the House who were able to get legislation approved. To charges of absenteeism Alfalfa Bill replied that he had responded to 188 of the 214 House roll calls, the best record of the six Democratic congressmen from Oklahoma.[83] Two days before the primary a news release from Washington revealed that the Dunbar Chautauqua Bureau had asked him to appear on the circuit with a guarantee of $85.00 for each speech. The story, with a large picture, hit the front pages at a most opportune moment. By means of such free publicity he was able to report a total campaign expenditure of only $491.70.[84]

Murray led the field in the Fourth Congressional District race, receiving 5,150 votes to 4,425 for H. H. Smith, who ran a surprising second. Barrett received only 1,811 votes, and Roddie 4,070.[85] Smith asked for a recount of the ballots, charging that Murray had won by fraud. The recount was denied, and the congressman quickly returned to Washington to work on the cotton problem.[86]

Gubernatorial nominee Robert L. Williams and the entire Democratic ticket in Oklahoma were running scared in 1914, but not Murray. The size of the Socialist vote in 1912 haunted the Democrats, and it appeared that the third party was much stronger in the Third, Seventh and Murray's own Fourth Congressional Dis-

[82] *Muskogee Times-Democrat*, June 25, 1914.

[83] *Bristow Record*, June 26, 1914; *Tishomingo Leader*, July 3, 1914; *Shawnee Daily News-Herald*, July 17, 22, 1914; political pamphlet, July 7, 1914, Murray Coll., OHS Library.

[84] *Shawnee Daily News-Herald*, Aug. 2, 1914; *Harlow's Weekly*, Aug. 8, 1914.

[85] Winters, *Directory of the State of Oklahoma*, 107.

[86] *Tishomingo Leader*, Sept. 18, 1914.

tricts. Williams wrote him in August for suggestions to be included in the state platform, and the congressman urged Williams to avoid details, to support the President by name, to praise the tariff and the Federal Reserve, and to call for rural-credits legislation.[87] However, as the campaign progressed, Williams and the other party leaders panicked at the apparent success of Republican John Fields's canvass and the growing Socialist strength. Williams wrote Murray a terse letter asking him to get a leave from Champ Clark and return to Oklahoma at once. When the congressman failed to reply, Williams wrote again, begging him to help in the campaign. Alfalfa Bill did not return and indifferently sent a $50.00 contribution to Democratic headquarters.[88] After Congress adjourned, he stayed in Washington for a while and then, at the request of the White House, went to New Jersey to campaign for Congressman Walsh of Wilson's home district.[89] The election returns in November indicate that Williams had reason for fright and that Murray had been almost too complacent.

In the Fourth District Murray received 13,758 votes; James Dennis Flynn, the Republican, 9,415; and Marion Hughes, the Socialist nominee, 9,198. Williams won by a margin of less than 5,000 votes over Fields; Fred Holt, the Socialist candidate for governor, held the balance of power with 52,703 votes. In the Third District and the Seventh District the Socialist congressional candidates polled more ballots than the Republican nominees.[90] Some historians have seen the national results of 1914 as a conservative protest against the New Freedom, but Oklahoma voters apparently felt that the program had not gone far enough.

The triumphant congressman accomplished very little during the lame-duck session of the Sixty-third Congress, which met from December 7, 1914, to March 4, 1915. The war in Europe, which had begun in August, 1914, led to discussions of submarine warfare, neutrality, preparedness, and armed shipping, but Wilson

[87] Robert L. Williams to Murray, Aug. 24, 1914; Murray to Williams, Aug. 26, 1914; Murray Coll., Univ. of Okla. Library.

[88] Williams to Murray Sept. 25, Oct. 4, 1914, Murray Coll., OHS Library.

[89] *Chandler Tribune*, Oct. 1, 1914; *Shawnee Daily News-Herald*, Oct. 27, 1914.

[90] Winters, *Directory of the State of Oklahoma*, 104–105.

delayed action on these matters until the fall of 1915. Many of the issues debated were mere extensions of the arguments of the second session.

Murray and the southern bloc attempted again to pass the rural-credits measure, but the bill was defeated, 80 to 237, with most of the votes for the bill coming from men like Barkley, Byrnes, Rayburn, McKeller, Henry, and Murray.[91] Alfalfa Bill addressed the Farmers' Union convention in Washington in January, 1915, and advocated an independent rural-credits program, to be controlled by the farmers. To him, it was "better fifty years of rural credits than a whole century of tenant agriculture."[92] However, Congress adjourned without providing aid to the farmers.

During the summer the congressman became a star performer on the Chautauqua circuit. He spoke fifty times in Wisconsin, Indiana, Ohio, and Iowa, earning $4,250 in sixty-four days. Wearing a linen duster, he went from town to town displaying his colorful oratory with his address "The Philosophy of the Plow." Old Chautauquans remember him as the champion coffee drinker on the circuit; he kept a pot of hot coffee on a table beside him, straining the black liquid through his mustache and a wad of tobacco. The Dunbar Chautauqua Bureau knew a rural crowd pleaser, and Murray did not let the people down. He was the hit of the tour, which was extended to the Southwest.[93]

He spent the fall in Tishomingo before returning to Washington for the opening of the Sixty-fourth Congress in December, 1915. He could look back upon the last three years with great satisfaction. His election to Congress in 1912 and re-election in 1914 had given him a solid place in Oklahoma politics. The three sessions of Congress revealed his total commitment to the southern bloc and their efforts to aid rural America. Murray voted for nearly all of Wilson's New Freedom proposals, balking only on the Panama tolls measure,

[91] *Congressional Record*, 63 Cong., 3 sess., 1914, LII, Pt. 1, 29–30.

[92] *Ibid.*, 64 Cong., 2 sess., 1917, LIV, Pt. 6, 290–91.

[93] *Harlow's Weekly*, Feb. 6, 1915; Murray, *Memoirs*, II, 379–80; Harry P. Harrison and Karl Detzer, *Culture under Canvas* (New York, Hastings House, Publishers, 1958), 232; Harry Dunbar to Murray, Apr. 23, 1915, Murray Coll., OHS Library; undated newspaper clipping, Murray Coll., Univ. of Okla. Library.

and his name should be included among the progressive members of the Democratic party in Congress. His position on foreign affairs, particularly with regard to Mexico, showed his streak of jingoism and flag-waving patriotism. In the next Congress Murray would no longer be an opponent of President Wilson's foreign policy but one of his most vocal supporters on the issues of preparedness and intervention. No major piece of legislation carried his name, but the farmers of Oklahoma felt that Murray's agrarian philosophy was an answer to their problems. However, when he began to devote all his time to the preparedness issue, the voters would reject him.

MURRAY AND THE PREPAREDNESS ISSUE

VI

In the fall of 1915, as he looked forward to his second term in Congress, the representative from the Fourth District had no idea that the next three years would bring his most devastating political defeats. After surmounting many obstacles, he faced the world with great confidence. Alice and the children had moved to Washington, and the family resided at 1464 Monroe Street, Northwest, in a comfortable if unpretentious home. The Murray family spent many happy hours in and around the Capital, and those hours were fondly remembered by the children as well as by their parents. There were times, even after they were all living in the national Capital, when the family was separated. Murray was often away on speaking engagements. In the fall of 1915 Alice wrote to her husband, who was at Ames, Iowa, on a Chautauqua tour, that she was eager for him to hurry home: "The old boys are alright. Their old ma gets the benefit of all their deviltry."[1]

When Bill Murray was at home, the boys had fewer opportunities for deviltry. Bill and Alice did little entertaining, and most of their activities centered around their children. The older boys had paper routes and belonged to a boy-scout troop, and on Saturday mornings the congressman would take the children in turn to the House floor, where they met their father's colleagues. During warm weather they would go to a swimming pool near the present Lincoln Memorial, and there they learned to swim. It was a great treat for the older boys when their father allowed them to swim in the Potomac River. There were, of course, more serious moments, such as the time little Burbank started a fire in the linen closet.

Any man as dedicated as Alfalfa Bill to the cause of public

[1] Alice Murray to Murray, Aug. 16, 1915, Murray Coll., Univ. of Okla. Library.

130

education would be deeply concerned about the education of his own children. The congressman had become an avid book collector, and the Murray home was full of books. The children read recent publications, as well as books long out of print, which their father purchased at Lowdermilk's bookstore. They could find on their shelves such works as Washington Irving's biography of George Washington, William H. Prescott's histories of the Spanish conquistadors, Theodore Roosevelt's travel adventures on the Amazon, and the works of Thomas Malthus and John Stuart Mill. The children were constantly urged to achieve their highest potential in school, and Murray was able to motivate them to study hard.

He practiced his pet educational theories on the children. He told them that the study of geometry was extremely valuable in exercising the mind. One of his favorite teaching devices was a geometric problem. For example, to help the children understand logic, he would take them outside, draw a circle in the dirt with a stick, and ask them to prove that a triangle always has 180 degrees in the sum of its angles. Each child was given a chance to prove the theorem and explain his deductions.

Now that Alice and the children were in Washington, the congressman had no direct contact with his tenants in Johnston County. He sent them detailed instructions by mail. The letters and the clauses in the tenants' leases directed their daily activities and their farming methods. He insisted that all plowing had to follow the contour of the earth to prevent erosion and that only selected seeds were to be planted. Particular fertilizers were prescribed for certain crops, and the best tools and machinery were furnished. At one time eighteen families worked Murray's lands, and he provided each of them with a sturdy home of solid oak. The Murray tenants were loyal to him, and he benefited from the ever-increasing production through larger rent payments.[2] The war in Europe had brought higher prices for farm commodities, and the owner and his tenants made substantial profits. Despite his use of tenants, Alfalfa Bill continued to work for federal legislation to help tenant farmers purchase land of their own.

[2] Johnston Murray, interview of Dec. 29, 1965; Burbank Murray, interview of Feb. 10, 1966.

Murray attended the opening-day ceremony of the Sixty-fourth Congress on December 6, 1915, and began to push for a preparedness program and for rural credits. President Wilson, facing a serious contest for re-election in 1916, hoped to use this legislative session to create a new political coalition. He could, perhaps, ensure a Democratic victory if he could avoid the question of war in Europe by standing for armed neutrality and at the same time enact additional reforms. Reversing his previous opposition, Wilson now called for a rural-credit law, abolition of child labor, woman suffrage, and additional regulatory agencies. Congress gave Wilson these measures but divided sharply on his diplomacy. Murray stood with the President on both his domestic program and his foreign policy.

The day after the session opened, Murray wrote Governor Robert L. Williams that he intended to devote full time to national issues and was withdrawing from Oklahoma affairs.[3] Alfalfa Bill had become deeply interested in the European war. Thirty years later he wrote in his *Memoirs* that he had been granted access by Secretary of State Bryan to the State Department "secret archives" in 1913. In the archives he claimed that he had discovered that war would break out the following year, 1914,[4] though this statement is open to serious question. During a series of speeches in Oklahoma in 1915 he urged a greater preparedness effort. According to the congressman, German submarine warfare was destroying American ships and threatening American neutrality. He rejoiced that United States merchant ships had been armed and given permission to return German fire. Many of Murray's political allies in the West and South had joined Bryan in opposing armed neutrality and the preparedness program. Bryan had resigned from the Cabinet on June 8, 1915, because of Wilson's strong stand against Germany when the *Lusitania* was sunk. Oklahomans generally supported Bryan's position rather than that of their Fourth District representative. For example, a petition from the small western Oklahoma town of

[3] Murray to Robert L. Williams, Dec. 7, 1915, Murray Coll., Univ. of Okla. Library.
[4] Murray, *Memoirs*, II, 210–11.

Weatherford, signed by more than one hundred farmers, was sent to Bryan congratulating him on his resignation. The farmers were antiwar, arguing that the United States had to remain absolutely neutral and refuse to sell munitions to all countries.[5] Murray rejected this view, and, according to correspondent J. W. Flenner, he was the only congressman from Oklahoma who "declared that he will probably swallow the administration's preparedness program, hook, line and sinker."[6]

Some Oklahomans favored Murray's endorsement of the President's preparedness program. Henry S. Johnston wrote him that the United States must teach patriotism and begin to build up its defenses.[7] Several county Democratic conventions in Murray's district endorsed his stand on the issue and commended his loyalty to the Administration.[8] The metropolitan press of Oklahoma, usually opposed to him, also supported Murray's position.

On March 25, 1916, Murray delivered an address to the House attacking the opponents of preparedness. He charged that the pacifists' hope of perpetual peace was impossible and that none of the great world religions gave substance to this hope. He praised efforts for disarmament, arbitration, and commissions of inquiry in international disputes but disavowed the idea of a world court; a world court could not end selfishness and greed, the causes of wars. The congressman attacked the concept of the "brotherhood of man," claiming that it was simply another way of saying "mongrelization." Southern states like Oklahoma had laws to prevent miscegenation because, contended Murray, the fourth generations of mixed parentage were sterile. He had formed this fallacious idea from reading the works of Luther Burbank. He argued that the United States should stay armed but neutral and remain out of any alliances leading to a "Federation of the World."[9]

In another House speech, on April 5, he repeated and expanded

[5] Petition from George W. Cornell to William Jennings Bryan, June 14, 1915, Bryan Coll., Library of Congress.

[6] *Muskogee Times-Democrat*, Jan. 3, 1916.

[7] Henry S. Johnston to Murray, Feb. 4, 1916, Johnston Coll., Univ. of Okla. Library.

[8] *Chandler Tribune*, Apr. 6, 1916.

[9] *Congressional Record*, 64 Cong., 1 sess., 1916, LIII, Pt. 14, 636–40.

his views. Speaking on "Adequate Preparedness," Murray said he did not fear either the loss of votes or political defeat on the question but did fear for the future of the country if a preparedness program was not enacted. For every nation self-defense was both right and a duty, though preparedness did not mean a large standing army or compulsory military service, he contended, only an increase in the size of the National Guard. Alfalfa Bill advocated enlistment of volunteers for the Army and a naval building program to be conducted in federally owned naval yards.[10] Murray and others in and out of Congress were making every effort to convince the nation of the need to prepare for war.

There was growing interest in the formation of a league of nations to serve as a parliament of the world to debate, arbitrate, and limit international strife. Murray opposed this idea. Such an organization would be controlled by nonwhites and non-Christians, he argued, and would mean the end of American sovereignty and of immigration-restriction laws. Even the Carnegie peace foundation was a dangerous threat to the white race, proclaimed the congressman.[11] This was one of the few times Murray used racism to bolster his position on a significant issue.

Although President Wilson disagreed with Murray about the proposed world organization, he doubtless welcomed Murray's vote against the McLemore resolution on March 7, 1916. In their respective chambers Representative Jeff McLemore of Texas and Senator Thomas P. Gore of Oklahoma introduced resolutions requesting the President to warn all Americans not to travel on armed merchant ships. Wilson opposed the resolutions as discourteous to Great Britain and other friendly countries.[12] Moreover, the President felt that Americans had the right to travel on armed merchant ships regardless of German threats. On March 7 Murray and 181 other Democrats followed the lead of the President, and the resolution was tabled by a vote of 276 to 142.[13]

The Oklahoma Democratic convention met in Oklahoma City

[10] *Ibid.*, 698–714.   [11] *Ibid.*, Pt. 3, 2407–408.

[12] Arthur S. Link, *Wilson: Confusions and Crises, 1915–1916* (Princeton, Princeton University Press, 1964), 167–70.

[13] *Congressional Record*, 64 Cong., 1 sess., 1916, LIII, Pt. 4, 3720.

in April, 1916, and Murray appeared for two main reasons: to praise Wilson's preparedness program and to get himself elected as a delegate to the Democratic national convention.[14] At the state convention he received a tremendous reception; the crowd began calling him to the platform before he was scheduled to speak. He acknowledged the cheers and left the stage, but continuing applause brought him back to make a speech on preparedness which one reporter said "simply sizzled with good, old-fashioned patriotism."[15] The delegates were obviously surprised and dismayed by Murray's total commitment to Wilson's foreign policy; they hissed and booed his remarks, marring the otherwise harmonious meeting. The angry congressman denounced those who had hissed him as a "bunch of mollycoddles and pacifists."[16] The delegates calmed down the next day and elected him a delegate-at-large to the convention. Henry S. Johnston wrote Murray to explain that the delegates had been very restless and that he and others felt the speech was splendid.[17]

As war tension mounted, nationalist groups in the United States began to support their native countries. Recognizing this fragmentation of the public, Murray spoke to the House on June 28 and declared, "I am neutral." Though a Scotsman at heart, he said, he was an American first, and, though Germany had a great civilization, that country must be defeated. He asked that all naturalized citizens put American needs first, even though they sympathized with their former homelands.[18] This speech displeased the large German, Czech, Slovakian, and Bohemian populations in the northern counties of his district and would deprive Murray of their support in the coming election.

Murray also supported Wilson's domestic program by voting for the child-labor bill and for the Adamson Act, which gave railroad workers the eight-hour day.[19] During the debate on a Puerto Rican

---

[14] *Muskogee Times Democrat*, Mar. 27, 1916.
[15] *Daily Oklahoman*, Apr. 12, 13, 1916.
[16] *Muskogee Daily Phoenix*, Aug. 8, 1918; *Ada Weekly News*, Apr. 13, 1916.
[17] Johnston to Murray, Apr. 26, 1916, Johnston Coll., Univ. of Okla. Library.
[18] *Congressional Record*, 64 Cong., 1 sess., 1916, LIII, Pt. 15, 1290–91.
[19] *Ibid.*, Pt. 2, 2035, Pt. 13, 13608.

government bill, Murray offered a number of amendments, most of which were of a minor nature. Two of these amendments were similar to those he proposed for the Jones Bill of 1914; one prohibited religious tests, and the other provided for just compensation when private property was taken by the government. The amendments were defeated when other congressmen pointed out that the provisions were already included in the bill.[20] Again and again the congressman from the Fourth District failed to do his homework and hindered the progress of the House with irrelevant obstructions.

News that Wilson had recognized the need for long-term credits for farmers elated Murray. Since 1913 he had been a member of the congressional bloc which had worked to enact a rural-credits program of federally supported long-term farm loans at low interest rates. As has been seen, until 1916 Wilson opposed any form of federal loans to farmers, but now no one doubted the need for farm credit; the question was how the federal government should provide for it. The Rural Credits Bill introduced in the Sixty-fourth Congress differed from those which had been proposed in the Sixty-third. Instead of provisions for floating government bonds and lending the money to banks to be passed on to farmers, the new plan created the Federal Farm Loan Board to govern twelve Federal Land Banks. The Land Banks were to sell tax-exempt bonds and use the proceeds for loans to farm-credit co-operatives established by the farmers. When Senator Henry Hollis of New Hampshire and Representative A. F. Lever of South Carolina showed their proposed bill to Wilson, he approved it immediately.[21]

Murray also championed the Rural Credits Bill but maintained that it had to be expanded. When the House met in the Committee of the Whole to discuss the measure, he introduced an amendment to aid tenant farmers. The amendment authorized farm-home cooperatives to be formed by families who owned no real estate and who had incomes of less than $1,000 per year. Each family would be authorized to borrow as much as $2,000 to purchase land, paying only 10 per cent down, and the balance would be covered by a loan

20 *Ibid.*, Pt. 8, 7493, Pt. 9, 8413–15.
21 Link, *Wilson: Confusions and Crises*, 345–50.

136

from the Federal Land Banks. Murray argued that the bill as it stood did not aid tenants; the homeless needed help, and, although this might be "paternal" legislation and "government aid," he was for it. The Oklahoma agrarian said he had supported aid to tenants during the past three years, and this bill would solve the problem, for even the "poor old darkey" needed to own a farm. In his opinion the 53,000 Socialist votes cast in Oklahoma in 1914 could be explained in terms of the tenant problem. His amendment, though supported by other southern congressmen, was defeated by a vote of 56 to 23.[22] The amendment had merit, and during the 1930's similar plans would be proposed by agencies trying to solve the dilemma of the southern tenant farmer. When the Hollis Bill came to a vote, it passed, 295 to 10, and Murray was among those voting for it.

His concern with tenancy in Oklahoma and the Socialist vote reflected the increasing size of both. Murray's congressional district alone contained 18,227 tenant families. In January, 1916, he introduced a new homestead bill to divide the remaining federal domain into tracts of 640 acres, to be sold at a low price to tenant farmers. There was enough land for 570,000 farms, Murray claimed. He summed up his agrarian philosophy in one sentence, "In my opinion the ultimate object of every law, both State and National, should be the building and the protection of American homes by the American citizen."[23] His analysis of the political ramifications of tenancy was correct, for in Oklahoma the Socialist party was strongest in the counties with high rates of tenancy.[24]

Criticism of Murray's support of the new homestead bill caused him to make a second speech on the subject. He refuted charges leveled against his proposal by the *Johnstown Democrat* of Pennsylvania and by the *Public*, a Chicago single-tax newspaper. In replying to the former, Murray contended that the original Homestead Act had not created tenancy, as the paper claimed, and to the latter he said that the single-tax plan was not fair to the farmers.

[22] *Congressional Record*, 64 Cong., 1 sess., 1916, LIII, Pt. 8, 7884–87.
[23] *Ibid.*, Pt. 14, 184.
[24] Donald Kenneth Pickens, "The Principles and Program of Oklahoma Socialism, 1900–1918" (Master's thesis, University of Oklahoma, 1957), 72.

Though he had vivid recollections of Henry George and his followers, who advocated a single tax on land, Alfalfa Bill favored a severely graduated land tax which could be used to break up large landholdings. After a long pseudohistorical account of the development of agriculture, Murray concluded with his favorite theme, "Civilization begins and ends with the plow."[25]

Again in an attempt to aid the farmer, Murray introduced two bills in the House to prohibit use of the mails by the stock and agricultural exchanges. These measures were designed to restrict the exchanges in their dealings in farm commodities and futures. He had long advocated laws to prevent gambling in agricultural products, and his opposition to the exchanges stemmed from his activities in the Farmers' Alliance and the Farmers' Union, both of which had sought their abolition. However, his proposals were never brought out of committee.[26]

Despite the gravity of the farm situation, Murray and Representatives Thomas and Barkley of Kentucky contributed a note of humor to the proceedings. During a rather tedious discussion of the declining tobacco market, Murray launched into a windy speech entitled "Tobacco, America's Civilizer," and when he yielded to a question, he was forced to agree that Americans were substituting "chewing the rag" for chewing tobacco. At this point Barkley spoke up:

> MR. BARKLEY. I want to find out what the gentleman's peculiar stimulant is.
> MR. MURRAY. My stimulant, sir, is tobacco smoked in the form of a cigar or in a pipe.
> MR. THOMAS. Why Mr. Chairman I have given him [Murray], since I have been here, at least $40 worth of chewing tobacco of the kind I now hold in my hand, because he will not buy a cent's worth.

Murray admitted that he borrowed chewing tobacco from Thomas and asked if his supply was now cut off. Thomas replied that either it had to be cut off or he had to have a salary increase.[27] This ex-

[25] *Congressional Record*, 64 Cong., 1 sess., 1916, LIII, Pt. 4, 3332–36.
[26] *Ibid.*, Pt. 3, 2919, 3109.　　　　　　[27] *Ibid.*, Pt. 4, 3860–61.

change reflected Murray's friendly relations with his colleagues as well as his tendency to bombastic oratory.

Murray continued to work hard for Oklahoma Indians through the Indian-affairs committee. He prepared reports on Creek oil lands and recommendations for more equitable division of the proceeds among the tribe's members.[28] Another report advocated allowing the United States Court of Claims to settle the case of Mansfield, McMurray, and Cornish versus the Choctaw and Chickasaw nations, which had long been the subject of bitter controversy. It was charged that the law firm had received unreasonable fees in cases involving the Indian-owned coal lands.[29] Murray successfully amended a bill dealing with the Five Civilized Tribes so that government funds could not be given to any sectarian group or institution. He opposed as wholly unrealistic that part of the bill which restricted child labor among the tribes. Children needed to work to develop character, he said, and described his sons' experiences selling newspapers in Washington. He opposed allowing children to work at jobs injurious to their health but offered an amendment to allow children under sixteen to work. The amendment was defeated.[30] When he introduced a bill to reimburse Douglas H. Johnston for expenses incurred during his tenure as Governor of the Chickasaws, Murray was returning favors granted to him by Johnston in the period from 1899 to 1905.[31] His efforts for the Indians were recognized six years after he left Congress, when he received a letter from Charles H. Burke, commissioner of Indian affairs in the Department of the Interior. Burke wrote: "My only regret is that you are not a member of the Oklahoma delegation in the congress. I have never hesitated to say that you were one man from that state that in season, and out of season, stood for legislation that would protect the Indians."[32] During his two congressional

28 U.S. Congress, House Committee on Indian Affairs, *Creek Nation Unallotted Lands*, 64 Cong., 1 sess., H.R. No. 868 (June 28, 1916).

29 U.S. Congress, House Committee on Indian Affairs, *Claims against the Choctaw and Chickasaw Nations*, 64 Cong., 1 sess., H.R. No. 658 (May 9, 1916).

30 *Congressional Record*, 64 Cong., 1 sess., 1916, LIII, Pt. 9, 8423.

31 *Ibid.*, Pt. 4, 3222.

32 Office of the Commissioner of Indian Affairs to Murray, Mar. 24, 1923, Murray Coll., OHS Library.

terms Murray worked arduously to help his Indian constituents in their struggles against fraud and greed.

On June 8 Murray asked for and received unanimous consent to deliver a five-minute speech. He astounded the House by launching an attack on Chief Justice Charles Evans Hughes. Hughes had been widely mentioned as the potential Republican Presidential nominee in 1916. Murray claimed that Hughes should resign or disclaim any intention of running for public office. He added further that a federal judge with life tenure and a fixed salary should not be on the bench if he was a candidate for any office; the judiciary was not a training school for politics. The House Republican minority responded quickly to this disparagement of Hughes, and the *New York Times* called the speech intemperate and ill-timed.[33] Undoubtedly Murray was warming up for his primary-election battle against Judge Tom D. McKeown, who was simultaneously a member of the bench and a candidate for Congress.

The following week Murray attended the Democratic national convention in St. Louis. The Oklahoma Democratic convention had made him a delegate-at-large with one-half vote but did not place him on the resolutions committee as he had requested. The meeting lacked the excitement of the Baltimore convention of 1912, for it was a foregone conclusion that Wilson would be renominated. Murray's only activity at the convention was to introduce a minor resolution.[34]

If the convention was marked by dullness, Murray's re-election campaign was just the opposite. The primary campaign in the Fourth District pitted Alfalfa Bill against two strong opponents, H. H. Smith of Shawnee, runner-up in the 1914 race, and Judge McKeown of Ada. By the first of April the two challengers were on the stump against the congressman.[35] As the race developed, Murray sized up his opposition and concluded that Smith probably had the Socialist vote and would run second while McKeown would

[33] *Congressional Record*, 64 Cong., 1 sess., 1916, LIII, Pt. 9, 9357–58; *New York Times*, June 9, 1916.

[34] *Official Report of the Proceedings of the Democratic National Convention Held in Saint Louis, Missouri* (Chicago, Democratic National Committee, 1916), 108.

[35] *Harlow's Weekly*, Apr. 1, 1916.

run third.[36] Murray's fear of the Socialist vote was well founded, for in his home county the registration figures showed 1,722 Democrats, 845 Socialists, and 672 Republicans. Equally important was the role played by Governor Robert L. Williams in the campaign. It was common knowledge in the Fourth District that Judge McKeown had entered the race at the urging of Williams and had the support of the Governor's wing of the party. By mid-May Murray realized that he was in danger of losing.[37]

The Governor and Murray had been on cordial terms as late as December, 1915, but by May, 1916, they were exchanging acrimonious letters and venting their feelings in the press. Murray and some of his supporters set out to prove that a former judge did not make a good executive or legislator. Though the charge was aimed at McKeown, it angered Williams, also a former judge. Through Williams' efforts Murray was kept off the platform committee at the Democratic national convention.[38] Murray's charges that McKeown was the Williams candidate were hotly denied by the Governor, but the congressman repeated the accusation and added that Williams had fought his election as a national-convention delegate.[39] The Governor continued to deny both charges, but the state press generally agreed that Murray was correct and that the Williams administration was trying to defeat him.

McKeown campaigned for an enlarged rural-credits program and for limitations on military spending. He attacked Murray's position on retaining some restrictions on payments to Indians, saying that all controls should be removed. When local officials of various counties began endorsing McKeown, the editor of the *Ada Weekly News* declared that the judge was ahead in the race.[40]

The other leading candidate, H. H. Smith, made demagogic appeals to various voting blocs in the district. In large newspaper

36 Murray to Claude Weaver, Feb. 26, 1916, Weaver Coll., Univ. of Okla. Library.

37 *Johnston County Capital-Democrat*, May 11, 1916.

38 Dale and Morrison, *Pioneer Judge*, 252.

39 Williams to Murray, May 18, 1916; Murray to Williams, May 23, 1916; Murray Coll., OHS Library; Williams to Murray, June 1, 1916, Murray Coll., Univ. of Okla. Library.

40 *Chandler Tribune*, May 18, 27, 1916; *Shawnee Daily News-Herald*, July 9, 1916; *Ada Weekly News*, July 27, 1916.

advertisements he declared that the Indians should be given all of their money immediately, without restrictions. He utterly opposed the preparedness program, stating that $750,000,000 for defense was idiotic; instead, he said, $250,000,000 should be spent on farm roads. Campaigning with a musical group, Smith said that if he was elected he would get Shawnee a new federal court building.[41] Both Smith and McKeown rightly sensed that the people of the district were antiwar and antipreparedness.

Across the nation the Democratic party was generally avoiding the issues of war and preparedness and stressing peace and prosperity. Murray refused to follow this tactic, arguing that the country must arm whether to maintain its neutrality or to prepare for eventual entry into the war. He made an extensive tour of the district in July, speaking on preparedness, rural credits, and foreign affairs. He called for McKeown and Smith to take meaningful stands on preparedness, saying that he stood by President Wilson and his program.[42] Addressing attentive crowds in the July heat, he said that McKeown lacked the temperament to be a congressman, though he was a good judge on the bench. Murray stressed his own seniority in the House and his close ties to Wilson, claiming that the President had wanted him on the resolutions committee at the Democratic national convention to ensure a strong preparedness plank. At the conclusion of his speeches Murray usually spent all of the question period defending his position on preparedness.[43]

In an open letter to his constituents Murray stressed the progressive legislation passed by Congress since March, 1913. He boasted of his record in support of the Underwood Tariff, the Clayton Antitrust Act, the Smith-Lever Act, the Child Welfare Bureau, the Rural Credits Act, and immigration restriction.[44] W. P. French, Murray's congressional secretary, wrote a widely published letter describing the congressman's committee work and his parliamentary successes on the floor of the House.[45]

[41] *Johnston County Capital-Democrat*, June 15, 22, 29, July 13, 1916.
[42] *Shawnee Daily News-Herald*, July 12, 1916.
[43] *Ibid.*, July 30, 1916.
[44] *Ibid.*, July 13, 1916.
[45] "An Old Neighbor's Estimate of Congressman Murray," June 1, 1916, Murray Coll., Univ. of Okla. Library.

The main issue, however, was preparedness, not Murray's record. Murray could not overcome the intense feeling in the district against this program.[46]

Throughout most of the state the Democratic primary was regarded with apathy by the voters. What interest there was focused on the Fourth District race, where all three candidates were campaigning at breakneck speed. When the returns were tallied on August 1, McKeown won the nomination. He received 5,682 votes to Murray's 5,403, Smith's 4,079, and Earl Powers' 279.[47] Murray claimed that illegal ballots and false returns in Okfuskee and Seminole counties had defeated him, but a recount failed to alter the results. Murray then announced his support of McKeown in the general election.[48] The state press agreed that Murray's stand on preparedness had caused his defeat.[49]

Murray returned to Washington after the primary, working in his office until Congress reconvened. On December 4, 1916, the lame-duck session of the Sixty-fourth Congress assembled. Meeting from December, 1916, until March, 1917, Congress accomplished little in the area of domestic legislation, for, as America's entry into the European war drew closer, all eyes were focused on foreign affairs. The Sixty-fourth Congress adjourned on March 4, and the Sixty-fifth assembled on April 2, to vote for war with Germany. Ironically, McKeown's first vote was for war, and Alfalfa Bill praised this action by the man who had defeated him.

Murray showed little interest in the work of the second session. Discouraged by his defeat, he resigned from his committees and did not enter into the foreign-affairs debates.[50] When the Indian appropriations bill came up for consideration, he did take the floor to advocate better treatment of the Indians. They were making better progress without government supervision, he claimed, and

[46] An example of the antipreparedness feeling is a petition to Murray from the International Association of Machinists, Choctaw Lodge No. 155, Shawnee, Oklahoma, Murray Coll., OHS Library.

[47] Winters, *Directory of the State of Oklahoma,* 102.

[48] Murray, *Memoirs,* II, 224–25; *Johnston County Capital-Democrat,* Aug. 10, 1916.

[49] *Muskogee Times-Democrat,* Aug. 3, 1916.

[50] *Congressional Record,* 64 Cong., 2 sess., 1917, LIV, Pt. 3, 2213; Pt. 4, 3909.

the government really had no Indian policy.[51] He secured an appropriation of $50,000 for the construction of two dormitories for the Chickasaws at Murray College in Tishomingo.[52] The appropriation blocked efforts by some Oklahoma legislators to close the college. The state had earlier closed two of the agricultural colleges, and Murray felt that this action was another way Governor Williams was attacking him.

On February 1, 1917, he introduced a curious piece of legislation concerning cumulative voting. Always an opponent of woman suffrage, he had been concerned with the growing strength of those who advocated giving women the right to vote. He also disliked the Supreme Court ruling which had declared Oklahoma's grandfather clause unconstitutional. He proposed a constitutional amendment which would give a married man two votes and a third vote if he had two or more dependent children. All voters with an eighth-grade education would receive an additional vote, as would veterans. The states were to classify and register voters, and no citizen would be denied the franchise because of sex, place of origin, religion, race, or previous servitude. The amendment would solve the problem of the Negro voter in the South, Murray said, for only the "stable" Negro would qualify. The bonus votes would aid the farmers, prevent Negro domination, help control the slum vote in the cities, and dilute the effects of granting suffrage to women. This bizarre proposal never got out of the House judiciary committee.[53]

Even though he advocated illiberal measures like the voting proposal, the Oklahoman also gave his support to necessary social legislation. He favored a system of old-age pensions sponsored by the federal government and voted for a committee to investigate the possibility of creating a federal unemployment-insurance system.[54] Murray's records in the two sessions of Congress were paradoxical; he made unwarranted and trivial proposals, but he also supported sound legislation. His voting record reflected his agrarian bent and intense personal convictions growing out of his education and rural background.

[51] Ibid., 1916, LIII, Pt. 2, 1916–18.   [52] Ibid., LIV, Pt. 1, 227–28.
[53] Ibid., Pt. 6, 269–70.   [54] Ibid., Pt. 4, 3545; Pt. 3, 2654.

On the last day of the session Murray made his final speech before the House. He expressed his sadness in leaving Congress and spoke of the past four years and the friendships he had formed. He praised Speaker Champ Clark as a good friend and urged Clark's nomination for the Presidency in the future.[55] In a letter to his constituents he wrote that he was returning to private life. He referred to the many beneficial laws which Congress had enacted in the past four years and said that he was proud to have been a member of the bodies responsible for them.[56]

The past four years had been very pleasant for Murray. He loved Washington, the House, and his associations with Wilson, Bryan, Clark, and others. In many respects this period was a high point in his career. Though his positions often reflected narrowness of mind, particularly in racial matters, he had an admirable voting record on New Freedom legislation. Though he stood for the agrarian position on each bill and introduced and supported amendments designed to aid his rural constituents, on final passage he generally stood with the progressives of both parties.

Murray returned to Tishomingo and began reorganizing his farms and building a new house southeast of town. For a whole month he remained out of politics, rejecting proposals that he seek an elective office in 1918.[57] Then he announced that he would probably run for governor. After commenting upon his quick change of direction, the editor of *Harlow's Weekly* said, "Murray probably has the strongest friends and the bitterest enemies of any politician in the state, and his presence will determine the character of any campaign in which he is a party." The other probable candidate, J. B. A. Robertson, had been defeated in the 1914 gubernatorial primary, but the editor felt that many voters who did not care for Robertson would support him against Murray.[58]

After an initial meeting in Ada a group of Murray's supporters gathered in Shawnee to organize a draft-Murray effort. The candi-

[55] *Ibid.*, Pt. 5, 5033.
[56] Murray to "My Constituents," Mar. 4, 1917, Murray Coll., Univ. of Okla. Library.
[57] *Harlow's Weekly*, Mar. 14, 1917.
[58] *Ibid.*, Apr. 11, 1917.

date about to be "drafted" had written several hundred letters suggesting the meeting. Nearly all the supporters were from the Fourth District, and many were postmasters who owed their jobs to him. Presided over by Douglas Johnston, the meeting had a small attendance.[59] Undaunted, however, the group published a pamphlet, "Draft Murray for Governor Is the Wise Course for Oklahoma Democrats," and ran advertisements in newspapers urging him to run. The chairmanship of the committee passed to Ben F. Harrison, a long-term Murray supporter, constitutional-convention member, and former state secretary of state.[60]

In response to the draft Murray addressed a letter to the people of Oklahoma saying that he felt he should retire from politics but that if a state-wide convention on his behalf were to be held he would be forced to make the race. To create interest in his candidacy he embarked on twelve tours about the state, delivering a speech titled "The Safety of a Wise Foreign Policy." Nearly every night during July and August, 1917, he spoke out for the war effort, urging Oklahomans to work harder.[61]

Murray's patriotic speeches aroused little enthusiasm among the voters, many of whom still opposed the war. Oklahoma had the distinction of being the only state in which large-scale armed resistance to the war effort took place. The "Green Corn Rebellion," staged by Indians, Negroes, and tenant farmers in two counties of Murray's former congressional district, was partly a reaction against military conscription. On his tour of eastern Oklahoma sparse crowds gathered to hear him, and a speech in Muskogee was canceled because of the small turnout.[62]

Despite the lack of interest in his candidacy, Murray issued a platform calling for free textbooks for school children, a strengthened rural-credits law, and the use of convict labor on state highways.[63] Though he announced that, as in 1910, he would depend on

[59] *Ibid.*, June 20, 1917.
[60] "Draft Murray for Governor," Murray Coll., Univ. of Okla. Library; *Johnston County Capital-Democrat*, July 5, 1917.
[61] *Harlow's Weekly*, June 27, July 18, 25, 1917; *Johnston County Capital-Democrat*, July 5, 1917; *Muskogee Daily Phoenix*, Aug. 19, 1917.
[62] *Harlow's Weekly*, Sept. 5, 1917.　　　[63] *Ibid.*, Sept. 26, 1917.

small contributions to finance his campaign, he visited some old friends in Ardmore who happened to be wealthy oilmen, and his platform contained nothing they would oppose. Speculation that he might withdraw coupled with his antagonism toward Governor Williams hindered the development of his campaign.[64]

Murray did not withdraw, and by the end of January, 1918, his home-town newspaper announced that he was definitely in the race and had the necessary campaign funds.[65] The *Daily Ardmoreite* endorsed him, and he built a base of strength in Ardmore and surrounding Carter County. Murray-for-governor clubs were established by February in the Third and Fourth Congressional Districts and soon spread into the First District. His old political allies, the members of the Sequoyah and Oklahoma constitutional conventions and the first legislature, organized his campaign. Henry S. Johnston led the Murray group in Perry, and the campaign advisory committee included Ben Harrison, A. H. Ellis, D. H. McDougal, Milas Lassiter, John Kroutil, Malcolm E. Rosser, and Cap Mitchell, all veterans of Murray's earlier campaigns. His only editorial support came from small-town papers, such as the *Shattuck Monitor* and the *Shawnee Daily News-Herald*.[66] His chief opponents, J. B. A. Robertson and Secretary of the Treasury William Alexander, received the blessings of the urban press, and Robertson was conceded an early lead.

A candidate for governor twice before, Robertson had been a Lincoln County political leader for many years. Though a pale campaigner, he conducted a clean and thorough canvass. He received the active support of Governor Williams.[67] His platform contained no innovations; he advocated an end to the tenant system, an enlarged road-building program, maintenance of the gas and oil taxes at their current level, and enforcement of prohibition. Throughout the campaign the press agreed that Robertson would be an easy winner.[68]

[64] *Ibid.*, Nov. 21, 1917.

[65] *Johnston County Capital-Democrat*, quoted in *Harlow's Weekly*, Jan. 23, 1918.

[66] *Harlow's Weekly*, Jan. 30, Feb. 20, 1918; *Daily Ardmoreite*, June 13, 1918.

[67] Dale and Morrison, *Pioneer Judge*, 274.

[68] *Cordell Beacon*, Apr. 18, 1918; *Chandler Tribune*, May 2, June 6, 1918; *Daily Ardmoreite*, June 23, 1918.

In their campaigns both Robertson and Alexander generally ignored Murray. In fact, the Murray campaign lagged so badly that he issued a second platform, shifting the emphasis from state issues to "winning the war." He emphasized his support of Wilson's program, and in his speeches he often devoted only five minutes to state matters and spent the remaining time on the war.[69] Taking a swing at those who had opposed him in 1916, he said that only men who had favored preparedness should be elected. The sluggishness of the campaign came partly from competition with the third Liberty Loan drive, and Murray waited until the drive ended before beginning a strenuous speaking tour. He denounced the International Workers of the World for opposing the war, and his newspaper appeals said he wanted to be "Oklahoma's War Governor." According to his advertisements, he knew how to end the war and how to protect the boys on the battle line.[70]

The voters remained disinterested in politics throughout the summer of 1918, and all three candidates found it difficult to attract audiences for their speeches. Even the newspapers were unusually quiet; the *Tulsa Democrat*, the leading paper in that city, carried no important political news until the July 21 issue.[71] Generally the newspapers reported Murray's speeches favorably, although three-fourths of them supported Robertson.[72] Neither Murray's speeches on the war effort nor Robertson's platitudinous addresses fired the electorate. The apathy caused even staunchly Democratic editors to predict a light vote after the most listless campaign in the state's history.[73]

Only in the last week of the campaign did the candidates treat the voters to the personal charges and spirited rivalry which had marked earlier primary elections. Alfalfa Bill's cumulative-voting proposal was cited as "proof" of his unworthiness for office, and both Robertson and Alexander brought up the charge that Murray

[69] "Proposed Platform of William H. Murray," Murray Coll., Univ. of Okla. Library; *Harlow's Weekly*, May 29, 1918.

[70] *Daily Ardmoreite*, June 13, 1918; *Cordell Beacon*, July 18, 1918.

[71] *Muskogee Daily Phoenix*, May 14, 1918; *Tulsa Democrat*, July 21, 1918.

[72] *Harlow's Weekly*, July 3, 1918; *Chandler Tribune*, July 4, 1918.

[73] *Cordell Beacon*, July 25, 1918; *Lawton News*, July 25, 1918; *Tulsa Democrat*, July 28, 1918.

had opposed the defunct grandfather clause. In his last speech Murray stopped dwelling on the war effort long enough to defend his record on the grandfather clause.[74] Even these last-minute personal attacks failed to excite the voters.

Robertson won the race easily, receiving more votes than Murray and Alexander together. Robertson received 48,568 votes; Murray, 24,283; and Alexander, 22,670. Four other candidates received a total of 12,398 votes.[75] Murray won a majority of the votes in only three of the seventy-seven counties. He had not found a winning issue, his organization had been weak, and the shift to a second platform had been unsuccessful. The two consecutive defeats left him thoroughly discouraged with politics and physically exhausted.

During the rest of 1918 and throughout 1919 Murray would often be mentioned for political office. His old friend O. A. Brewer wrote him that he should run for the state senate in 1920 and then run again for governor in 1922. Rumors spread that he would run for Congress from the Fourth District in 1920, but Murray quelled the rumors by announcing that he would not run for any office.[76]

After the campaign Alfalfa Bill returned to his farm, where a bumper crop and high prices brought him a large profit. He repaid Senator Robert L. Owen the $1,500 he had borrowed in 1912 to run for Congress, and he sold 280 acres of land for $100 per acre and used this money and $20,000 in rent payments received from his tenants to pay off his other debts.[77] He still owned 1,600 acres of bottom land, of which 1,100 acres were being worked by tenants. Though he could now afford to buy a car, he refused to do so, saying that the five-mile walk into Tishomingo was good for his sons, who needed to learn the value of money. The boys also worked on the farm during the summer months to learn thrift and the virtues of hard work.[78]

---

[74] *Daily Ardmoreite*, July 28, 29, Aug. 6, 1918; *Muskogee Times-Democrat*, Aug. 2, 3, 1918; *Lawton News*, Aug. 6, 1918.

[75] Winters, *Directory of the State of Oklahoma*, 98.

[76] O. A. Brewer to Murray, Apr. 4, 1919, Murray Coll., OHS Library; *Harlow's Weekly*, Nov. 19, Dec. 3, 1919.

[77] Murray, *Memoirs*, II, 236.   [78] *Ibid.*, I, 278–79.

In spite of his financial prosperity, Murray was restless. After thirteen years in Oklahoma politics success in farming proved to be a poor substitute for public life. In 1898, after political defeat and failure in journalism and law, he had started over in a new territory. Now there were no more frontiers in the United States. Rural America was losing its dominance, and the way of life to which Alfalfa Bill had devoted himself was disappearing. He feared for the future of democracy in the United States and forcefully expressed his despair: "The American people once ascending the peaks of civilization have missed the road and are now descending through the dismal canyons to the fogbound seashore where neither harbor, pilot nor lighthouse can be found."[79]

For Murray, there was only one way to preserve the agricultural society, and that was to find a new frontier. Alfalfa Bill decided to go to South America.

[79] *Daily Oklahoman*, May 9, 1920.

✪

COLONIZER IN BOLIVIA

VII

Thᴇʀᴇ ɪs ɴo concrete evidence about when or how Murray first became fascinated by South America. It may have been during the time he sold Atlases to farmers in central Texas and spent his evenings reading the books.[1] His interest may have developed from his romance with Lita Rakestraw, the Corsicana girl to whom he was briefly engaged. Lita's father was a former Confederate officer who had lived in Villa Americana, Brazil, for a while after the Civil War, and he may have told Alfalfa Bill about South America.[2] Another possible source of his interest may have been Willis Offenbarger, a casual Texas friend who had been born in Brazil and who told him romantic tales of Latin America.[3] In his biography of Murray, Gordon Hines wrote that when Murray decided to leave Fort Worth in 1898 he flipped a coin to determine whether he would go to the Indian Territory or to South America. In his *Memoirs* Murray does not mention the coin story but claims that he made his first trip to South America to rest and regain his health.[4] He had exhibited great interest in South America as a congressman and had read Theodore Roosevelt's book about his adventures on the Amazon River.[5]

Alfalfa Bill spent the early months of 1919 preparing for his first journey to South America. He read a number of books about

[1] Murray, *Memoirs*, I, 164; Hines, *Alfalfa Bill*, 51.
[2] Murray, *Memoirs*, I, 191–92; Hines, *Alfalfa Bill*, 83–84.
[3] Hines, *Alfalfa Bill*, 78–79.
[4] *Ibid.*, 101; Murray, *Memoirs*, II, 234. The discussion of the colony in the *Memoirs* (II, 233–357) is a mixture of home remedies for travel ailments, anecdotes about transportation facilities, narratives about fellow travelers, and amusing, if often erroneous, geographical and historical comments.
[5] Burbank Murray, interview of Feb. 10, 1966.

151

the continent, including a volume by Paul Walle on Bolivia.[6] To assure himself a welcome by Latin Americans, he obtained letters of recommendation from Cardinal Gibbons of Baltimore, Speaker of the House Champ Clark, Vice-President Thomas Marshall, a number of railroad and bank presidents, and former Governor Charles N. Haskell.[7] Murray recognized the dangers inherent in his proposed travels and prepared a will leaving his farm properties to Alice and the children.[8] With these preparations completed, he left for New Orleans.

Traveling on board the U.S.S. *Albenguarres* of the United Fruit Lines, Murray went first to Panama and then to Peru. He made an extensive trip by train and boat from Lima to Lake Titicaca and then to La Paz, Bolivia. From La Paz he traveled to Buenos Aires, Argentina, then up the Paraná River to Paraguay, and ultimately to the interior of Brazil. He was intrigued by the Gran Chaco, an area of Paraguay, Bolivia, and Argentina. He decided to return to La Paz and obtain a concession of half a million acres in a portion of northeastern Chaco, where he hoped to start an agricultural colony. The population of the area was small, and only a few Europeans were settled there. The terrain reminded Murray of Texas and Oklahoma, and he felt that this was the frontier for which he had been searching.[9]

The idea of an agricultural colony in Bolivia was not a new one. The Bolivian government had tried to foster the development of English and German colonies for a number of years. To attract immigrants to the Chaco, the Bolivians had made 100,000 square

[6] Murray, *Memoirs*, II, 236; Paul Walle, *Bolivia, Its People and Its Resources, Its Railways, Mines, and Rubber Forests* (trans. by Bernard Miall), (London, T. F. Unwin, 1914); Anna Gwin Pickens, "The Murray Colonies of Bolivia" (Master's thesis, University of Chicago, 1948), 29. The Pickens study is a sound presentation of Murray's Bolivian colony based upon the sources available in 1948. Unfortunately the writer of the study was denied access to the confidential correspondence in the State Department files on the Murray colony, and a significant manuscript source, the Marion Unger Collection (see note 45) was not yet available.

[7] Murray, *Memoirs*, II, 275; letter of introduction from Cardinal Gibbons, Apr. 4, 1919; Charles N. Haskell to William H. Murray, July 25, 1922 ; Murray Coll., Univ. of Okla. Library.

[8] Last Will and Testament, Apr. 2, 1919, Murray Coll., Univ. of Okla. Library.

[9] Murray, *Memoirs*, II, 259–61.

miles of land available for settlement under the land law of 1905. One person could acquire as much as 45,000 acres at ten cents an acre.[10] The Bolivian government wanted foreigners in the Chaco for political as well as economic reasons. In this region the boundary between Paraguay and Bolivia had never been firmly established, and in the continuing dispute Bolivia wanted the support of other powers, which the presence of their citizens might provide. This quarrel would ultimately lead to war between Paraguay and Bolivia in the 1930's.

Murray obtained the services of the law firm of Kelley and Fletcher of Cochabamba, Bolivia, to negotiate with the government for the concession. He proposed to pay $39,000 for 300,000 acres and placed $10,000 in escrow with the W. R. Grace Company. The law firm agreed to obtain the concession before April 1, 1920.[11] Expecting prompt action by the Bolivian government, Murray announced the formation of the colony and began advertising for settlers.[12] However, he found the Bolivian government slow to act, and he returned to Tishomingo in late August, hoping that the concession would soon be granted.[13] A governmental crisis in Bolivia prevented serious consideration of the proposal in 1919 and 1920.

From the beginning of his colonization venture Murray made every effort to keep the United States Department of State completely informed of his activities and plans. On October 18, 1919, he sent Secretary of State Robert Lansing a copy of the proposed concession bill and asked for the department's reactions to the plan.[14] Lansing replied that such concessions were sometimes involved in border disputes and warned Murray to be careful.[15] In a second letter on December 1 Murray promised to keep Lansing

[10] W. W. R., "Bolivia Today and Tomorrow," *Pan American Magazine*, Vol. XXX (December, 1919), 58–68.

[11] Contract between Murray and Kelly and Fletcher, Aug. 11, 1919, Murray Coll., Univ. of Okla. Library.

[12] *Woodward News-Bulletin*, Apr. 11, 1919; *Guymon Herald*, Apr. 10, 1919.

[13] *Johnston County Capital-Democrat*, Sept. 4, 1919.

[14] Murray to Robert Lansing, Oct. 19, 1919, File 824.52, "The Murray Colonization Project" (Washington, D.C., National Archives, Diplomatic, Legal, and Fiscal Branch). Hereafter cited as File 824.52, National Archives. This collection includes all correspondence, confidential and nonconfidential, relating to the Murray colony.

[15] Lansing to Murray, Oct. 21, 1919, File 824.52, National Archives.

informed of his actions and sent him copies of the prospectus, contracts, and other documents.[16] His complete candor with the department later proved beneficial and distinguished his venture from others that were less than honest.

During the spring of 1920 Murray continued to publicize his colonization plan. The *Daily Oklahoman* featured an article on "Murray's Promised Land." Alfalfa Bill reported that he had a large tract in Bolivia upon which he planned to establish a co-operative farm community. It was not a "new democracy" or a political experiment, he said, but a return to pioneer life. The settlement would be divided into 640-acre sections with a common cattle range. There would be collective work on fences and roads and collective purchasing. It would be a community free of strife and turmoil; the rules governing the paradise were to be the Ten Commandments.[17]

The colonizing project was thwarted when Bolivia reported that Paraguay had established a fort on the river on which Murray planned to bring in his colonists. Deciding to investigate the matter, he sailed from New York for Rio de Janeiro on June 12. Hoping to find an overland route to the proposed colony, he traveled to the Mato Grosso region of Brazil.[18] He visited Villa Americana, where his friend Captain Rakestraw had lived, but found the land route to the colony impassable.[19] The threat of war between Bolivia and Paraguay grew more ominous, and so he booked passage from Buenos Aires back to New York.[20] Returning to Tishomingo, he announced that the colonization plan had failed because of the boundary dispute and that he had lost $4,500 on the two trips.[21] He canceled the venture and returned the deposits prospective colonists had sent to him.

After the devastating Democratic defeat in November, 1920, Alfalfa Bill decided that he had no future in Oklahoma politics. The

[16] Murray to Lansing, Dec. 1, 1919, File 824.52, National Archives.
[17] *Daily Oklahoman*, May 9, 1920.
[18] Murray to Alice Murray, June 19, 1920, Murray Coll., Univ. of Okla. Library.
[19] Murray, *Memoirs*, II, 261.
[20] U.S.S. *Callao*, Passenger List—First Class, Sept. 2, 1920, Murray Coll., Univ. of Okla. Library.
[21] *Johnston County Capital-Democrat*, Oct. 7, 1920.

failure of his Bolivian scheme had not quenched his desire to establish an agricultural colony in South America, and in July, 1921, he left on a third trip, this time to Peru.[22] Armed with a letter of introduction from his old friend Milas Lassater, now president of the Federal Land Bank at Wichita, Kansas, he made preliminary arrangements for a concession in Peru.[23] After a brief trip through the interior of the country he drew up a prospectus for "The Murray Colony of Peru" and sent it to the farmers who had signed up for the Bolivian venture. Peru was actually a better place for his colony than Bolivia, Murray claimed. Returning to Oklahoma, he announced that a tract of 247,000 acres had been acquired and that homesites would sell for $300. He suggested that a minimum of $2,400 was necessary to establish a farm. He planned to take the first contingent of farmers on January 1, 1923, he said, after making it perfectly clear that no Socialists would be allowed.[24]

When Murray discovered that the Peruvian government was moving slowly in granting the concession, he postponed the departure date and returned to Peru. In March, 1922, he obtained an audience with Peruvian President Augusto Leguía and secured a contract for the concession. The government agreed to send a ship to New Orleans for the colonists and to build a road to the proposed site. When the Peruvians failed to complete the road, Murray abandoned the project and once again returned to the United States.[25]

He had not given up his dreams, however. In September, 1922, he returned to South America. The Chaco still held his imagination, and he gained permission from the Bolivian government to explore the public lands in the region. For three months he traveled through the Chaco, ultimately deciding to arrange for a concession at the abandoned mission of Aguayrenda, twelve miles northeast of Yacuiba in the department of Tarija. He returned to La Paz and met with President Bautista Saavedra to discuss the possibility of a

---

[22] Murray to Alice Murray, July 26, 1921, Murray Coll., Univ. of Okla. Library.

[23] Milas Lassater to the President of Peru, July 7, 1921, Murray Coll., Univ. of Okla. Library.

[24] "Prospectus of Murray Colony of Peru," Murray Coll., Univ. of Okla. Library; *Daily Oklahoman*, Dec. 25, 1921.

[25] Murray, *Memoirs*, II, 262–63.

land grant.[26] Murray petitioned the government for a concession in the foothills of the Chaco, which he described as "ideal" for colonization. He asked for a total of 450,000 acres and agreed to build fifty kilometers of roads and to develop cattle ranching and cultivate cotton. He asked the government to grant him a trade monopoly in the concession, to exempt cotton gins and machinery from import tariffs, and to prohibit the sale of liquor in the area. He promised that all colonists would be financially solvent and would be white people of European descent.[27]

The Murray proposal received the enthusiastic endorsement of Jesse S. Cottrell, the American minister in La Paz. A former newspaperman, Cottrell had known Murray in Washington. He wrote Secretary of State Charles Evans Hughes that Murray was planning ahead and had a well-defined program. The minister described the land Murray wanted as similar to the middle-western plains of the United States.[28] Murray continued to have Cottrell's support during the next six years.

Alfalfa Bill met with Hernando Siles, minister of war and colonization, on December 14, 1922, and with President Saavedra on December 16, and both men approved his project.[29] Saavedra sent the concession bill to the Bolivian congress, but the body adjourned in December without acting upon it. Though the prospects for an agricultural colony in Bolivia seemed very bright and high profits were possible, according to the *Bulletin of the Pan American Union*,[30] the congress was very reluctant to grant the concession because of the small amount Murray was offering to pay for such a sizable tract of land.[31] Even when he reduced his request to a

[26] *Mensaje del Presidente de la República al Congreso Nacional de 1922* (La Paz, Litografías e Imprentas Unidas, 1922), 63–64. Hereafter cited as *Mensaje del Presidente, [date]*.

[27] Pickens, "The Murray Colonies of Bolivia," 50–55.

[28] Jesse S. Cottrell to the Secretary of State, Nov. 25, 1922, File 824.52, National Archives.

[29] Hernando Siles to Murray, Dec. 14, 1922; Private Secretary of President Saavedra to Murray, Dec. 15, 1922; Murray Coll., Univ. of Okla. Library.

[30] Frederick L. Hoffman, "American Business Opportunities in Bolivia," *Bulletin of the Pan American Union,* Vol. LV (August, 1922), 167–69.

[31] *Memoria de Guerra y Colonización, 1923* (La Paz, Intendencia de Guerra— Talleres Recreo, 1924), 12–13. Hereafter cited as *Memoria, [date]*.

little over 100,000 acres, the congress refused to act. Still hoping to make the necessary arrangements, Murray left La Paz in early February, 1923, and returned to Tishomingo, where he began to recruit colonists.[32]

After two months Murray once more returned to Bolivia, arriving in La Paz on May 1.[33] Three weeks later the congress granted the concession to *el conocido colonizador norteamericano*, and the report of the minister of colonization glowed with optimism.[34] Murray obtained a ninety-nine-year lease on 42,000 acres of land in the Itau, Aguayrenda, and Aguayrendita area of southern Bolivia, and he made an initial payment to the government of $1,800.[35] After many trips and a four-year delay, he finally had his concession.

Murray continued to keep the State Department informed of his activities and reported the signing of the contract to Secretary of State Hughes. Writing from La Paz, Murray told Hughes that he had given Cottrell a copy of the contract and that he would send the department copies of advertisements for colonists. A second assistant secretary of state replied to his letter, saying only that the papers were now part of the department's permanent records.[36]

Cottrell sent a long dispatch to Hughes describing Murray's proposition and the details of the concession. Besides the 42,000 acres covered by the lease, Murray also had an option to lease an additional 200,000 acres. He had guaranteed to have twenty-five families on the lands by December 31, 1925, but Cottrell reported that thirty-five families were already planning to come to Bolivia and that Murray intended to sell them plots of 80 to 150 acres at sixty cents an acre. According to the agreement, machinery and supplies could be brought into the colony duty-free, and exports were free from taxation for five years. The land to be settled was

32 Doyle C. McDonough to the Secretary of State, Feb. 5, 1923, File 824.52, National Archives.

33 *Daily Oklahoman*, Apr. 11, 1923; Murray to Alice Murray, May 2, 1923, Murray Coll., Univ. of Okla. Library.

34 *Memoria, 1924,* 5–7.

35 *Anuario Administrativo de 1923* (La Paz, Litografías e Imprentas Unidas, 1924), 370–73; Testimonio, May 25, 1923, File 824.52, National Archives.

36 Murray to Charles Evans Hughes, May 26, 1923; Alvey A. Adee to Murray, July 3, 1923; File 824.52, National Archives.

fertile, well watered, and well timbered and was only twelve miles from the Argentine Central Railroad. Cottrell sent Hughes copies of the lease and Murray's receipt, which he asked to have placed in the State Department file.[37]

By now the colony was receiving widespread newspaper coverage in the United States. Alfalfa Bill's reputation, the romantic appeal of South America, and American interest in foreign investment possibilities made the colony good newspaper copy. The *Dallas Morning News* of July 1, 1923, carried a long article and four pictures of Murray and scenes in Bolivia.[38] The *Daily Oklahoman* devoted almost a full page to describe an occasion "When 'Alfalfa Bill' Wore a Boiled Shirt." After obtaining the concession, Murray had given a gala party at the Gringo Club in La Paz, complete with dress suits, roses, and champagne.

Back in Tishomingo in July, Murray told a reporter that all the arrangements had been made for tools, seed, and equipment for the colony. Alice served the newspaperman maté tea, which her husband had brought back from South America, and said that she was also making preparations to go to Bolivia. Murray declared he would never re-enter politics and wanted only to find willing pioneers for his colony.[39]

One of the most extensive articles about Murray and the colony was printed by the *Providence Sunday Journal* of Providence, Rhode Island. Reporter Franklin Bickford wrote that Alfalfa Bill had two hundred farmers ready to depart for the colony. He quoted Murray as saying, "I would like to have the reputation of establishing the first important colony in South America on a permanent basis." Bickford told about Murray's trips and the protracted negotiations and described the area to be settled. The mission of Aguayrenda was one hundred miles from Villa Montes, the nearest Bolivian town of consequence, and although only a few white people lived in the area, corn and sugar cane were being raised by forty to fifty Indian families. Most of the land was being used to

---

[37] Cottrell to Hughes, May 29, 1923, File 824.52, National Archives.
[38] *Dallas Morning News*, July 1, 1923.
[39] *Daily Oklahoman*, July 8, 1923.

graze cattle and sheep, which had grown fat from the fine pasturage. The article did not suggest the development of an agricultural utopia in Bolivia, though it was generally favorable to Murray and his scheme.[40]

While he was in Tishomingo, Murray issued "The Prospectus for Murray Colonies of Central South Bolivia; South America." The prospectus contained a detailed description of his plans and statements by three Tishomingo bankers attesting to his honesty and character. He told prospective colonists that they would need at least $1,800 in order to take part, that only families were allowed to go, and that firm rules were to be established about personal conduct, liquor, education, and the division of labor. The lands were described at length, and he noted that irrigation would be necessary and that the railroad connection was still under construction. Anyone reading the prospectus could hardly overlook Murray's honesty and candor in describing the primitive conditions and the need for colonists to endure hardship and hard work. This was no Eden they were going to, but a frontier area not unlike the Great Plains in the 1870's and 1880's.[41]

Continuing to keep the State Department informed, he sent copies of the prospectus and application form to Secretary Hughes. A copy of the official proclamation as printed in *La Reforma* of La Paz was included.[42] Hughes also received regular reports from Joseph Flack, temporary chargé d'affaires in La Paz.

On August 28, 1923, the Bolivian chamber of deputies adopted a resolution urging President Saavedra to cancel the concession. Flack discussed the problem with Julio Alborta, a Bolivian who had helped Murray with the negotiations, and Alborta reported that the president could lease the lands without the approval of the chamber, though he could not sell them. President Saavedra told the chamber that the Murray contract was legal, and he was supported by Minister of War and Colonization Siles and by the administra-

40 *Providence Sunday Journal*, July 22, 1923.

41 "The Prospectus for Murray Colonies of Central South Bolivia; South America," July 21, 1923, Murray Coll., Univ. of Okla. Library.

42 Murray to Hughes, Aug. 12, 1923; prospectus and blank application forms; clipping from *La Reforma* (La Paz), June 17, 1923; File 824.52, National Archives.

tion newspapers, *La Reforma* and *La República*. The leaders of the opposition in the chamber were Senator José Estenssoro from the Chaco and Senator Mogro Moreno of the department of Tarija, who wanted to embarrass the Saavedra government. Siles argued that the concession would help develop the area, but Estenssoro claimed that many Indians would lose their lands.[43] After five days of debate the lease was finally approved by a vote of 7 to 3.

By January, 1924, Murray had obtained enough families to begin final plans for their departure. He issued three sets of instructions telling the settlers how to pack their goods and obtain their passports, the limits on their baggage, and other details. The final instructions of March 1 contained information about the price of goods he planned to sell at a general store in the colony.[44] Murray sent his son Johnston to Bolivia ahead of the main party to procure mules for the last portion of the trip and to buy supplies. In La Paz young Murray bought $8,400 worth of clothing, drugs, hardware, plows, sewing machines, and other goods and shipped them on to Aguayrenda.[45]

In answer to many inquiries about Murray and his colony, the State Department issued a memorandum stating that the project was being conducted in good faith, with honest motives, and was wholly feasible. In response to a Post Office Department request for information, the State Department said that there was no need for an investigation of possible mail fraud. However, the report did note that the colonists, rather than Murray, were obliged to secure title to the lands.[46] Other favorable comments on the

[43] Joseph Flack to Hughes, Sept. 3, 17, 25, 1923, File 824.52, National Archives; *La República* (La Paz), Aug. 29, 1923; *Redactore del H. Senado Nacional*, 1923, I, 79–81, quoted in Benigno Carrasco, *Hernando Siles* (La Paz, Editorial del Estado, 1961), 291–99.

[44] "Second Circular of Instructions," Jan. 12, 1924, File 824.52, National Archives; "Final Instructions," Mar. 1, 1924, Murray Coll., Univ. of Okla. Library.

[45] Marion Draughon Murray to her father, Apr. 18, 1924, Unger Collection (Norman, University of Oklahoma Library, Division of Manuscripts). Hereafter cited as Unger Coll., Univ. of Okla. Library. In 1961 Mrs. Marion Unger, Johnston Murray's former wife, gave to the University of Oklahoma an extensive collection of letters, drawings, and photographs relating to the time she spent at the Murray colony in Bolivia. The letters are illustrated with marginal sketches and maps. The collection is a remarkable and colorful view of life in the colony.

[46] Memorandum, Division of Latin American Affairs, Jan. 31, 1924, File 824.52, National Archives.

colony were printed by the *Bulletin of the Pan American Union* and by the *West Coast Leader* of Lima, Peru, which reported that Murray had been well received in the department of Tarija.[47] With these words of reassurance the band of twentieth-century pioneers departed for Bolivia on May 4, 1924.

They traveled on a special train to New Orleans, where they boarded ship. After a long voyage they debarked at Antofagasta, Chile.[48] A special railroad car took them from Antofagasta to Argentina. The last part of the trip turned into a nightmare. The eighty-six colonists, particularly the forty-nine children, found the high altitude wearing, and Johnston Murray had been unable to acquire mules for the last part of the trip. Forced to travel through Argentina by rail, the settlers were delayed by Argentine customs officials and were compelled to stay in extremely poor facilities for several days. Finally they were allowed to complete the last few miles to their destination, and D. C. McDonough, the American consul in La Paz, cabled the State Department of their safe arrival.[49]

The settlers moved into the whitewashed school-dormitory building of the old mission, sleeping on blankets on a dirt floor while their farms were being surveyed. In addition to Alfalfa Bill, his wife, and his two youngest children, the older Murray sons also joined the venture and brought their families. The other settlers included twenty-nine adults and forty-five children.[50] The number of small children proved to be a serious problem, though the initial presence of a doctor and a dentist alleviated some of the hardships.

Shortly after their arrival, several families became homesick, and the situation at the mission grew unpleasant. Defective drain-

[47] "Bolivia," *Bulletin of the Pan American Union*, Vol. LVII (December, 1923), 608; *West Coast Leader* (Lima), Feb. 26, 1924, cited in Pickens, "The Murray Colonies of Bolivia," 34.

[48] Alice Murray to "Dear Folks at Home," May 26, 1924, Murray Coll., Univ. of Okla. Library.

[49] Cottrell to Hughes, June 5, 1924, File 824.52, National Archives; *Commerce Reports*, Vol. III (July 7, 1924), 10 (Washington, D.C., U.S. Government Printing Office, 1924).

[50] *South Pacific Mail* (Valparaiso), June 12, 1924, cited in Pickens, "The Murray Colonies of Bolivia," 107; Marion Murray to her father, June 20, 23, 1924, Unger Coll., Univ. of Okla. Library.

age led to a shortage of good water, and insects became a serious menace. The goods shipped from New Orleans and La Paz failed to arrive. Murray wrote to Jesse Cottrell about the offensive behavior of Argentine officials who had physically threatened some of the colonists. Local Bolivian officials proved very helpful, but Johnston Murray had to pay the Argentine customs agent five pesos for each loaded mule brought into Bolivia. Murray asked Cottrell to investigate. Cottrell did so but failed to obtain any help from the Argentine minister in La Paz other than a promise to look into the matter.[51]

The rain, the insects, and the primitive shelter caused some of the colonists to return to the United States. When two of the families decided to leave, Murray gave them the money for their passage. Another family also departed, and when they passed through Valparaiso, Chile, they told the American consul, C. F. Deichman, their version of the situation at the colony. They said that Murray had made fantastic promises, that the Indians held the best land, and that the remainder was poor and dry. They claimed that though they had lost $8,000 they were able to return home, while another family was stranded without funds.[52] Deichman sent the State Department extremely critical reports on the colony during the next five years, though his only source of information was the stories of homeward-bound settlers.

Conditions were steadily deteriorating throughout all of Bolivia in 1924, as McDonough reported in a letter to Secretary of State Hughes. Cottrell reported that Murray was trying very hard to prevent further trouble at the colony. In commenting on the Deichman report, Cottrell wrote that Murray was honest, that he had a sincere pioneer urge, and that, "while self-educated," he appeared to be "shrewd and a good practical farmer." The land was dry for half the year, but Cottrell believed that crops would grow and that the railroad would soon be completed. The charges made by the

[51] Murray to Cottrell, June 29, 1924; Cottrell to Hughes, July 23, 1924; File 824.52, National Archives.
[52] C. F. Deichman, "Results of Colonization Project of Colonel William H. Murray in Southeastern Bolivia," July 25, 1924, File 824.52, National Archives.

William H. Murray, president of the Oklahoma constitutional
convention, 1906.

Mary Alice Hearrell (later Mrs. William H. Murray), in the 1890's.

Murray reading law in the hammock between the pecan trees at Twelve Mile Prairie, about 1905.

The Murrays entertaining a guest in the yard of their home at Twelve Mile Prairie.

Alfalfa Bill dictates to his secretary on the front porch of the farm-
house at Twelve Mile Prairie, about 1905.

Murray surveys his colony at Aguayrenda, Bolivia, about 1925.

Governor Murray addresses a typical campaign audience in the 1930's.

Before a delegation of firemen the Governor signs a firemen's pension bill.

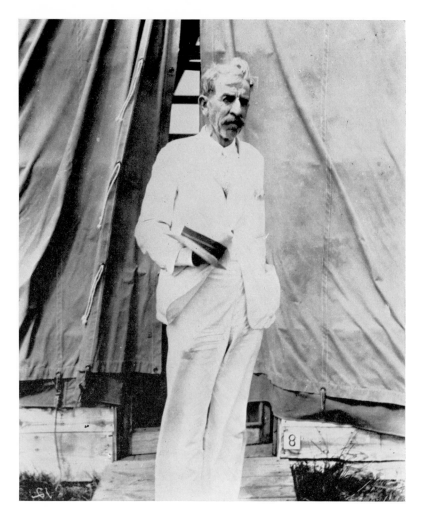

Clad in a wrinkled white cotton suit, Governor Murray inspects a
National Guard encampment, about 1931.

family in Valparaiso were untrue, he said. While there were many insects and weather was dry, the colony could not yet be called either a success or a failure. Consul McDonough agreed with the minister, saying that a problem had arisen with Indian squatters but that the Bolivian government was favorably disposed to Murray. If any colony had a chance of succeeding in Bolivia, he felt that Murray's venture would do so.[53] President Saavedra told the congress that the colony was developing well and that the government should help make the transition easier for the colonists. Saavedra felt that the quota of twenty-five families by the end of December, 1925, would be exceeded. His report was quite enthusiastic.[54]

Johnston Murray's wife, Marion, wrote to relatives that the unfavorable rumors about the colony being circulated in Oklahoma by one family were simply not true. No one else wanted to return to the United States, she wrote, there was no head tax on livestock, the Indians had no deeds, and Murray had been very generous to the settlers. He had employed over one hundred Indians to do much of the hard labor, and his general store was prospering.[55] Colonist W. C. Pitner sent a letter to the *West Coast Leader* praising Murray and reporting that the sugar cane looked promising and that homes were under construction.[56] For a few weeks it appeared that the situation had improved. Then more serious problems arose. The rainy season had been brief, the drought continued, and a plague of locusts attacked the colony.

It became obvious quite soon that the colonists lacked Murray's pioneer spirit. Pitner reversed his position and, together with Robert Gallentine, wrote to Cottrell pleading for help. Both men claimed

---

[53] D. C. McDonough to Hughes, Aug. 1, 1924; Cottrell to Hughes, Oct. 2, 1924; D. C. McDonough, "Colonization Project of Colonel William H. Murray in Southeastern Bolivia," Oct. 18, 1924; File 824.52, National Archives; Porfirio Díaz Machicao, *Historia de Bolivia, Saavedra, 1920–1925* (La Paz, Alfonso Tejerina, 1954), 172–73.

[54] *Mensaje del Presidente, 1924,* 51.

[55] Marion Murray to her father, Sept. 21, Oct. 20, 1924; Marion Murray to her family, Oct. 19, 1924; Unger Coll., Univ. of Okla. Library.

[56] *West Coast Leader,* Dec. 2, 1924.

that Murray had misrepresented conditions, that there were no schools or doctors, and that all the other farmers but two had left.[57] Alfalfa Bill tried to refute these charges in a letter to C. O. Gates, the brother of colonists Ervin and Warren Gates. He contended that there was no problem with land titles or the Indians and that all was going well.[58] His opinion was not shared by Gallentine, who wrote another letter to Cottrell in which he complained of being ill and without food and said he wanted to go home.[59]

Meanwhile, work at the colony continued. Cotton was planted, and though it was a very dry year, the wells supplied enough water for irrigation.[60] However, when members of the second band of colonists departed soon after arriving, Warren and Ervin Gates also left the colony and told the *Buenos Aires Herald* that only two families remained. The venture was a disaster, they said, and the last two families wanted to leave but were without funds.[61] C. O. Gates wrote to the State Department saying that Murray had mistreated his brothers and had defrauded them. The Gates brothers claimed that Murray cursed them, charged exorbitant prices at his store, and treated the colonists like peons, though the brothers admitted that some of their information was secondhand.[62]

In response to an unfavorable article in the *Buenos Aires Herald*, Murray wrote the editor that there was no truth in this story. He contended that some members of his first group of colonists did not want to work and that hard work was necessary in a virgin territory. Murray said that some of the colonists had indicated on the voyage to Chile that they did not plan to work. One colonist's wife had admitted that they were "movers," who had never settled in one place very long. The editor declined to accept Mur-

---

[57] W. C. Pitner and Robert Gallentine to Cottrell, Dec. 31, 1924, File 824.52, National Archives.

[58] *Johnston County Capital-Democrat*, Jan. 8, 1925.

[59] Gallentine to Cottrell, Jan. 9, 1925, File 824.52, National Archives.

[60] Marion Murray to her family, Jan. 25, 1925, Unger Coll., Univ. of Okla. Library.

[61] *New York Times*, Feb. 1, 1925.

[62] Warren Gates to C. O. Gates, Dec. 22, 1924; C. O. Gates to the State Department, Feb. 8, 1925, File 824.52, National Archives.

ray's version of the affair and claimed that the colony was a sordid venture which needed to be exposed.[63]

In April, 1925, the Gallentine and Pitner families, who had continued to ask for help from the State Department, suddenly appeared in Buenos Aires, where they booked third-class passage to New York on the steamer *Voltaire*. On board the ship they told a story of mistreatment, disease, starvation, and threats by Murray. Only by getting help from employees of Standard Oil Company in Argentina had they been able to escape from Bolivia, they said. Both men claimed to have lost sixty pounds and to have been stranded by Murray in a jungle where their crops had failed. The ship's passengers raised $674 to help pay for the two men's fares back to Oklahoma. On arriving in Oklahoma, they repeated their story, which was printed throughout the state. Neither Pitner nor Gallentine revealed that on February 27 Murray had loaned them $362.80 and $875.00 respectively.[64]

The State Department continued to receive complaints about the colony. The president of the United States Chamber of Commerce in Argentina protested that Murray's failure reflected on all American businessmen. The chargé d'affaires in Buenos Aires, Benjamin Shaw, interviewed the editor of the *Buenos Aires Herald* and repeated the accusations made by him. The paper reported that the last family had departed, leaving only Alfalfa Bill, his sons, and their families.[65]

Murray returned to Tishomingo in July, 1925, to purchase a cotton gin and gather a new group of colonists. In a report on the colony's first year he claimed that the land was better than he had thought and that cotton crops and gardens were flourishing. Local markets were purchasing their beans and corn, and despite the

[63] *Buenos Aires Herald*, Mar. 11, 14, 1925.

[64] Gallentine to the State Department, Mar. 31, 1925, File 824.52, National Archives; *New York Times*, Apr. 6, 1925; *Daily Oklahoman*, Apr. 6, 1925; note for $362.80 signed by W. C. Pitner and note for $875.00 signed by Robert Gallentine, Feb. 27, 1925, Murray Coll., Univ. of Okla. Library.

[65] Willard T. Clark to the American Consul at La Paz, Feb. 12, 1925; Benjamin Thaw, Jr., to Hughes, June 4, 1925; newspaper clipping, *Buenos Aires Herald*, June 18, 1925; File 824.52, National Archives.

serious setbacks of the first year he had great hopes for the future. Marion, Johnston's wife, shared her father-in-law's optimism about the cotton crop. More than one hundred acres had been cleared and were being planted by Indian labor. The cotton produced over a bale an acre, and the merchants in Tucumán, Argentina, had offered to buy both their cotton and their corn.[66]

On his way back to the United States Murray had stopped in La Paz to see Cottrell, who was by now less optimistic about the future of the colony. He had begun to agree with Consul Deichman at Valparaiso, who urged the State Department to stop Murray's attempt to bring a third group of colonists to Bolivia. The Bolivian government remained favorable; spokesmen said that the colony was expanding and that other colonies were to be established. But the United States State Department did not accept this appraisal, and when more adverse consular reports were received, the Division of Latin American Affairs formally labeled the scheme a failure.[67]

Meanwhile, Murray was having trouble obtaining new colonists. Close to bankruptcy, he was forced to borrow $500 from Roy Johnson of Ardmore before returning to Bolivia. He wrote a long letter to Secretary of State Hughes discussing the more recent problems of the colony. He denied the charges made by some of the former colonists and included in his letter newspaper clippings of statements by Warren Gates and Pitner praising the colony. Murray's charge that many of the colonists failed to do their share of the work was supported by Gabriel Martin in an article in the *South Pacific Mail* of Valparaiso. Martin reported that many of the colonists were surprised to find that they were supposed to labor in this Bolivian "paradise."[68]

---

[66] "Murray Colony of Bolivia to All Interested Therein," June 14, 1925, Murray Coll., Univ. of Okla. Library; Marion Murray to her father, Feb. 12, Mar. 22, 1925; Marion Murray to her family, Feb. 14, May 29, 1925; Unger Coll., Univ. of Okla. Library.

[67] Cottrell to Hughes, May 23, 1925; C. F. Deichman to Hughes, May 25, June 15, 1925; W. Roswell Barker to Hughes, Apr. 1, May 5, 1925; Memorandum from the Division of Latin American Affairs, Mar. 21, 1925; File 824.52, National Archives.

[68] Murray to Hughes, July 1, 1925, File 824.52, National Archives; *South Pacific Mail*, Nov. 12, 1925, cited in Pickens, "The Murray Colonies of Bolivia," 113–14.

Despite the apparent failure of the colony, the Bolivian government remained hopeful that it would eventually succeed. Felipe Guzmán, the new minister of war and colonization, told the congress that establishing a colony was a delicate procedure and that the government should give Murray more help. Since one of the main problems was getting the settlers through customs, where language difficulties were magnified, he urged the government to commission Julio Alborta to go to New Orleans and accompany the next group of settlers.[69] Instead of blaming Murray for the problems, the Bolivian government believed they were the result of transplanting families to a primitive area. Drought, locusts, and quarrels between Murray and the farmers had added to the difficulties.[70] Murray's family agreed with this view.

Alice Murray steadfastly defended her husband's actions, saying that he had been blamed for everything. She accepted the rugged existence with few complaints, and her letters to relatives in Oklahoma were filled with optimism. The Murrays' three married sons lived close by, and Alice and her daughters-in-law prepared a varied diet of deer, turkey, and sometimes parrot. When Alfalfa Bill returned to the colony, efforts were redoubled to fence the land and increase cotton production. Johnston and his brother William did the cultivating, since the Indians did not know how to operate a plow. The cotton gin arrived, as did a mechanic to put it into operation. In March, 1926, Alice felt that the future looked much brighter.[71]

Marion Murray wrote that the crops were prospering. The forty-five Indian families renting land in the colony had produced a sizable corn crop, and the forage had yielded three cuttings. The alfalfa was sold for a dollar a bale, and Murray's gin was busy baling cotton. Conditions had so improved that the colonizer decided to hire a farm manager and move to one of the towns. The Murray

[69] *Anexos al Mensaje del Excelentisimo señor Presidente Constitucional Provisorio de la República* (La Paz, Talleres Gráficas de la Intendencia de Guerra, 1926), 30–31.

[70] *Memoria, 1926*, 10–12.

[71] Alice Murray to "Still," July 10, 1925; Alice Murray to "Nita," Mar. 21, 1926; Murray Coll., Univ. of Okla. Library; *Daily Oklahoman*, June 20, 1926.

sons planned to stay on the land even though the Bolivian government had refused to give them clear title to it.[72] In a candid letter Marion wrote that in spite of the brighter prospects she wished Murray would give up the colony. She said that her father-in-law should have been living in 1726 or 1826, for in 1926 people would not accept the hardships of pioneer life.[73]

In the fall of 1926 the situation at the settlement deteriorated rapidly. The Indians were unable to pay their rents, and the Murrays had to accept horses and even rock salt as payment. All the sons had lost their investments. Finally the Murrays moved to Aguayrenda, where a son was born to Johnston and Marion. In January, 1927, came word that the government had canceled the concession.[74] At that time Marion wrote that Alfalfa Bill seemed to be failing in health. She said that he looked "awfully queer," and appeared to be "losing his grip." He brooded about losing all of his money, as well as that of his sons.[75] He had been ill, as had nearly all members of the family, and had possibly contracted malaria. He received some severe burns when he fell into a hole filled with live coals in which stumps were being burned.[76] Tired and discouraged, Alfalfa Bill seemed to be losing his spark and drive.

Murray went to La Paz to negotiate with the government for an extension of the concession or for payment for the improvements. He was pleased by his talks with Hernando Siles, who was now president of Bolivia. However, the Siles government was being threatened by a revolution, and by the end of May the entire country was under a state of siege. The government then became hostile to Murray. He wrote to Cottrell protesting the cancellation of the concession and the refusal of the Bolivian government to pay the

[72] Marion Murray to her family, Jan. 1, Mar. 25, Apr. 22, 1926, Unger Coll., Univ. of Okla. Library.

[73] Marion Murray to her family, Apr. 29, Sept. 2, 1926, Unger Coll., Univ. of Okla. Library.

[74] Marion Murray to her family, Sept. 14, 21, Oct. 13, 1926, Unger Coll., Univ. of Okla. Library; *Mensaje del Presidente, 1926*, 68.

[75] Marion Murray to her family, Jan. 13, Apr. 7, 1927, Unger Coll., Univ. of Okla. Library.

[76] Burbank Murray, interview of Feb. 10, 1966.

transportation charges on the cotton gin. He also charged that the government had not carried out its agreement to remove the squatters and to give him a clear title to the land.[77] Cottrell sent a seven-page report to Secretary of State Frank Kellogg, in which he sympathized with Murray's plight but expressed a desire to keep the legation out of the affair. Murray was about to lose $80,000, wrote Cottrell, but then colonization was a dangerous investment. Cottrell also reported that former President Saavedra owned lands near the concession and wanted to add it to his holdings. He added that only the general store had proved profitable, and even this operation had alienated local merchants. Kellogg responded by advising Cottrell to render only informal assistance.[78]

At this low point Murray characteristically came up with a new plan: a prospectus for the El Gran Chaco Cattle Corporation of Bolivia. He was to be the president, and Sam R. Hawks, a hotel operator from Clinton, Oklahoma, was to serve as secretary and sales agent. The two men proposed to raise $250,000 to launch the venture. The Murray sons and their wives did not favor the proposal and urged Alfalfa Bill to return to Oklahoma and run for the senate or the governorship in 1930.

The cattle corporation never developed, but a change in attitude by the Bolivian government encouraged the colonists' hopes about cotton production.[79] Suddenly the local officials stopped pressing them and removed some of the squatters from the lands. President Siles reported to the congress that, though Murray had a firm commitment to bring in twenty-five families, the contract should be modified to remove this stipulation and reduce the acreage. The concession, reduced to 7,500 acres, would be operated by Indians trained by Murray to work the lands and operate the cotton gin. The change in attitude came about because the dispute between

[77] Murray to Cottrell, Jan. [?], 1927, [?], 1927, File 824.52, National Archives.
[78] Cottrell to Frank Kellogg, Mar. 5, 1927; Kellogg to Cottrell, Apr. 18, 1927; File 824.52, National Archives.
[79] Marion Murray to her family, Apr. 9, 1927, Unger Coll., Univ. of Okla. Library; "Prospectus of El Gran Chaco Cattle Corporation of Bolivia, South America"; Sam Hawks to Murray, Apr. 11, 1927; Murray Coll., Univ. of Okla. Library.

Bolivia and Paraguay over the Chaco was worsening and the Bolivian government needed Murray's presence to help validate its claims to the region.[80]

Not realizing that they were being used as pawns in the border dispute, the Murrays rejoiced in the new spirit of co-operation. Cottrell also seemed encouraged, though he expressed concern that neither Julio Alborta nor Vincente Mendoza López, Murray's lawyer, had been paid for their services. The store was causing further problems, for Murray was using his lease to import goods duty-free for resale in the store. According to Cottrell, Alborta said that "Colonel Murray was a peculiar man and felt that everybody was trying to take advantage of him."[81] Ironically, the August, 1927, issue of the *Bulletin of the Pan American Union* featured an article on the opportunities for colonization in Bolivia, stressing that only small capital investments were needed because the good climate and cheap labor assured large profits. In this remarkable article the author noted that, though colonization in Bolivia was still in its infancy, irrigated alfalfa was already being grown.[82] No doubt the Murrays would have been more reserved in their comments on Bolivian colonization.

At the end of 1927 some members of the Murray family abandoned Bolivia. Marion Murray and her infant son left to return to her parents' home. Even Murray was tempted to return to Oklahoma. His old friend and political ally Henry S. Johnston had been elected governor in 1926, and he asked Alfalfa Bill to return as his legal adviser.[83] Murray declined the offer and tried to continue producing cotton with Indian labor.

As the boundary dispute with Paraguay grew more ominous, the government of Bolivia used its administration-controlled press to

[80] Murray to Cottrell, June 24, 1927, File 824.52, National Archives; *Mensaje del Presidente, 1927,* 79–80; *Memoria, 1927,* 122–25.

[81] Marion Murray to her family, July 26, 1927, Unger Coll., Univ. of Okla. Library; Cottrell to Kellogg, May 9, June 30, 1927, File 824.52, National Archives.

[82] David Weeks, "Colonization Opportunities in Bolivia," *Bulletin of the Pan American Union,* Vol. LXI (August, 1927), 786.

[83] Henry S. Johnston to Murray, Nov. 17, 1926, Murray Coll., Univ. of Okla. Library.

praise the colony.[84] The *Memoria* of 1928 reported the delivery of baled cotton in La Paz and lauded the success of the endeavor. The government agreed to reduce the import duty on materials brought into Bolivia by Murray, but in return he had to agree to buy and gin all of the cotton grown locally.[85] Finally, on August 6, 1928, President Siles canceled the concession, though he agreed to permit Murray to continue operating the cotton gin.[86] A month later, still maintaining the myth of the success of the colony, the Bolivian vice-consul in New York City wrote an article praising the fine work of Murray in the Chaco.[87]

The boundary dispute brought an end to Murray's dreams. The Bolivian army drafted Indian men and boys living on his land and commandeered his mules and other livestock. Using what money he had left, Murray bought passage to the United States for himself, his wife, and his two youngest children. Johnston, Massena, and William would remain in Bolivia to work until they had enough money to return home. As late as March, 1929, Murray had faith in the ultimate success of the colony, but the termination of the contract with the Bolivian government ended further hope.[88]

On July 24, 1929, the Murrays left Aguayrenda for New Orleans and after a long and arduous journey arrived in Tishomingo on August 22.[89] Murray was welcomed home by a throng of well-wishers. Though he had been out of the state for ten years, his name still attracted attention.

From the beginning Alfalfa Bill's dream of an agricultural colony had been based on the false premise that he could implement his agrarian philosophy in an isolated area of a country suffering from internal political chaos and external pressures. Nor could he find other men willing to endure the hardships of pioneer life. The land

[84] *El País* (La Paz), Mar. 28, 1928; *La Razón* (La Paz), Mar. 25, 1928.

[85] *Memoria, 1928,* 153–56.

[86] *Mensaje del Presidente, 1928,* 96–97.

[87] Emeterio Cano de la Vega, "The Colonization of the Chaco—the Work of Colonel Murray," *Bolivia: A Bi-Monthly Survey,* Vol. II (September, 1928), 22–23.

[88] *Bartlesville Morning Examiner,* Mar. 19, 1929.

[89] Diary of Alice Murray, July 15–Aug. 16, 1929, Murray Coll., Univ. of Okla. Library.

and the potential remain, and one historian has suggested that this region still offers Bolivia its greatest hope for agricultural development.[90]

The Bolivian debacle never made Murray bitter. In the 1940's he wrote nostalgically of the years in South America and suggested to friends that he would like to try the colonization project again. The agricultural frontier of the nineteenth century was gone, but Alfalfa Bill never gave up his dream of recreating a land of yeoman farmers.

[90] Hubert Herring, *A History of Latin America* (New York, Alfred A. Knopf, 1961), 566.

172

THE GUBERNATORIAL CAMPAIGN OF 1930

VIII

AUGUST, 1929, seemed an unpropitious time for Alfalfa Bill Murray to launch his gubernatorial campaign. The oil and real-estate boom of the 1920's had given the state a façade of great prosperity. The profiles of Oklahoma City and Tulsa had been pierced by rising skyscrapers, and even smaller towns like Enid could boast of multistory buildings. Though agriculture had shared less fully in the boom, farm property values had increased sufficiently to give rural people a feeling of security. The economic glow was extinguished in less than sixty days, when the October, 1929, Wall Street crash destroyed the illusion of prosperity in Oklahoma and the nation. The worst depression in the history of the country, while a disaster for millions, gave Murray unexpected assistance in his efforts to return to Oklahoma politics.

During his ten-year absence the Oklahoma Democratic party had suffered from internal strife and Republican victories to a degree never experienced before or since. Beginning in 1919, when Republican John Harreld won a special election for the Fifth District congressional seat, Democratic candidates marched down the road to defeat. The following year Warren G. Harding became the first Republican Presidential nominee to carry the state, and Harreld became its first Republican senator. Five of the eight congressmen were Republicans, and the Republican party also gained control of the State House of Representatives. Even the Oklahoma Supreme Court and the Corporation Commission acquired Republican party members in the sweep. If the Democrats felt that this was a disaster, the worst was yet to come.

In 1922 Democrat Jack Walton, mayor of Oklahoma City, won the governorship on an anti–Ku Klux Klan platform. The Klan had become a powerful force in the state, and Walton won only through the active support of the Farmer-Labor Reconstruction League. The league, patterned after the Non-Partisan League of North Dakota, represented a new bloc of voters within the Democratic party. Socialist opposition to American entry into the World War had virtually destroyed the party in Oklahoma. Almost in a body the former Socialists joined the Democratic party and helped to form the league and nominate Walton. The Democrats won a sweeping victory in November, 1922.

The next year Walton became Oklahoma's first governor to be impeached. His misuse of the governor's power of pardon and parole, suspension of the writ of habeas corpus, and repeated declarations of martial law, among other charges, led to his trial and conviction. Martin Trapp, the lieutenant governor, succeeded Walton and tried to restore party prestige.

In the 1924 primary Walton won the nomination for the Senate seat being vacated by Robert L. Owen. In the general election, though Democratic Presidential nominee John W. Davis carried the state, Walton was defeated by W. B. Pine, who became Oklahoma's second Republican senator.

The Democratic party appeared to be regaining solidarity in 1926, when Henry S. Johnston won the governorship and Elmer Thomas of Lawton defeated John Harreld in his bid for re-election to the Senate. But even this victory was a hollow one, for in 1928 Johnston endorsed the wet, Catholic Al Smith, and the state voted overwhelmingly for the dry, Protestant Herbert Hoover. The Republicans almost recaptured the State House of Representatives and won three of the congressional races. The twelfth legislature met on January 20, 1929, and impeached Johnston on charges of incompetency. He was soon convicted and removed from office. The large Republican minority in the legislature had joined a group of insurgent Democrats to put Lieutenant Governor William J. Holloway in the Governor's office. Holloway acknowledged the minority-party support by appointing Republican oilman-philanthropist Lew Wentz as chairman of the Highway Commission. In 1929 the Democrats were still deeply torn by the

Johnston impeachment and the disastrous election of the previous year.

From 1919 until 1929 Murray's name was often mentioned in Oklahoma politics. The former congressman often made his views known, but he took no active part in the political wars. In 1920 he issued a broadside entitled "Murray on Cause of Defeat," in which he declared that in order to win in 1922 the Democrats had to stop slandering each other and work to obtain a broader federal program of farm credits.[1] Many observers felt that this was the opening gun in a campaign for the governorship, but the growth of the Ku Klux Klan, the decline of farm prices, and his activities in Bolivia kept Murray out of the race. During visits to Oklahoma in 1920 and 1921 he gave a series of lectures at Murray State College on "Written Constitutional Government," in which he called for a return of the government to the Constitution, a theme he would repeat for the next thirty-six years.[2] The following year he contributed a column to the *Johnston County Capital-Democrat* titled "The Farm and Farmers," but his discussions of politics and agriculture added little to what he had already said and written. In 1922 he refused to enter the political maelstrom created by the league and the Klan and wrote to Campbell Russell, a member of the Corporation Commission, that in justice to his family he could not spend the large sums of money which campaigning required. He said that the costs prohibited honest men from running and that the rise of the Klan demonstrated the lack of honesty in state politics.[3] After Walton's election a group of Okmulgee Democrats formed a Murray-for-governor club, but he refused to aid them.[4] If, in 1926, Murray had returned to Oklahoma to become Governor Johnston's legal adviser,[5] the Governor's impeachment might have been forestalled.

Impeachments, the Reconstruction League, the Klan, internecine

1 "Murray on Cause of Defeat," Nov. 12, 1920, broadside, Murray Coll., Univ. of Okla. Library.

2 *Harlow's Weekly*, Dec. 17, 1920.

3 Murray to Campbell Russell, July 20, 1922, Campbell Russell Collection (Norman, University of Oklahoma Library, Division of Manuscripts).

4 *Oklahoma City Times*, Nov. 22, 1922.

5 Henry S. Johnston to Murray, Nov. 17, 1926; Johnston to Murray, Nov. 4, 1927; Johnston Coll., Univ. of Okla. Library.

primary wars, and Republican victories ripped apart the Democratic leadership. In one way or another nearly every important leader was identified with the chaos. Only one well-known politician had avoided the fray, the man who had been in Bolivia, Alfalfa Bill. The stage was set for his return to politics, and the depression gave him the issues upon which to campaign.

Even before the Murrays returned to Tishomingo from Bolivia, the rural newspapers of Oklahoma had begun to speculate that the former leader was about to re-enter the political arena.[6] A few days after they reached their old home, Johnston called on Murray to brief him about the political situation. Murray publicly deplored Johnston's impeachment.[7] To gather firsthand information, he began to tour the state giving speeches on Bolivia. His intentions were made clear in a fifty-five-page brochure, paid for by Ardmore oilman Roy Johnson and issued by friends in Tishomingo. The brochure praised Murray and his previous activities in the state.[8] Now all that was needed was to put the old organization together again. A call for reunions was issued.

Just as they had in 1910 and 1918, the former members of the constitutional conventions and the first legislature rallied to Murray's call. Judge A. L. Beckett, former constitutional-convention delegate, organized a reunion on September 17, at Okmulgee, where Alfalfa Bill met with former governors Charles N. Haskell, Robert L. Williams, and Johnston. A mock session of the convention revived memories of Murray's role in writing the state constitution. A reunion of the members of the first house of representatives took place on September 26 in Oklahoma City.[9] The rural press gave extensive coverage to the reunions,[10] and by the first week of October Murray's name was being widely mentioned in connection with the 1930 primary races for the Senate and for the governorship.

Throughout September and October Murray continued his trav-

[6] *Harlow's Weekly*, July 20, 1929.

[7] *Oklahoma City Times*, Aug. 24, 1929.

[8] *Brief Biography of Murray (Alfalfa Bill)* (Ardmore, McLean Printing Co., 1929).

[9] *Okmulgee Daily News*, Sept. 22, 1929; *Oklahoma City Times*, Sept. 26, 1929.

[10] *Harlow's Weekly*, Oct. 5, 1929.

els over the state giving speeches about his adventures in Bolivia. In each town he got in touch with old political friends. At a typical meeting in Ardmore Murray conferred with local leaders R. M. McCool and U. T. Rexroat, while denying Roy Johnson's report that he planned to run for governor.[11] In fact, he commented that politics did not interest him. Then he continued on to Ada, Stillwater, Madill, and other towns. When he visited his father, Uriah Dow Murray, now living in Oklahoma City, an *Oklahoma City Times* reporter described Alfalfa Bill's early life for readers who might not remember the long-absent politician.[12] As a result of these trips Murray decided not to run against Republican W. B. Pine for the Senate, and by the first of November he was in the gubernatorial race.

Murray formally announced his candidacy in January, 1930. Many editors were predicting that the campaign would be so slanderous that no Democrat could win. Murray commented, "I would be nominated if the primary election be held tomorrow; I will be nominated in August. The country folk is aroused."[13] In his platform he attacked big business and the School Land Commission, and he pledged to appoint only honest officials, adhere to the constitution, restore the good name of the state, and embark upon an extensive road-building program. His platform included planks advocating economy in government, greater control over public utilities, and equal rights for all, including Negroes. He promised that "the poor and weak shall have my especial care for the rich and strong can usually protect themselves."[14] The metropolitan press ignored Murray's announcement, and R. M. McClintock, a leading political journalist, failed even to mention his name in connection with the gubernatorial race.[15]

The campaign got off to such a slow start that for the first two

---

11 *Daily Oklahoman*, Aug. 29, 1929.

12 *Oklahoma City Times*, Sept. 5, 1929.

13 *Daily Oklahoman*, Dec. 5, 1929; *Muskogee Daily Phoenix*, Dec. 8, 1929; *Harlow's Weekly*, Jan. 4, 1930.

14 Platform of William H. Murray, Jan. 8, 1930, Murray Coll., Univ. of Okla. Library.

15 *Cordell Beacon*, Jan. 9, 1930.

months of 1930 it appeared that Murray might be forced out of the primary. In March, however, he gained needed support when the *McAlester Democrat* and a group of old-time labor leaders endorsed him. He had been under attack from labor unions since 1908, and in March, 1930, Tulsa labor leader William McClaren spoke against him in a radio address, but a definite shift on the part of organized labor was taking place.[16]

Murray faced formidable opposition in the gubernatorial primary. Frank M. Buttram, a millionaire oilman from Oklahoma City, was his principal opponent. Buttram ran as a conservative candidate, pledging to restore order to the state government. One of the most able men in the race was Congressman Ed Howard of Tulsa, and Alfalfa Bill feared him more than any of the other candidates.[17] Former Governor Martin Trapp, Secretary of the Treasury A. S. J. Shaw, and William Darnell were also candidates. When Darnell withdrew, many of his Farmers' Union backers transferred their support to Murray.

Murray selected a diverse group of men for his campaign staff. Sam Hawks, Clinton hotel operator, became his campaign manager, assisted by O. A. Brewer, a long-term Democratic politician. Claude Weaver, Murray's companion in Congress in 1913 and 1914, headed the Oklahoma City Murray club. The advertising committee included Luther Langston, who had been a leader of the Socialist party and its candidate in the race against Murray in the congressional election of 1912.[18] Other members of the campaign organization included Judge James R. Armstrong and former Superintendent of Public Instruction R. H. Wilson, both of whom had been leaders in the Johnston administration.

Early in the campaign funds were too limited for Murray to make much use of radio, and so the main agency for disseminating his views became the *Blue Valley Farmer*, a small country weekly. It was published at Roff by L. N. Sheldon, a former Socialist and founder of the Oklahoma Non-Partisan League. O. A. Brewer purchased the paper, which at that time had only 430 subscribers, to

[16] *Harlow's Weekly*, Mar. 22, 1930.
[17] Murray, *Memoirs*, II, 375.　　　　　[18] *Daily Oklahoman*, Mar. 16, 1930.

obtain its mailing rights, and it became the focal point of Murray's efforts and a legend in Oklahoma. Published when money was available and distributed by volunteers, the *Blue Valley Farmer* was Alfalfa Bill's voice, with Hawks as the president of the company and Brewer as the manager and treasurer. The Sage of Tishomingo had to have newspaper coverage. He had been endorsed by fourteen weeklies, but he was still being ignored by the large-city newspapers, and his opponents had received eighty-four editorial endorsements.[19] The *Daily Oklahoman* and the *Oklahoma City Times*, owned by E. K. Gaylord's Oklahoma Publishing Company, supported Buttram; the *Tulsa World* endorsed Howard; and the *Oklahoma News*, owned by the Scripps-Howard chain, supported Trapp.

Murray, Brewer, and Hawks concentrated on circulating the *Blue Valley Farmer* in two or three counties each week, particularly in areas where Murray was to speak. They used the same copy, changing only the first page, for several weeks, after which all the contents were changed. Ultimately the paper appeared in every part of the state. Murray claimed that it forced Darnell out of the race by capturing the support of the Farmers' Union.[20] Sheldon reported one press run of 450,000 issues and an average monthly circulation of 300,000, with a total cost of $37,000.[21] This large expenditure led to speculation that a paving contractor was Murray's financial angel.[22] The *Cordell Beacon*, in commenting on the *Blue Valley Farmer*, stated:

> The chief charge against Buttram is his alleged excessive use of money. Yet it costs more to print and distribute one issue of the paper, than Murray is allowed legally for the entire campaign. Besides this, it is alleged that he [Murray] has in his headquarters men like J. Luther Langston, L. N. Sheldon, and O. A. Brewer, who have never been known to work in a campaign except for money.[23]

19 *Muskogee Daily Phoenix*, Mar. 30, 1930.
20 Murray, tape-recorded interview of Nov. 20, 1952, OHS Library.
21 L. N. Sheldon, interview by Hermione B. Briscoe, July 20, 1938, cited in Hermione B. Briscoe, "The 1938 Oklahoma Gubernatorial Campaign as Presented by a Group of State Newspapers" (Master's thesis, University of Oklahoma, 1939), 186.
22 *Tulsa Tribune*, July 13, 1930.
23 *Cordell Beacon*, May 15, 1930.

Throughout the campaign Murray played the role of the poor underdog despite increasingly large expenditures. He called his canvass a "cheese and crackers campaign," alluding to a large cake of cheese given to him by Bill Hunsford of Tahlequah. Carrying the cheese and a box of crackers from town to town, Alfalfa Bill focused his campaign on two issues: tax equalization through a gross income tax on individuals and corporations and economy in government. As the depression worsened in the spring of 1930, he told the press that he had started his campaign with $42 borrowed from the First National Bank of Tishomingo, a statement designed to win the sympathy of financially disabled Oklahomans.[24]

Murray promised to alleviate the grave economic conditions by lowering ad valorem taxes on farms, ranches, homes, and small businesses. He advocated free seed for destitute farmers and a state road-building program to provide jobs. His speeches featured sharp personal attacks on his opponents, especially Buttram, Trapp, Howard, and Shaw. Trapp, Howard, and Shaw had served terms as state treasurer, and Murray labeled them the "state house gang." He did not criticize his most-feared opponent, Congressman Howard, in Howard's home district. He simply cautioned the voters that a vote for Howard would be lost because the congressman lacked support elsewhere in the state. A rumor circulated by Murray's opponents suggested that a state which suffered three gubernatorial impeachments would lose its statehood, the implication being that Murray would be impeached. In rebutting the story, Alfalfa Bill emphasized his record as a lawyer, president of the constitutional convention, speaker of the first house, and congressman.

While the urban press continued to ignore his campaign, Murray steadily built up rural and small-town support. Darnell's organization melted away when Murray launched an extensive speaking tour.[25] The Buttram forces covered the state with newspaper advertisements and billboards, but voters were less favorably impressed by his Horatio Alger autobiography than by Alfalfa Bill's

---

[24] Murray, *Memoirs*, II, 365.
[25] *Harlow's Weekly*, Mar. 1, 1930; *Oklahoma City Times*, Mar. 6, 1930.

proposal to eliminate the state property tax. The prospect of a 75 to 80 per cent cut in the property tax appealed to farmers who had no markets for their crops and to homeowners who had large mortgage payments.[26] The leaders of the Farmers' Union, primarily President John Simpson, opposed the idea of a gross income tax, favoring a net income tax. But voters were not concerned with semantics.[27]

Murray also gained the support of the Oklahoma Federation of Labor, which reversed its 1910 condemnatory resolutions. This support greatly improved his chances for victory. Langston, one of his chief advisers, had been secretary of the federation in 1910, when Murray was bitterly denounced by the organization. Now Langston's labor connections became an important source of strength.[28] Murray wooed Joe C. Campbell, president of the federation, in a letter which advocated a liberal industrial commission, a state-controlled unemployment-compensation fund, a program of old-age assistance, a state minimum wage, the eight-hour day for women, and an increased appropriation for the labor department.[29] The federation's leadership endorsed him, and the secretary-treasurer, Victor S. Purdy, sent out letters to local labor leaders on Murray's behalf. Purdy said that Alfalfa Bill had been a champion of labor at the constitutional convention and in the first legislature. He pointed out that Murray had received the endorsement of the trades councils of Oklahoma City, Tulsa, Muskogee, and Okmulgee. Purdy claimed that Murray represented the common people while Buttram represented only the wealthy.[30]

This accusation became a theme of the campaign. Buttram seemed likely to poll the most votes and thus would remain in the contest if a runoff primary became necessary. He was a rich, educated businessman who attracted support from the upper middle

26 *Johnston County Capital-Democrat*, Mar. 6, 1930.

27 *Harlow's Weekly*, Apr. 5, 1930.

28 *Oklahoma City Times*, Aug. 7, 1930.

29 Murray to Joe C. Campbell, June 16, 1930, Oklahoma Federation of Labor Coll., Univ. of Okla. Library.

30 Victor S. Purdy to Walter Longstreet, Aug. 8, 1930; Purdy to Ben Sharp, Aug. 8, 1930; Oklahoma State Federation of Labor Coll., Univ. of Okla. Library.

and upper classes. Murray used Buttram's apparent strength to weaken him by pointedly describing to audiences Buttram's large mansion and accusing the oilman of failing to pay his taxes. Though Murray kept Trapp and Shaw under attack, Buttram now became his real target. The front page of the *Blue Valley Farmer* carried a continuous series of barbs at the oilman, accusing him of listing his taxable personal property at $820 when he lived in a mansion full of art objects and Persian rugs.[31] When Alfalfa Bill claimed that Buttram owned stock in the Oklahoma Publishing Company and the *Tulsa Tribune*, editors E. K. Gaylord and Richard Lloyd Jones denied the story in editorials entitled "An Unconscionable Liar Seeks the Governorship."[32] Buttram was also hurt by the presence among his supporters of many Hoover Democrats of 1928, a fact that Murray made clear in his speeches. As the campaign neared its close in mid-July, rumors grew that Trapp, Buttram, or Howard would withdraw to solidify the anti-Murray vote, but all three stayed in the race.[33]

Murray, now being referred to by some writers as "the court-house-lawn Socrates," continued to preach tax reform through the elimination of the state property tax and the creation of a state tax commission to equalize county property valuations. In a Tulsa radio speech he expressed fear of the growth of the rich at the expense of the poor, but he said the answer was not mob rule. Farmers were suffering more than any other group, and only a reduction in taxes and governmental spending could help them. His proposals for a gross income tax, free school textbooks, and governmental economy were designed to win broad support for him.[34] He promised to use state funds to aid weak rural school districts and advocated a three-billion-dollar federal road program to employ the jobless.[35]

The campaign progressed so well that Murray wrote Alice at

[31] *Blue Valley Farmer*, June 26, July 24, 1930.
[32] *Daily Oklahoman*, July 1, 1930.
[33] *Johnston County Capital-Democrat*, July 17, 1930.
[34] A. L. Beckett, *The Speeches of William Henry Murray* (Oklahoma City, Harlow Publishing Co., 1931), 186–94.
[35] *Cordell Beacon*, June 12, 1930.

the end of June that he was confident of victory. He wrote from Tulsa, "Have been well and holding up better than any previous campaign due to extreme care to diet and habits." Burbank was ready to go to college, and Alfalfa Bill told Alice that their youngest son should apply to Dartmouth College at once; even at the height of the campaign he was concerned about his children. About the campaign, he wrote that everything was fine and that "abuse from opponents will start soon, but even this helps."[36] Murray knew that his campaign had gained great momentum and that he had pulled far ahead.

Throughout the summer the metropolitan press refused to accept Murray as a major contender. In May W. T. Huff, political correspondent for the *Muskogee Daily Phoenix*, wrote that Murray was doing very poorly in "Little Dixie," the rock-ribbed Democratic area of southeastern Oklahoma. At the end of July the *Daily Oklahoman* still contended that Trapp, Howard, and Buttram were leading.[37] But the editor of the *Muskogee Daily Phoenix* had come to believe that Alfalfa Bill had forged ahead: "Economic conditions are favorable to the Tishomingo candidate. Farmers who have seen prices go to smash and workers out of a job don't stop to do much reasoning. Murray presents himself as a fellow sufferer."[38]

The editor's analysis proved correct; on July 29 Murray not only led his opponents but also received almost twice as many votes as his closest competitor, Frank Buttram, whom he would meet in the runoff election. The results gave Murray 134,243 votes; Buttram, 69,501; Howard, 50,671; Trapp, 38,641; and Shaw, 25,572.[39] Howard led in the counties of his own congressional district, while Shaw and Trapp carried a few scattered counties. Buttram led in Oklahoma, Kay, Logan, Muskogee, Garfield, Blaine, and Sequoyah counties, demonstrating his strength in Oklahoma City, Ponca City, Enid, Blackwell, Guthrie, and Muskogee. Murray carried fifty-four counties representing every section of the state, running best, of course, in the rural areas. For example, in

36 Murray to Alice Murray, June 29, 1930, Murray Coll., Univ. of Okla. Library.
37 *Muskogee Daily Phoenix*, May 11, 1930; *Daily Oklahoman*, July 25, 1930.
38 *Muskogee Daily Phoenix*, June 27, 1930.
39 Winters, *Directory of the State of Oklahoma*, 73.

Washita County in western Oklahoma, Buttram won in the town of Cordell by a small margin, but Murray carried the rural precincts by majorities of three and four to one.[40] Many factors contributed to Alfalfa Bill's enormous success, but, as the editor of the *New York Times* suggested, he simply reaped the harvest of economic discontent.[41]

Stunned by the size of Murray's lead, veteran Democratic leaders shifted to his cause. The Trapp supporters moved into his camp, as did Eugene Lorton, editor of the *Tulsa World* and former Howard supporter, and both Howard and Shaw asked their organizations to work for Murray.[42]

The Buttram leaders moved quickly to stop the bandwagon. The principal gun in the Buttram arsenal was the Oklahoma Publishing Company. Owner-editor E. K. Gaylord determined to destroy Murray by one of the most unrestrained journalistic attacks in Oklahoma's political history. Using his papers, the *Daily Oklahoman* and the *Oklahoma City Times*, termed by Murray "The Twin Harlots of Fourth and Broadway," Gaylord published a series of front-page editorials and ran stories by Edith Johnson. Miss Johnson and Gaylord claimed that Murray's election would drive out industry, lead to a spoils system, and destroy small merchants. Not content with attacks on his program, Miss Johnson wrote that Alfalfa Bill despised soap and water, lived in a house with dirt floors and outdoor plumbing, wore dirty shirts, ate hot cakes and sirup with his hands, and wore two pairs of trousers in the winter.[43] When she charged that his underwear showed below his trouser cuffs, Murray replied, "I want to assure you that I do not know as much about her underwear, and if I did, I would be too much a gentleman to tell it."[44] Referring to her as a "bachelor lady," he inquired of his audiences where she got her information: "How'd she know? I stay at Oklahoma City hotels once in a while —but I sleep alone. Maybe she works in a hotel laundry."[45] The

[40] *Cordell Beacon*, July 31, 1930.
[41] *New York Times*, Aug. 1, 1930.
[42] *Harlow's Weekly*, Aug. 2, 1930.
[43] *Daily Oklahoman, Oklahoma City Times*, Aug. 1–12, 1930.
[44] Murray, *Memoirs*, II, 380.   [45] Hines, *Alfalfa Bill*, 274.

Gaylord-Johnson articles backfired. The state press became indignant, and farmers whose homes lacked indoor plumbing and the unemployed who lived on dirt floors became even more sympathetic to Murray.[46] Political columnists working for the metropolitan newspapers wrote that he had slipped in the polls, Buttram was moving ahead, and the bandwagon had stopped. These comments were either absolute fabrications or reflections of extremely poor judgment in light of the results.

In the runoff primary Murray had two antagonists to face, Buttram and senatorial candidate Charles Wrightsman. In the spring Murray had tried to sell advertising space in the *Blue Valley Farmer* to Wrightsman, a Tulsa oil millionaire. Rebuffed, Alfalfa Bill wired former Senator Thomas P. Gore in Washington, asking him to return to Oklahoma and run for the Senate. Eager to re-enter politics after his defeat in 1920, Gore returned and won a place in the senatorial runoff primary against Wrightsman. Gore attached himself to Murray, and the two "poor boys" took on the "rich men." Buttram was hurt by Wrightsman, who in badly delivered speeches managed to antagonize voters with stories about his butler giving handouts to the poor at the rear entrance of his home.

On August 12, the day of the runoff, rural voters flocked to the polls to give Murray an almost two-to-one victory over Buttram, while Gore defeated Wrightsman by a smaller, though comfortable, margin. Buttram carried only Oklahoma and Muskogee counties, losing Tulsa by 200 votes. In the Republican primary State Senator Ira Hill of Cherokee, a competent but lackluster politician, had won the gubernatorial nomination, and the popular Republican Senator W. B. Pine was renominated.

Murray and Gore now began their final drives for the offices they had coveted so long. Immediately after the second primary the Gaylord newspapers endorsed Hill for governor. Small-town editors castigated Gaylord for deserting the Democratic party.[47] Other Democratic papers, such as the *Walters Herald* and the *Payne*

---

[46] *McAlester Democrat*, Aug. 4, 1930; *Johnston County Capital-Democrat*, Aug. 7, 1930.

[47] *Durant News*, Aug. 14, 1930.

County News, came out for Murray as the ranks of the Democrats closed.[48] Hill offered an alternative to Murray's program of reduced taxes in the form of a bond issue of fifteen million dollars to build a state road system and employ the jobless. The Sage of Tishomingo said that this was not enough money and that the amount of interest to be paid made the plan prohibitive. The *Blue Valley Farmer* attacked Hill as a banker and was particularly hard on oilmen W. G. Skelly and Lew Wentz, who were Hill's principal backers. Murray's strategy in the general election was the same as in the primary—to make his opponents take the defensive and appear as millionaire villains.[49] He threatened to organize a boycott of Skelly Oil Company gasoline stations when Skelly helped subsidize Hill's campaign paper, the *Spotlight*.[50]

Alfalfa Bill not only began to broaden his support in the general-election campaign but also took control of the party machinery. In September he was greatly pleased by the actions of the Federation of Labor, which formally repealed its 1910 resolutions, praised his program for its dedication to humanitarian progress, and pledged its support to him.[51] Ten days later, when the state Democratic convention met in Tulsa, Murray won complete control. Delegates warmly applauded his convention speech, cheered his fulminations against Hill, and endorsed the income tax and his plan to repeal the state property tax. Six of the defeated gubernatorial candidates appeared on the platform with Governor Holloway to pledge him their support. Later, when the newspapers began to press the state Democratic committee to stop the sale of advertising in the *Blue Valley Farmer*, the committee refused to intervene. Sam Hawks became manager of state party headquarters and supervised the general-election campaign. Even farm leader John Simpson reversed his earlier stand and endorsed the nominee.[52]

[48] *Blue Valley Farmer*, Aug. 21, 1930.
[49] *Ibid.*, Sept. 25, Oct. 2, 1930; *Harlow's Weekly*, Sept. 13, 1930.
[50] *Blue Valley Farmer*, Oct. 2, 1930.
[51] *Official Proceedings of the Twenty-seventh Annual Convention of the Oklahoma State Federation of Labor*, Sept. 8–10, 1930.
[52] *Muskogee Daily Phoenix*, Sept. 17, 1930; *Daily Oklahoman*, Sept. 18, 1930; *Johnston County Capital-Democrat*, Sept. 18, 1930; *Harlow's Weekly*, Sept. 13, 20, 1930.

During the campaign Murray, in a surprise move, savagely attacked the state educational system. His former opponent, Frank Buttram, was a regent of the University of Oklahoma, and Murray's criticism of that institution was especially vehement. In August he declared that the university's graduates were less competent than those of the Oklahoma Agricultural and Mechanical College at Stillwater. Speaking in October to the League of Young Democrats, he said: "The University wants an appropriation of $5,000,000 for buildings, including $150,000 for a swimming pool. Well so far as I am concerned they can go to the creek to swim. . . . You can't get through life by graduating from football, baseball or highballs."[53] The candidate remembered that College Hill Institute did not have a swimming pool and saw no need for building one at the university in the midst of a depression.

Hill's organization retaliated by printing a broadside, "Football, Baseball and Highballs," which declared that Murray intended to destroy the university and end athletics in the state schools. Alfalfa Bill also attacked the North Central Association, which accredited Oklahoma schools, declaring that the state should control its own institutions. At Muskogee, Alva, and Tonkawa he announced, "I would like to see a return to the old McGuffey Readers."[54] The average Oklahoman was not concerned about a swimming pool for the university but did like Murray's free-textbook proposal and his announced goal of economy in state spending.

Murray made a direct appeal for the Negro vote in the general-election campaign. Speaking at the all-Negro town of Boley, he criticized the use of the word "colored" as improper when used to refer to Negroes and commented that the word "nigger" applied to "stingy" people, both black and white; he would use "Negro" to refer to his black friends. He endorsed the "intelligent humane Southern view" of race, which held that whites should eat, sleep, and attend schools where Negroes were not present. However, whites must guarantee the Negro his rights to life, liberty, and the

53 *Muskogee Daily Phoenix*, Oct. 22, 1930.
54 *Johnston County Capital-Democrat*, Oct. 9, 1930; *Oklahoma City Times*, Oct. 28, 1930.

pursuit of happiness; equal rights in the courts; and protection from mob violence. Negroes should be given a chance to rise by their own efforts, said the candidate, and he urged Negroes to develop a pride in their race, for racial pride and peaceful racial relations would allow the Negro to make great strides forward.[55] Oklahoma Negroes were generally Republican, and the *Black Dispatch*, the leading Negro paper in Oklahoma City, denounced Murray's speech as a vote-getting device.[56] It was a rather blatant attempt to win Negro votes, but Murray was the first Democratic politician in years to seek their support openly.

As the fall campaign wore on, the crowds of farmers attending Murray's speeches grew larger. In the cities, however, little political activity took place, and the voters appeared apathetic.[57] Murray continued to aid Gore in his Senate race, and the *Blue Valley Farmer* devoted several issues almost entirely to him.[58] The former Texas Populist tied his campaign to Alfalfa Bill's, and the results of the general election demonstrated his wisdom in doing so.

Murray defeated Hill by 301,921 votes to 208,575, while Gore led Pine by fewer than 24,000 votes.[59] Hill carried only thirteen of the traditionally Republican counties and Oklahoma County. With one exception the entire Democratic ticket was elected; only Republican Congressman M. C. Garber of the Eighth District survived. In describing the tide that swept the state, Murray wrote, "The flames ignited by economic errors, now consuming the huts and cabins of the poor, will eventually destroy the mansions and palaces of the rich, and the rich seem not to comprehend the truth."[60] While the violence Murray predicted failed to occur, voters had given notice that they opposed government by millionaire oilmen, whether Democratic or Republican. After the election Alfalfa Bill returned to Tishomingo to rest, but not without making a final judgment on the election: "I cannot see why people voted

[55] Murray, *Memoirs*, III, 474–79.
[56] *Black Dispatch* (Oklahoma City), Oct. 21, 1930.
[57] *Harlow's Weekly*, Oct. 18, Nov. 1, 1930.
[58] *Blue Valley Farmer*, Oct. 9, 1930.
[59] Winters, *Directory of the State of Oklahoma*, 72.
[60] Murray, *Memoirs*, III, 484.

for me as they did in many instances and then failed to vote for friendly candidates to the legislature."[61] He recognized that his program would face rough sledding when the legislature convened in January.

Throughout November and December Murray stayed in Tishomingo and refused to see visitors.[62] Tired from his strenuous campagn, the sixty-one-year-old victor turned over to Lieutenant Governor–elect Robert Burns all the ceremonial tasks before the inauguration. The campaign had lasted over a year, and he needed the time to rest and prepare a detailed program for the legislature. In an attempt to quiet growing fears that he meant to destroy the state school system, he contributed an editorial to the *Blue Valley Farmer* advocating more state financial aid to schools.[63]

In a year's time Bill Murray had won three major political victories. Untouched by the conflicts of the 1920's and unhampered by great wealth, he had pledged to aid the common people who were suffering from the effects of the first year of the depression. He spoke their language, he knew their needs, and they had voted for him. During the next four years he would try to meet the problems of the depression and would constantly and sincerely seek to lighten the burdens of the common man.

[61] *Blue Valley Farmer*, Nov. 6, 1930.
[62] *Harlow's Weekly*, Nov. 29, 1930.
[63] *Blue Valley Farmer*, Nov. 13, 1930.

✪

DEPRESSION GOVERNOR

IX

O<small>N THE MORNING</small> of January 12, 1931, over twelve thousand spectators gathered before the steps of the capitol building for Alfalfa Bill Murray's inauguration. The ceremony and the Governor's address set the tone of the new administration. Uriah Dow Murray, ninety-one years old, acting in his capacity as a notary public, swore in his son as Oklahoma's ninth governor. Chief Millett Hoy Koy Bitty of the Comanche Nation offered a prayer. Then, in the freezing weather, the Governor delivered his inaugural address. Many of those in the audience had lost or were losing their homes and farms; many others were unemployed. To them Murray said, "I shall honestly and honorably represent those who choose to call themselves the 'better element,' but this is one time when Oklahoma Indians, niggers and po' white folks are going to have a fair-minded Governor too."[1] To those who wondered how Murray planned to carry out this promise, he said that it was very simple: "Running a government is very much like running a farm."[2] To show the entire state that a man of the people now resided in the governor's mansion, the inaugural ball turned into a square dance, for which Alfalfa Bill acted as a caller.[3]

The "better element" of the Sooner State often contended that the next four years was one long square dance, with the state government performing turns as directed by Alfalfa Bill. But to the rural folk, the city laborers, and the economically distressed, Murray appeared to be trying to do something for them. They knew he was not working for the oil companies, the owners of toll bridges,

[1] Hines, *Alfalfa Bill*, 277.
[2] *Ibid.*, 278.
[3] *Muskogee Daily Phoenix*, Jan. 13, 1931.

the banks, or the savings-and-loan companies. He had a program to relieve the burdens of the people who looked to him for help. A man who had to borrow $250 to attend his own inauguration knew what poverty was.[4] Murray spelled out his legislative proposals on January 13, in his first message to the thirteenth legislature.

The first address by the Governor indicated clearly what the aim of the administration would be—tax relief for the farmers and the homeowners. Murray devoted the major portion of his speech to the question of taxation. He called for the creation of a state tax commission which would equalize the property valuations of the seventy-seven counties. Property valuations and tax bases varied widely from county to county, and Murray felt that equalization would ensure fair taxation and also reduce property taxes. He asked for an income tax on individuals and corporations at one-half the federal rate, with the proceeds to go to the public schools. Murray wanted mortgages and bank deposits placed on the property-tax rolls and asked the legislature to repeal the law exempting fraternal organizations from property taxes. To prevent losses of revenue from nonpayment of taxes, he recommended that oil and natural-gas taxes be collected by the pipeline companies and paid directly to the state. A special tax would be levied to provide free seed to tenant farmers, and all state and county employees should pay a gross income tax. The basic elements of this wholesale reorganization of the state tax structure were the tax commission, the income tax, and repeal of the state property tax. These reforms were necessary and most desirable, but, as Murray realized, they would be fought by the corporations and upper-income groups.

He advocated a drastic reduction of expenditures through the elimination of many agencies and boards. He said that the Fish and Game Department and the Highway Commission were unconstitutional and had to be reorganized. The cost of higher education should be cut by eliminating duplicate courses at the University of Oklahoma and the Oklahoma Agricultural and Mechanical College. He asked that six state departments be combined and that seven agencies he abolished. The attorney general had eleven as-

[4] *Daily Oklahoman*, Apr. 23, 1931.

sistants; they should be reduced to five. The state examiner and inspector's office had sixteen assistants; six would suffice. He felt that the state could get by with a two-year budget of $26,475,000, a considerably smaller budget than that of the preceding biennium.

There was corruption in the state government, announced the Governor, and it had to be eradicated. He asked for a corrupt-practices act and a new employee expense-claims procedure. No fees should be paid to members of the legislature, and a law should be passed to prohibit any person from being the beneficiary of funds appropriated while he was a member of the legislature. Murray had always been concerned about the activities of lobbyists and thought they made "use of women, particularly those of care-less and loose character." His solution to the problem of lobbies, a remarkably ingenious idea, was to keep the legislators out of the hotels where they might be tempted. The hotels were "filled with lobbyists, who used poker games, liquor and women and even money for bribery." He asked for a large appropriation to build on the capitol grounds a state office building containing a dormitory for legislators. There they could work on bills, hold committee meetings, and do their work without interruption. Needless to say, the members did not applaud this portion of the address.

In his first address Murray did not dwell on the important prob-lem of the crisis in oil prices. He closed his speech by saying: "I was expected to say something on this question. I have not done so for the reason I desire to make a second mental trial of my solution to the problem."[5] Before the end of the summer he would make national headlines with his solution.

Murray's first address to the legislature was followed by an-other shorter and less startling one. He appeared before the legis-lature on February 4 to ask for long-needed reforms in the state judiciary and in county government. He wanted a reduction in the number of state district courts and rotation of judges. He also asked for the consolidation of a number of county offices and the adoption of the county-manager form of government. All township

[5] *First Message of Governor William H. Murray to the Thirteenth Legislature,* Jan. 12, 1931.

governments should be eliminated, he said, and he hoped that the seventy-seven counties could be combined into fifteen or twenty. Another, far less meritorious, "reform" he requested was a law providing that county attorneys would be paid only for convictions.

He called for educational changes which would reduce expenditures and yet improve the schools. He wanted an appropriation of two million dollars for free textbooks in the public schools and a new textbook commission to select the books to be purchased. All common schools with fewer than seventy pupils should be closed and consolidated. No state money should be expended to promote competitive athletics, which Murray believed were needless frills.

Anticipating the New Deal by four years, he asked for a state system of old-age pensions. The pension fund would be created through monthly contributions by wage earners. As an alternative he suggested that businesses should be compelled to form their own retirement program.[6]

He concluded his second address by complimenting the representatives and senators for their admirable behavior during the first month of the session. Their conduct had been sensible and sober. But now they needed to go to work to enact his program. He declared: "The roll will be called and the fire bells will be rung before this is over. When you have stopped me you can brag about it. But wait until you do."[7]

The members of the house, all of whom had been elected in the Murray sweep, were amenable to the Governor and had elected his choice for speaker, former constitutional-convention member Carlton Weaver.[8] But the senate had acquired great power during the administration of William J. Holloway. Half of the senators were holdovers from the 1928 election. They had helped impeach Henry S. Johnston and were almost solidly against Murray's program. The senate would block some of the reforms vitally needed by the state, but it would also hold Murray in check on several occasions when no other governmental agency could do so.

[6] *Second Message of Governor William H. Murray to the Thirteenth Legislature,* Feb. 4, 1931.

[7] *Oklahoma City Times,* Feb. 5, 1931.

[8] *Harlow's Weekly,* Jan. 10, 1931.

Tax reform, the essence of the Murray program, was the first item of business for the legislature. The first bill, the tax-commission measure, breezed through the house in three hours with only one dissenting vote. On January 14 the senate approved the bill by a vote of 33 to 10.[9] The Oklahoma Tax Commission was the first and most enduring achievement of the Murray administration. Operating through three-member county equalization boards, the commission balanced the property valuations over the state. By June, 1931, the county boards had lowered ad valorem taxes 20 to 25 per cent.[10] "Look at your tax receipts," became Murray's rejoinder to those who criticized his efforts.

The income-tax proposal also moved rapidly through the house. An income tax of 2 per cent on earnings of $1,800 a year, graduated to a 10 per cent levy on incomes of over $3,600, was approved. The senate rejected this proposal, giving Murray's program a temporary setback.[11] Other new revenue measures were enacted to help prevent fiscal chaos. The legislature passed laws providing for a new method of collecting the gross-production tax on oil and levied a new $.01 per gallon gasoline tax. An inheritance tax and a corporation license fee also brought in new revenues. However, these new sources of funds failed to make up for the income lost when the property tax was reduced. The Tax Commission raised the valuation of corporate property by $65,000,000, but the overall valuation shrank by $141,000,000.[12]

The senate continued to block the income-tax proposal and other portions of the Murray financial program. The Governor made his reactions quite clear: "I'm inclined to think the Constitutional Convention made one serious error. Four year terms for senators are too long; they have too much time to build up dangerous machines. I think I'll offer a constitutional amendment to the voters cutting the terms of senators to two years."[13] When a delegation of senators came to the Governor's office to discuss the tax plan, he became so angry that he broke the glass top on his desk.

[9] *Ibid.*, Jan. 10, 17, 1931.
[10] *Ibid.*, June 20, 1931.
[11] *Ibid.*, Jan. 24, Feb. 7, 1931.
[12] Dale and Wardell, *History of Oklahoma*, 354; Hines, *Alfalfa Bill*, 283.
[13] Hines, *Alfalfa Bill*, 284.

When the senate still refused to act, Murray tried to enlist the support of various pressure groups. He spoke to the Oklahoma Education Association and asked for their help. To the ten thousand teachers of the state he declared, "Any objection to a law passed to tax the least-taxed class of the state in order to feed those thousands by the roadside, is a menace to the state, laying the foundation for the decline of government."[14] But the teachers failed to respond, and the Governor was finally forced to compromise with the senate.

The upper chamber finally approved an income tax, but the rates were far lower than those Murray desired. Corporations also had to pay income taxes for the first time, but the senate gave oil companies a 27½ per cent depletion allowance and exempted insurance companies and building-and-loan associations. However, the tax put a larger share of corporate earnings into the state treasury.[15] A new tax code was adopted which ended many inequalities and established modern auditing procedures.

Every one of the twenty-four tax measures Murray requested passed the house, but the senate's refusal to accept many of them meant that the state still faced serious financial problems. Throughout the spring of 1931 expenses mounted and revenues tumbled. Murray's request for a budget of $26,475,000 was ignored; the legislature appropriated over $35,000,000. The Governor forced department heads to return to the treasurer over $3,000,000 of the additional appropriations. To meet its debts, the state issued warrants of questionable value, and Oklahoma City banks began to discount them. Fearing that the state's credit was being destroyed, the Governor finally persuaded the banks to redeem the warrants at par value. Although the state debt continued to grow, reaching almost $8,000,000, Murray tried to hold expenses down by vetoing a large number of appropriations and by eliminating state jobs.[16] If the senate had enacted Murray's income-tax plan, the state would have ended the budgetary period in the black.

The Murray tax reforms that were enacted were the most comprehensive in the state's history, and constituted an important

14 *Muskogee Times-Democrat*, Feb. 6, 1931.
15 *Harlow's Weekly*, Apr. 4, 1931.   16 *Oklahoma City Times*, Apr. 20, 22, 1931.

victory for the Governor and the people. Many injustices were eliminated, particularly in the collection of corporate and natural-resources taxes. The small property owners found their taxes greatly reduced. The farmers of the state, who had paid most of the county and state property taxes, hailed Murray as a hero.[17]

The Governor was not satisfied that only a portion of his program had been enacted and used the initiative procedure to place his defeated or amended tax recommendations and other proposals before the voters. In what became known as the "firebells campaign," Murray and his partisans attempted to win public support for his program at a special election called for December 18, 1931. The "firebells" proposals originally included an income tax, a constitutional budget officer appointed by the governor, an escheat law permitting state seizure of lands owned by corporations, a new board of education with a $2,000,000 appropriation for free textbooks, and a law forbidding the legislature to appropriate funds in excess of the amounts requested by departments. Murray made a drive to organize firebells clubs at the precinct level, and within three weeks a large organization had been formed.[18] State employees were asked to contribute $7,000 to the campaign. At first Murray said they were not required to make donations,[19] but a few days later he asked for at least a $2.00 donation from each employee.[20] On October 24 a state-wide drive by Murray tax-reform clubs obtained 165,000 signatures on the petitions. Three constitutional amendments provided for the budget director, limitations on city and county tax rates, and escheatment of corporate lands. Four referred laws included the income tax, a $.01 gasoline tax for relief funds, free textbooks, and reduction of wheat and cotton acreage.[21] Murray toured the state to stir up support for the measures, and large crowds greeted him with bursts of fire bells and sirens.[22]

---

[17] W. N. Redwine to William H. Murray, Apr. 10, 1931, W. N. Redwine Collection (Norman, University of Oklahoma Library, Division of Manuscripts). Hereafter cited as Redwine Coll., Univ. of Okla. Library.

[18] *Harlow's Weekly*, May 23, June 6, 1931; *Daily Ardmoreite*, May 8, 1931.

[19] *Oklahoma City Times*, Oct. 9, 1931.

[20] *New York Times*, Oct. 18, 1931.

[21] *Harlow's Weekly*, Oct. 17, 31, 1931.

[22] *Muskogee Daily Phoenix*, Oct. 28, 29, 1931.

196

Opposition mobilized quickly to defeat his proposals. The Kansas-Oklahoma division of the Mid-Continent Oil and Gas Association financed the campaign against them.[23] Other opponents included the Oklahoma Publishing Company, sixty-four of the seventy-seven boards of county commissioners, the Republican party, and the Citizens League, a front for oil producers led by Attorney-General J. Berry King.[24] The legislature opposed the budget-officer plan, fearing a loss of control over state finances. The county commissioners were angered by the loss of county revenues when the county equalization boards lowered property taxes.

In early December Murray removed three of the proposals from the ballot, retaining only the income tax, free textbooks, the budget officer, and the escheatment of corporation-owned lands. State Superintendent of Public Instruction John Vaughn, who was to be excluded from the proposed textbook commission, led the school administrators in attacks on the "firebells" issues, saying that the school bells would be silenced if the measures passed. Schoolmen were incensed by the economy drives, which had caused many of them to suffer losses in pay.

On election day, December 18, weather conditions benefited Murray's opponents. Rain, sleet, snow, and mud kept the rural voters at home. Some of the measures carried in fifty or more of the counties, but the urban vote defeated them. Rural counties could not roll up sufficient majorities to counteract heavy opposition in the cities. The income tax was defeated by a vote of 208,144 to 235,918; the escheat measure, by 202,353 to 240,028; free textbooks, by 196,579 to 245,743; and the budget officer, by 194,274 to 245,794.[25] Though defeated, Murray fought for the measures when the next legislature met in January, 1933, and placed the other three "firebells" issues—the gasoline tax, limits on cotton and wheat acreage, and restrictions on city and county taxes—on the ballot in 1932. Murray's proposals were genuinely needed in Oklahoma. Budgetary reform was long overdue, the state needed a

23 *Ibid.*, Nov. 1, 1931.
24 *Harlow's Weekly*, Nov. 7, 1931.
25 Winters, *Directory of the State of Oklahoma*, 185; *Harlow's Weekly*, Dec. 26, 1931.

free-textbook system, and the income-tax law passed by the legislature needed to be strengthened. In campaigning for the measures,
Alfalfa Bill was not playing the role of a demagogue but was acting
as a Governor working to solve basic problems.

As governor of one of the leading petroleum states, Murray faced
the dilemma of simultaneous oil-price declines and ever increasing
production. Oilmen were divided about the question of prorating—
limiting production and marketing below capacity. The depression
and the opening of the east Texas oil field had drastically lowered
the price of crude oil. Oklahoma and California had prorated oil
in 1930 and had successfully limited production, but the east Texas
field had increased its output fiftyfold in the same year. In January,
1931, Murray was uncertain about what steps to take, but he opposed repealing the proration law. Independent producers, such as
Champlin Refining Company of Enid, needed cash immediately to
remain solvent and were materially aided when the United States
Supreme Court ruled against production curtailment by the states.[26]
The price of oil promptly fell, and by July 11 was selling for $.22 a
barrel. In an attempt to halt runaway production some companies
voluntarily ceased operations, and on July 27 more than three
thousand oilmen met in Tulsa to call for closing all the oil fields.

On August 4, 1931, Murray called out the National Guard to
turn off the flow of oil in Oklahoma.[27] With the guard in control of
the fields Murray announced that there would be a production
limitation of 77,000 barrels per day when the fields were reopened.
There were 3,106 martial-law areas in the fields, fifty feet in di-
ameter around each well. Many operators defied the guardsmen,
who in some cases were forced to use bayonets to enforce the shutdown. Wells and pipelines were also closed, a procedure that H. F.
Sinclair of the Sinclair Oil Corporation had called a "policy of
strangulation."[28] The Sinclair, Champlin, and Wilcox oil companies
opposed proration, but other operators pleaded for the governors

[26] C. B. Glasscock, *Then Came Oil: The Story of the Last Frontier* (Indianapolis,
The Bobbs-Merrill Co., 1938), 307–308.
[27] *Executive Proclamation No. 1460*, Aug. 4, 1931.
[28] *New York Times*, Feb. 19, 1931.

of Kansas, Texas, Arkansas, Louisiana, and New Mexico to adopt similar restrictions.[29] Murray announced that the guardsmen would stay in the fields until the price of oil reached $1.00 a barrel. He commissioned Cicero Murray, a distant cousin, a colonel in the guard, and gave him control of the Oklahoma City field. The guardsmen were paid by a tax on the oil production, which saved the general budget this additional expense. The Oklahoma Publishing Company immediately charged the Governor and his relative with "running hot oil," which they both denied.

Murray felt that the only way to solve the oil problem was for representatives of the oil-producing states to meet and agree on a uniform proration policy. He called such a meeting at Fort Worth, Texas, on March 1, 1931. Murray, Governor Sterling of Texas, Alfred M. Landon, representing Kansas, and a representative of New Mexico met and asked President Herbert Hoover to urge the major oil companies to limit production and oil imports. Alfalfa Bill also called on his fellow governors to shut down the wells of companies importing foreign oil. The federal government responded favorably to the request, which led Murray to call another meeting for March 9, at Texarkana, Texas. At this and succeeding meetings Oklahoma was represented by Cicero Murray, who had no official state office and was not on the state payroll. Cicero became chairman of the Oil States Advisory Committee, the name given to the conference, and a third gathering of the committee formulated the basis of the interstate oil compact.[30]

Cicero Murray's role in the oil controversy prompted considerable criticism in the legislature. State Senator H. P. Daugherty asked for an investigation of Cicero's trips to Texarkana and Washington. As newspaper criticism mounted over this unofficial delegation of power, and later over Cicero's management of the oil fields held by the National Guard, both the Governor and his cousin denied any wrongdoing. In his *Memoirs* Murray admitted that

[29] *Daily Oklahoman*, July 11, 1931.
[30] *New York Times*, Mar. 2, 4, 1931; *Tulsa Tribune*, July 13, 1931; Donald R. McCoy, "Alfred M. Landon and the Oil Troubles of 1930–32," *Kansas Historical Quarterly*, Vol. XXXI (Summer, 1965), 113–37.

some "hot oil" had been run but blamed it on the lack of enough guardsmen to control the three thousand producing wells.[31]

After the Governor deployed the guard in August, Cicero was given the title "proration umpire," and the guard stayed in the fields until an oil-conservation law was passed by the fourteenth legislature. Murray kept the oil wells closed until the Corporation Commission could regain control. On August 6, 1931, a federal court upheld the proration law, giving Murray legal support for his actions.[32] When Governor Ross Sterling threatened to follow Murray's lead and call out the Texas guard, the legislature of that state also passed a proration law. On August 24, 1931, the Phillips Petroleum Company bid $1.00 a barrel for Oklahoma crude oil, and Cicero Murray announced that when that price was firmly established military control would be lifted.[33] Phillips withdrew the bid on September 18, and the price fell to $.70, but on October 10 the Governor accepted the $.70 offer, and for the first time in two months Oklahoma's oil began flowing in quantity. The National Guard remained in the oil fields a total of 618 days to prevent excess production.[34]

Murray received national publicity from his use of the guard in the oil fields and in other crises, such as the Red River bridge episode. The "bridge war" came about when Texas and Oklahoma built three free highway bridges across the Red River at Ryan, Oklahoma, and at Denison and Gainesville, Texas. At the Denison and Gainesville crossings there were also toll bridges, and the owners of the toll bridges obtained an injunction against the state of Texas, from which they had received their charters, to prevent the opening of the free bridges. When Governor Sterling refused to open the Texas end of the bridges until the suit was settled, Murray threatened to open them, but was restrained from carrying out his threat by a federal court order. Alfalfa Bill declared that Oklahoma, which was not a party to the toll-bridge contract, had the right to open the bridges, for, according to the Louisiana Purchase treaty with France in 1803, Oklahoma held title to both sides of the river.

[31] Murray, *Memoirs*, II, 504–509.   [32] *Daily Oklahoman*, Aug. 5, 6, 1931.
[33] *Ibid.*, Aug. 24, 1931.   [34] *Harlow's Weekly*, Oct. 10, 1931.

If this argument was found invalid by the courts, he said, he would take one-half of each bridge—not one-half to the middle of the river, but one lane all the way across. On July 16 Murray disregarded the restraining order and issued an executive order opening the three bridges. Two days later he had the highway department plow up the approaches to the toll bridges. Governor Sterling then sent companies of Texas rangers to keep the Texas end of the free bridges closed. Murray retaliated by asking the women of both states to meet at the bridges, cross them, and hold quilting bees, expressing doubt that the rangers would fire on them. The toll-bridge owners, meanwhile, were still collecting tolls from motorists who approached the bridges on the Texas side and neglecting to tell them that the Oklahoma end was impassable.[35] Murray then acted to resolve the problem by using what was becoming his favorite tool of state.

On July 24 he called out the National Guard and established martial law around the bridges. The bridge companies brought in United States marshals to carry out the federal court order, but Adjutant General Charles Barrett of Oklahoma refused to be enjoined. The next day Murray went to the bridge at Denison and personally took charge. State and national papers published photographs of "Horatio at the Bridge," wearing a khaki uniform, surrounded by armed guardsmen, and holding conferences with his officers. The guardsmen opened the free bridges, and traffic moved across the Red River. The federal court in Texas, lacking power to remove the guardsmen, rescinded the order closing the free bridges. Murray earned the thanks of the citizens of both states, who overwhelmingly favored the free bridges. A later court ruling established the southern boundary of Oklahoma at the south bank of the river, upholding the claim of the Governor.[36] Once again he had used the National Guard and martial law in answer to the people's demands for governmental activity of some kind to combat the worsening depression.

[35] *Durant Weekly News*, July 12, 24, 1931; *Daily Oklahoman*, July 17, 18, 22, 1931; *Harlow's Weekly*, July 25, 1931.
[36] *Daily Oklahoman*, July 24, 25, 26, Aug. 6, 1931; *Durant Weekly News*, Aug. 7, 1931; *Harlow's Weekly*, Aug. 1, 1931; *New York Times*, Aug. 7, 1931.

Murray received still more publicity from his spectacular battle with Lew Wentz, Republican chairman of the Highway Commission. Appointed to the commission by Governor Holloway, the oilman-philanthropist had made a creditable effort to build a state highway system. In his campaign for governor Alfalfa Bill had labeled Wentz his "enemy number one." Wentz was constantly under fire from the *Blue Valley Farmer*, and after the inauguration the Governor moved to oust him. Long-term Murray men Sam Hawks and John McKeel were appointed to the commission when the two incumbent Democratic members resigned. Wentz refused to submit his resignation, though Hawks replaced him as chairman. The house passed a bill permitting the Governor to remove Wentz, but the senate refused to concur. The Highway Commission soon split over whether to use concrete or asphalt paving on state highways. Hawks and McKeel awarded an exclusive contract for concrete to the Portland Cement Company, for which McKeel had been an attorney. Wentz forced them to rescind their action and award the business to a Kansas firm which offered a lower price. The Murray appointees defended the first contract on the grounds that the money would have remained in Oklahoma.

Despite the Governor's every effort Wentz remained on the commission. Hawks and McKeel ignored him at meetings and by a vote of 2 to 1 overruled all his objections. When Wentz protested that McKeel was not buying all of the concrete from the Kansas firm, the charge went unanswered. Murray issued an executive order instructing the commission to build a farm-to-market road system and to pay a minimum of two dollars a day to all commission employees.[37] This order lost some of its humanitarian aspect when some of the employees reported that they had been fired for refusing to subscribe to the *Blue Valley Farmer*.[38] Wentz remained on the commission until April, 1932, when the Governor issued an executive order removing him and appointing Maud Thomas of Beaver in his place. Wentz refused to vacate his office, and attorneys Leon

[37] *Blue Valley Farmer*, Oct. 2, 16, 1930, Mar. 26, 1931; *Harlow's Weekly*, Jan. 31, Mar. 14, Apr. 18, Aug. 29, 1931; *Tulsa Tribune*, Feb. 20, 1931.
[38] *Oklahoma City Times*, Oct. 29, 1931.

Hirsh and J. B. A. Robertson, acting for Miss Thomas, obtained a restraining order against Wentz. The state supreme court ruled against Murray, however, and Wentz remained on the commission.

Seeing the futility of further conflict, Alfalfa Bill agreed to a truce, for the next legislature could create a new commission and enable him to remove Wentz. During the gubernatorial campaign Murray had demanded a reduction in the number of state employees, but between June, 1931, and September, 1932, the number of employees of the Highway Commission almost doubled. Despite the Governor's claim that "there was no graft" in the highway department, it was common knowledge that employees rebated a percentage of their salaries and were forced to subscribe to the *Blue Valley Farmer*.[39]

Like the highway employees, presidents and faculties of state institutions of higher learning were experiencing fear for their jobs. Murray's ideal of higher education was still College Hill Institute of the 1880's. He wanted "frills" abolished and attacked university professors who failed to teach eight hours a day, six days a week, twelve months a year. In his opinion, attendance at professional meetings was a waste of time, and the new student union building at the university was a "country club" for students.[40] He proposed that the university and the Agricultural and Mechanical College accept only juniors and seniors and that all students attend a junior college for two years. There were, he declared, too many college graduates in the state. President William Bennett Bizzell of the University of Oklahoma was accused of being a poor educational leader, of allowing drunkenness among the faculty, and of mismanaging funds. Murray sent Alva McDonald, a former United States marshal, to Norman to investigate "flagrant immorality and corruption." McDonald found no immorality but charged seven staff members with misusing funds. Bizzell called a meeting of the Board of Regents and answered the accusation of padded expense

---

39 *Harlow's Weekly*, Apr. 9, 1932; *Tulsa Tribune*, Nov. 9, 1932; Murray, *Memoirs*, II, 448.
40 *Blue Valley Farmer*, Feb. 12, 26, 1931.

accounts. McDonald's final 1,308-page report proved nothing, and all the charges were dismissed.[41]

Murray continued his vendetta with the university. He called for entrance examinations, which Bizzell opposed, and sent the National Guard to collect tickets at the 1931 Oklahoma-Nebraska football game, claiming that ticket money was mismanaged. The Governor removed Frank Buttram from the Board of Regents, charging that the University of Oklahoma Press had published Buttram's campaign materials in 1930. The Alumni Executive Council approved Raymond A. Tolbert, whom Murray appointed to fill Buttram's position.[42]

The state teachers' colleges also felt Murray's ire, and by June, 1931, he had replaced more educators than any Oklahoma governor except Jack Walton. The presidents of Central State College, Langston University, Southeastern State College, Northwestern State College, and Northeastern Oklahoma Junior College were removed.[43] Though Murray claimed to be an ardent supporter of higher education, people became skeptical when he ousted the head of the University Hospital in Oklahoma City and issued an executive order allowing chiropractors to practice there.[44]

During the firebells campaign Murray's secretary, Claude Weaver, sent a letter to President Bizzell strongly urging "voluntary" contributions to the firebells effort of at least two dollars per faculty member. The letter, reprinted in the *Nation*, brought national attention to Murray's educational policies.[45] When some faculty members at Southwestern State College attended meetings opposing the firebells issues, the Governor ousted President E. E. Brown and replaced him with an old friend. When state teachers' pay checks were two or three weeks late in 1932, Murray said it was the teachers' fault for defeating his initiated measures.[46]

[41] *Tulsa Tribune*, Mar. 26, 1931; *New York Times*, Mar. 27, 1931; *Harlow's Weekly*, Aug. 11, 1931.

[42] *Blue Valley Farmer*, Mar. 26, 1931; *Tulsa Tribune*, Mar. 30, 1931.

[43] *Daily Oklahoman*, Apr. 29, 1933.

[44] *Tulsa Tribune*, July 8, 1931.

[45] "Voluntary Contributions," *Nation*, Vol. CXXXIV (June 8, 1932), 652.

[46] *Blue Valley Farmer*, Oct. 13, 1932.

He wanted to reorganize the state higher educational system through a "co-ordinated board for the co-ordinated colleges of the greater university." This board would be the only degree-granting agency in the state and would give examinations, which, when passed, would lead to a degree. The plan was never taken seriously by the legislature, partly because Murray asked all the private institutions in the state to join the board.[47] It must be noted that Murray used $267,000 of relief funds to buy textbooks for the children of relief recipients. But this act could not counterbalance the grave harm he did to higher education in the state.

Like other governors, Murray had to meet the problem of providing aid to the unemployed. His program ranged from providing free textbooks to allotting ten unemployed men a half-acre each on the grounds between the governor's mansion and the capitol building, where they grew vegetables for their own use or for sale.[48] Murray urged Oklahoma farmers to increase production and sent Highway Commission trucks filled with unemployed men to the rural counties to work for the farmers in return for produce. When a relief fund of $400,000 was exhausted, Murray issued an executive order directing the highway department to use all of the $.01 gasoline-tax revenue in excess of $1,000,000 to hire unemployed men to build farm-to-market roads under the supervision of the highway engineers.[49] When the appropriation for free seed was used up, he exacted a "contribution" of 1.5 per cent of the salaries of state employees to replenish the fund. Realizing that the state could not provide all the funds needed, he called a relief conference to meet in Memphis, Tennessee, in the fall of 1931.[50]

Using his powers as governor, Murray tried to protect the economically oppressed from injustice and abuse. When police began arresting the unemployed for vagrancy, he threatened to extend martial law to city jails and free the prisoners. When Oklahoma City police placed ninety men in jail in one such arrest, Murray is-

---

[47] Murray, *Memoirs*, II, 548.
[48] *Muskogee Times-Democrat*, Feb. 26, 1931.
[49] *Harlow's Weekly*, July 18, 1931.
[50] The Memphis and St. Louis relief conferences will be discussed in Chapter XII.

sued an executive order dismissing the charges against the men.[51] The Oklahoma City health department forbade Saint Anthony Hospital to dispense food to unemployed men at the hospital kitchen, whereupon Murray intervened to have the department's order revoked. The health department tried to stop the sale of skimmed milk by the Oklahoma Co-operative Milk Association, and Murray placed a military zone around the home office and automobile of the co-operative's president so that the sale of inexpensive milk could continue. His plea for a federal relief program was answered after March, 1933, but, as will be seen, his use of federal funds led to a continuous battle with Franklin Roosevelt's New Deal agencies.

A state agency which Murray helped to create in 1908, the State School Land Commission, caused him trouble throughout his administration. He had warned the first legislature that corruption would result if the state continued to own farm lands, and his warning proved valid. From 1908 until 1931 no audits were made of the school lands or funds, and a former employee who admitted stealing $48,000 escaped punishment. The commission included the governor, the state auditor, the superintendent of public instruction, the president of the State Board of Agriculture, and the secretary of state. When Murray tried to have his friends A. L. Beckett and Joe Neely named commission secretary and land appraiser, the other members of the commission, led by Superintendent Vaughn, removed the Governor as chairman of the body.[52] Murray sent the Board of Public Affairs a letter requesting an investigation of the School Land Department, and an audit made in 1933 revealed thefts and frauds in the administration of the lands and funds.[53] Murray eventually secured a more honest administration of school properties, though the problem continued to exist long after his administration.

In the summer of 1931 Alfalfa Bill contributed to the emerging good-neighbor policy toward Latin America. On June 7 two deputy sheriffs in Carter County stopped a car containing three Mexican

[51] *Harlow's Weekly*, June 13, 1931.
[52] Murray, *Memoirs*, II, 474, 523–24.
[53] Murray to Board of Public Affairs, Apr. 24, 1931, Murray Coll., Univ. of Okla. Library; *Senate Journal, Fourteenth Legislature, 1933*, 391–92.

boys returning to their homes from Saint Benedict's College in Kansas. Without warrants the deputies ordered the boys out of the car and, when the young men ran, shot and killed two of them. One of the boys was related to the vice-president of Mexico, and the shootings could have seriously endangered United States relations with Mexico. Secretary of State Henry Stimson sent a telegram to Murray, requesting a "minute investigation" and asking the Governor to send the bodies on to Mexico.[54] In a letter to the county attorney of Carter County Murray denounced the killings as murder and demanded a thorough investigation. He ordered the attorney general and the Bureau of Criminal Investigation to aid in the prosecution.[55] The Governor sent a message of sympathy to the Mexican consul in Oklahoma City and notified Stimson of the steps he had taken. With Stimson's approval, the Governor purchased coffins for the bodies and provided an escort, made up of a National Guard colonel and his son Massena, to accompany the bodies to the border. Murray's prompt action brought letters of appreciation from Stimson, the Mexican chargé d'affaires in Washington, and other members of the State Department.[56]

Complications arose at the trial of the two deputies, when the jury in the case acquitted them. The county attorney blamed the Governor's special counsel, J. M. Springer, for failure to obtain a conviction, but Murray said that racial prejudice and a jury made up of friends of the two defendants caused the miscarriage of justice.[57] When the dean of Saint Benedict's College asked Murray to help create memorial scholarships for the boys, Murray replied that he could not do so because of the sectarian nature of the school. Instead, he arranged for two scholarships to be established at the Agricultural and Mechanical College in Stillwater.[58] Charles

54 Henry L. Stimson to Murray, telegram, June 8, 1931, Murray Coll., Univ. of Okla. Library.

55 Murray to the Carter County Attorney, June 8, 1931, Murray Coll., Univ. of Okla. Library.

56 Henry L. Stimson to Murray, June 9, 15, 22, 1931; W. K. Casl[?] to Murray, July 16, 1931; Murray Coll., Univ. of Okla. Library.

57 Marvin Shilling to Murray, Nov. 25, 1931; Murray to Henry L. Stimson, Nov. 25, 1931, Murray Coll., Univ. of Okla. Library.

58 Murray to Richard Burns, Dec. 7, 1931, Murray Coll., Univ. of Okla. Library.

Nutter, the Associated Press chief of staff in Mexico City, wrote the Governor that his statements and actions in regard to the deaths had been well received in Mexico. Nutter praised him for sending his son to the border and for his co-operation, which had prevented a "nasty diplomatic tangle."[59]

Murray also helped members of minority groups and organizations. On one occasion, when a mob was threatening to lynch three Negroes, he called out the National Guard to prevent violence.[60] Another incident involved his condemnation of the American Medical Association for trying to close a co-operative hospital at Elk City. This institution, organized in 1929 with support from the Farmers' Union, was operated by Michael Shadid. When the medical association used its influence to prevent Shadid from obtaining qualified doctors and interns, the Governor reacted in a typical manner. He wrote an article in the *Blue Valley Farmer* threatening to use his office against the association should it continue its campaign against the hospital.[61] Murray received the praise of the Oklahoma State Federation of Labor when he reappointed Thomas H. Doyle and Mat McElroy to the Industrial Commission in the face of bitter business opposition.[62]

Other people who received the concern and help of the Governor were the former constitutional-convention members and those who had served in the first legislature. Throughout his four-year term, no one could charge that Murray forgot his friends and relatives, for both groups quickly found places in the state government. The state senators would fulminate when the Governor failed to consult them on appointments, but their objections seldom deterred him from rewarding faithful friends of long standing. By the end of January, 1931, the surviving constitutional-convention delegates of 1907 were in control of the executive branch. Ben Harrison was state budget officer, Pete Hanraty was official guide, Charles H.

[59] Charles Nutter to Murray, Nov. 27, 1931, Murray Coll., Univ. of Okla. Library.
[60] Murray, *Memoirs*, II, 569.
[61] Michael A. Shadid, *A Doctor for the People* (New York, The Vanguard Press, 1939), 131–33; Michael Abraham Shadid, *Doctors of Today and Tomorrow* (Superior, Wisc., Cooperative Publishing Association, 1947), ix–xi.
[62] *Official Proceedings of the Twenty-eighth Annual Convention of the Oklahoma State Federation of Labor*, Sept. 14–16, 1931.

Pittman was Election Board secretary, W. D. Humphrey was state health commissioner, W. C. Hughes was a member of the Board of Affairs, and Jim Harris was a colonel on the Governor's staff.[63] Other former associates were acting as commissioner of health and superintendents of three institutions. Murray removed the heads of the state hospitals at Fort Supply and Clinton to appoint still more old friends. The Governor made two of his women supporters honorary colonels on his staff and announced they would wear bloomers for uniforms.[64]

In addition to old political friends, thirteen Murray relatives joined the patronage parade. Nephew Clive Murray became a member of the staff at Murray State College, son Massena became a lieutenant in the National Guard unit policing the oil fields, half brother W. C. Murray became a gasoline inspector, and six of Mrs. Murray's relatives received state jobs.[65] Twelve friends from Tishomingo were put on the state payroll as rangers, clerks, and stewards.[66] When the controversial subpenitentiary was built at Stringtown, old Tishomingo friend Joe Neely became the superintendent. A. H. Ellis, a long-term confidant, was named superintendent of the state orphanage at Pryor. Melvin Cornish, Murray's secretary, handled patronage requests, but the Governor made the ultimate decisions.[67]

Murray also used his position to gain control over the Democratic party in Oklahoma. He wanted R. M. McCool as state chairman and Robert Bellatti as secretary-treasurer, and the state central committee elected them unanimously.[68] In the counties local Murray leaders became county party chairmen and dispensers of patronage. For example, the warden of the state penitentiary at McAlester, a Murray appointee, named the new Pittsburg County chairman.[69]

---

[63] *Daily Oklahoman*, Jan. 25, 1931.
[64] *New York Times*, Jan. 20, 1931.
[65] *Oklahoma City Times*, Nov. 19, 1931.
[66] *Daily Ardmoreite*, Apr. 22, 1931.
[67] W. N. Redwine to Melvin Cornish, Apr. 12, 1932, Redwine Coll., Univ. of Okla. Library.
[68] *Harlow's Weekly*, May 9, 1931.
[69] W. N. Redwine to Melvin Cornish, Dec. 23, 1931, Redwine Coll., Univ. of Okla. Library.

Murray appointees were soon in the majority on many state boards, such as the State Board of Regents and the Board of Regents of the University of Oklahoma. Patronage was also used to punish opponents of the Governor, as when Albert Harrison, father of Luther Harrison of the Oklahoma Publishing Company, lost his job in the State Health Department.[70] Murray's patronage policy alienated the Oklahoma League of Young Democrats, who denounced the "reign of the old men" of the constitutional convention.[71]

Alfalfa Bill's policies also came under increasing fire as a result of certain tactics of the *Blue Valley Farmer*. In March, 1931, O. A. Brewer sold his interest in the paper to Murray and members of his family. L. N. Sheldon became the editor, though Murray wrote the front-page editorial each week. In August the Governor tried to sell $100,000 in first-mortgage bonds of the company to build a publishing plant, but the scheme fell through.[72] During the next four years the January, May, July, and September issues of the *Blue Valley Farmer* carried large advertisements from the state colleges and universities proclaiming the virtues of their campuses. Although this advertising was paid for from state funds, Murray saw no conflict of interest.[73] The circulation of the paper jumped enormously after January, 1931, when state employees found subscription blanks in their offices and administrators such as C. H. Pittman began to solicit subscriptions.[74] This newspaper venture was certainly proving more profitable than the *Navarro County News* of 1896.

Much of the bitter strife during Alfalfa Bill's tenure in office came as a consequence of dissension in the official family. The Governor's "cabinet" stood solidly against him, and he reserved his most acrimonious remarks for them. He was often much more agreeable to members of the legislature and could deal more effec-

[70] *Harlow's Weekly*, Apr. 18, 25, 1931.
[71] *Muskogee Daily Phoenix*, Feb. 22, 23, 1931.
[72] *Blue Valley Farmer*, Aug. 6, 1931.
[73] See, for example, *Blue Valley Farmer*, July 23, 1931.
[74] *Oklahoma City Times*, Apr. 23, 1931; Sheldon, interview of July 20, 1938, cited in Briscoe, "The 1938 Gubernatorial Campaign as Presented by a Group of State Newspapers," 186.

tively with senators than he could with state executives. Alfalfa Bill had special labels for the cabinet members, whom he called the "Wentz Warts": Attorney General J. Berry King was a "law clerk," Commissioner of Charities Mabel Bassett was "contemptuous," and Treasurer A. S. J. Shaw was "Jackass Shaw." These officials could not be controlled by the Governor, and by working in concert they thwarted him on several occasions. Together with the Governor they composed the membership of such boards as the School Land Commission, and they often simply prevented Murray from carrying out his program. In the firebells election and in the elections of 1932 and 1934 they worked against the Governor. The decentralization of power Murray had fought to achieve at the constitutional convention became an albatross around his neck.

When Bill Murray wanted to escape from the worries of the cabinet, Lew Wentz, or the National Guard, he trudged a block east on Twenty-third Street to the governor's mansion, where Alice and Jean waited. During his years as governor, Alfalfa Bill did not have to go to Tishomingo for refuge and rest with his family. Alice made the Governor's home as private as her husband wanted it, and yet maintained its public function. She had no desire to become part of the political life of her husband, believing that wives should stay out of their husbands' careers. However, she prepared dinners for visiting dignitaries, and she enjoyed entertaining. A natural person, she put her guests at ease with her quiet charm. Since there was a constant flow of visitors, she was never idle.

The Murray family made the mansion their home for four years, and during the holidays the house resounded with the noise of children and grandchildren. Alice's sisters helped her with social events, such as dances for Jean and Burbank. The youngest son was attending the University of Wisconsin—the Governor did not want anyone to say that his son had received special consideration from an Oklahoma school. Burbank occasionally brought fraternity brothers home, and the third-floor ballroom was often filled with young people.[75]

Only once did Alice enter the political world of her husband. She

[75] Burbank Murray, interview of Feb. 10, 1966.

211

was artistic and devoted many hours to various home crafts. At the urging of her husband, she invited a number of elderly ladies from over the state to a quilting bee at the mansion. The newspapers were filled with photographs of Alice and her guests making patchwork quilts. Society editors might lament the absence of graceful society from the mansion, but the common people of the state knew that the Murrays were "good folks." Bill Murray and his family never pretended to be anything other than what they were, and the average citizen heartily approved.

The first year of Murray's four-year term produced several accomplishments. The creation of the Tax Commission and the county excise boards were major reforms. The corporate income tax helped to strengthen weak school districts and equalize the tax burden. The Tax Commission was the most lasting achievement. Although critics attacked his appointments to the excise boards, his willingness to let the unemployed grow potatoes in the yard of the executive mansion, and his attacks on education, such matters did not arouse the average Oklahoman. The public stood with the Governor when he used the National Guard to close the oil fields and open the Red River bridges. Some politicians felt that his popularity had increased to the point where he could name the entire state ticket in 1932.[76] Of course, some citizens were angered by Murray's patronage appointments, by the role Cicero Murray played in the oil fields, by McKeel's concrete-purchasing policy, and by the means used to solicit advertisements and subscriptions for the *Blue Valley Farmer*. But most Oklahomans recognized the Governor as one of their own when he went out on the stump to tell an audience of farmers: "I am in favor of galluses, red galluses. Red galluses are the pure sign of a he-man."[77]

Several times during 1931 Murray seemed to become physically exhausted and to allow the pressures of office to tax his body and mind to the point that his behavior became quite eccentric. On August 7, 1931, his father died, and when Alfalfa Bill gave the

[76] Josh Lee to A. N. Boatman, Sept. 29, 1931, A. N. Boatman Collection (Norman, University of Oklahoma Library, Division of Manuscripts).
[77] *Muskogee Daily Phoenix*, Feb. 25, 1931.

eulogy at the funeral, he was visibly shaken. His fear of the "reds" prompted him to send the National Guard to Henryetta on May Day, when a stock of nitroglycerine was reported missing.[78] From the beginning of his administration Murray suspected plots against him from every side. He claimed that he was under the threat of impeachment and of physical violence and that spies were being used against him and might even assassinate him.[79] In his office he chained the chairs to the radiators to keep visitors at a distance. His secretary reported that by late afternoon of a long workday the Governor was likely to become extremely irritable. At the age of sixty-two, with the illnesses he had suffered in Bolivia only recently behind him and with the weight of a depression-ridden state on his shoulders, it is understandable that Murray sometimes behaved oddly during 1931 and the next three years.

Nor was the pace to slow down in 1932. For the next seven months Murray and his supporters would make every effort to reach the highest pinnacle of all.

[78] *Daily Oklahoman*, May 1, 1931.
[79] *New York Times*, Jan. 17, 1931.

213

☆

"BREAD, BUTTER, BACON, AND BEANS"

X

AMERICAN PRESIDENTIAL CAMPAIGNS have long been characterized by slogans used to promote candidates and platforms. Voters have been wooed by such phrases as "Fifty-four Forty or Fight," "Tippecanoe and Tyler Too," the "New Freedom," the "New Deal," and "I Like Ike." Probably no slogan ever summed up the personality and platform of a candidate as well as Alfalfa Bill Murray's "Bread, Butter, Bacon, and Beans." This mouth-watering slogan appeared in countless songs, poems, and pamphlets extolling the virtues of the "Alfalfa Statesman."

Seeing himself in the Lincoln tradition, Murray began his drive for the Presidential nomination shortly after his inauguration as governor. His campaign gained momentum from extensive press coverage of his colorful personal habits and political behavior. Throughout 1930 and 1931 national newspapers and journals publicized Murray's activities so widely that by 1932 he was probably the best-known governor in the United States, other than Franklin D. Roosevelt. Articles featuring Alfalfa Bill had appeared in *Collier's*, the *American Mercury*, the *New Republic*, the *Nation*, the *Commonweal*, the *Christian Century*, the *Literary Digest*, the *American Magazine*, the *Saturday Evening Post*, the *Outlook and Independent*, and many other popular magazines. Virtually every article included picturesque photographs of Murray, a wool scarf wrapped around his neck, a slouch hat pulled down over his eyes, seated at his desk issuing an executive order or proclaiming martial law.

Although the *Nation* and the *New Republic* had strongly criticized his actions with regard to the state educational system, other magazines emphasized his methods of getting things done. To an

American populace demanding governmental activity to halt the economic decline, Murray's use of the National Guard and defiance of the state legislature and the corporations had a certain appeal. The general reader probably laughed when Murray commented on the threat of impeachment. The *New York Times* quoted him as saying, "Try it on me and you'll find me a wild cat in a stump."[1] A *Collier's* editorial criticized his use of military force to seize the oil fields but said that the ends he sought were above reproach.[2] A month later the same journal compared him to the "midwestern radicals like the Populists and the Greenbackers."[3] George Milburn, writing in the *American Mercury*, damned Murray as a rural bumpkin, but William G. Shepherd reported in *Collier's* that he was well dressed and well groomed and not a "fiery uncouth yokel." Shepherd quoted Alfalfa Bill's definition of a public official as "an honest, wise, brave man—too honest to be bought; too wise to be deceived; too brave to be intimidated" and suggested that the Governor met the test.[4]

All the articles stressed Murray's frequently bizarre behavior, although Monsignor J. B. Dudek suggested in the *Commonweal* that many of his idiosyncrasies were designed to attract attention.[5] In the generally favorable article Monsignor Dudek quoted the Governor's favorite theme: "I hold that civilization begins and ends with the plow; that no government can stand without freedom for the farmer, both from physical and financial slavery. . . . Virgin wealth comes only from agriculture, the mines and other natural resources."[6] A Protestant journal, the *Christian Century*, also praised him, particularly his handling of the slaying of the two Mexican boys at Ardmore.[7]

[1] *New York Times*, Aug. 16, 1931.

[2] "Bayonet Business," *Collier's*, Vol. LXXXVIII (Sept. 26, 1931), 62.

[3] "The Old Ghost Walks," *Collier's*, Vol. LXXXVIII (Oct. 17, 1931), 70.

[4] George Milburn, "The Sage of Tishomingo," *American Mercury*, Vol. XXIII (May, 1931), 11–21; William G. Shepherd, "King of the Prairie," *Collier's*, Vol. LXXXVIII (Nov. 28, 1931), 45.

[5] J. B. Dudek, "Mr. Murray of Oklahoma: II," *Commonweal*, Vol. XV (Dec. 2, 1931), 124.

[6] J. B. Dudek, "Mr. Murray of Oklahoma: I," *Commonweal*, Vol. XV (Nov. 25, 1931), 91.

[7] "Oklahoma Knows She Has a Governor," *Christian Century*, Vol. XLVIII (Aug. 26, 1931), 1074.

A lengthy interview of Murray by George Milburn was head-lined "Victuals and Battles" in the *Saturday Evening Post*. Milburn quoted the Sage of Tishomingo's response to accusations of demagoguery:

> They have accused me time and again of being a demagogue. . . . Often when I'm making a public speech I'm actually making two speeches at the same time. I'm making one speech to the man who must be appealed to through his emotions and I'm making another one to the man who can understand what I'm talking about. So if that's demagoging, I'll have to plead guilty. But that's not my idea of what a demagogue is. A demagogue, to my notion, is a character in public life who deliberately makes promises to the people that he hasn't any idea of fulfilling, and appeals to the popular prejudice with an insincere purpose. No one has ever truthfully said that about me.[8]

In the *American Magazine* Jerome Beatty wrote a long article dwelling on Murray's comeback after the Bolivian failure. Beatty described Murray as dressed in a shiny, unpressed black suit sprinkled with cigar ashes, a shirt frayed at the collar and cuffs, and a thin black tie. Beatty concluded that Murray was neither a lunatic nor a Lincoln.[9]

Murray tried to cast himself in the Lincoln image when he spoke at the tomb of the "Great Emancipator" on February 11, 1931. Accompanied by newspaperman Walter Ferguson and by Roy Johnson and Cicero Murray, Alfalfa Bill went to Springfield, Illinois, to speak at memorial exercises at the Lincoln tomb. The Governor of Illinois and other dignitaries were mildly surprised when Murray appeared in formal evening attire provided by a member of his entourage. His speech, "The Philosophy of the History of Abraham Lincoln—Among Men Who Have Guarded Civilization," was an hour-long patriotic eulogy. He called for the perpetuation of Lincoln's high standards of character and for the

[8] William H. Murray as Told to George Milburn, "Victuals and Battles," *Saturday Evening Post*, Vol. CCIV (Dec. 19, 1931), 81.

[9] Jerome Beatty, "You Can Blaze Your Own Trail When You're Broke," *American Magazine*, Vol. CXII (September, 1931), 52–54, 142–45.

revival of the spirit of the Emancipator to free Americans from the slavery of concentrated wealth. He said that the nation needed Lincolnlike political leaders, placing himself among them by inference. When William Allen White later talked to Murray, the Kansas editor commented upon the Springfield speech and added, "I would not be surprised to see you in the White House someday."[10]

Other Kansans shared White's view of the Oklahoma Governor when he toured that state in February. He spoke in Emporia, Kansas, to six hundred members of the Rotary, Lions, and Kiwanis clubs gathered at a local hotel. He said again that the United States needed high-caliber leaders. He blamed the depression on the high cost of state and federal governments and the operations of the Federal Reserve System. Traveling on to Topeka, he addressed the legislature and the state Democratic convention. Appearing in a crowded chamber, he lectured the legislature on its duties and later told the convention that the Democrats had to restore the hope of "the little man."[11]

The Murray Presidential campaign accelerated in the spring of 1931. The *Blue Valley Farmer* featured articles on Murray as Presidential timber and asked readers to send in the names and addresses of Oklahomans now living in other states so that the paper could be sent to them. The candidate spoke at a Jefferson Day dinner in Joplin, Missouri, on April 13,[12] and the South Central Business Association of Kansas City provided him with a large audience when he spoke to that group in May. He told the businessmen: "It is silly to assume that the map of the United States is no wider than Wall Street. I object to any one section of the country controlling the prosperity of another section. . . . The only remedy is economy [in government] until it hurts. . . . You can't buy prosperity through boards and committees."[13] Tom Pendergast's publication, the *Missouri Democrat*, featured an article about the

10 *Harlow's Weekly*, Feb. 14, 21, 1931; *Illinois State Register* (Springfield), Feb. 11, 1931; *New York Times*, Feb. 13, 1931.
11 *Emporia Gazette*, Feb. 23, 1931; *Kansas City Journal-Post*, Feb. 23, 24, 1931; *Kansas City Times*, Feb. 24, 1931.
12 *Blue Valley Farmer*, Mar. 5, 1931; *Daily Ardmoreite*, Apr. 13, 1931.
13 *Missouri Democrat*, May 1, 1931.

speech, and a later edition included a picture of Murray and Pendergast man J. B. Shannon.[14]

The Governor visited California at the end of May to speak to an association of former Oklahomans living in the state. He arrived wearing a white cotton suit, white shoes, and a white hat, and he received a large number of people at the Biltmore Hotel in Los Angeles. Murray spoke in Los Angeles and San Francisco before going on to Salt Lake City and Denver.[15] After the stormy fireworks of the summer of 1931, which saw him fielding the National Guard on several occasions, the *New York Times* compared Alfalfa Bill with Andrew Jackson. During August he spoke at Fair Park in Dallas, to tell the people of his native state what to look for in a Presidential candidate.[16]

Murray recognized the economic plight of the nation and the need for increased relief funds at all levels of government. Aware of the publicity a relief gathering would bring, he called an unemployment conference of Mississippi Valley states to meet in Memphis, Tennessee, on August 23. Three hundred delegates attended the Mississippi Basin Unemployment Conference, which was chaired by Republican Representative Frank Reid of Illinois. Alfalfa Bill proposed that the conference endeavor to bring about increased federal spending on public works. In his keynote address he urged the delegates to concern themselves only with the question of relief, but the Oklahoma delegates turned the meeting into a Murray-for-President gathering. A number of political leaders attended the conference, including Senator Elmer Thomas of Oklahoma, Governor Woodring of Kansas, and representatives of the governors of Tennessee and Arkansas. A tentative program was formulated which called for additional relief projects like Muscle Shoals Dam and a rejection of the dole. Murray suggested that relief funds be obtained by placing a levy of 8 to 15 per cent on the salaries of governmental employees. When the meeting adjourned,

[14] *Ibid.*, May 8, 1931.
[15] *Daily Ardmoreite*, Apr. 9, 1931; *Los Angeles Times*, May 30, 1931.
[16] *New York Times*, Aug. 2, 1931; *Daily Oklahoman*, Aug. 6, 16, 1931.

Alfalfa Bill pronounced the conference a great success but said that "there was too darned much Murray."[17]

The next important appearance was a Labor Day parade and speech at Chicago in celebration of the fiftieth anniversary of the American Federation of Labor. Wearing a gray coat, brown trousers, white canvas shoes, suspenders, and a lavender tie, Murray led a parade of 50,000 through the city. To an audience of more than 100,000 at Soldier Field he spoke for an hour, stopping frequently to drink coffee from a Thermos. He attacked Wall Street and La Salle Street bankers, saying they had caused the depression. A great ovation greeted his demands that the government halt unemployment. If the government did not become responsive to the needs of the people, he declared, a revolution would take place in 1932. He advocated a tariff on all raw materials, increased foreign trade, and the assessment of taxes based upon the ability to pay.[18] Those who felt that the Sage of Tishomingo appealed only to farmers were surprised by the thunderous applause he received along the parade route and at Soldier Field.

In late September Murray campaigned among the farmers in speeches at Newton and Des Moines, Iowa, and at the Kansas State Fair in Hutchinson. At the Jasper County Fair in Newton he spoke to 3,000 farmers, who applauded his demands for a higher tariff on agricultural products. A large crowd gathered at the Sylvan Theater in Des Moines to hear him call for more patriotism and less politics in government. He said that the people were ready to fight for their homes and that President Hoover's relief committees were impotent.[19] After his Iowa appearances Murray went to St. Louis, where the Memphis conference had agreed to meet again on September 25. The second session attracted only ninety people, most of whom were Oklahomans. Congressman Reid of Illinois again

17 *Harlow's Weekly*, Aug. 29, 1931; *New York Times*, Aug. 24, 1931; *Daily Oklahoman*, Aug. 24, 27, 1931; *Commercial Appeal* (Memphis), Aug. 23, 24, 25, 1931; *Times-Picayune* (New Orleans), Aug. 25, 1931.
18 *Chicago Tribune*, Sept. 8, 1931; *Chicago Daily News*, Sept. 8, 1931; *New York Times*, Sept. 8, 1931.
19 *Des Moines Register*, Sept. 23, 24, 1931.

served as chairman, and Murray opened the meeting. Three members of Hoover's emergency committee spoke, but little was accomplished.[20] There was no planned program, and the resolutions simply called for aid to the farmers. Murray went on to Little Rock, Arkansas, where he addressed a large audience on national economic problems and possible solutions. He said that the next election would be decided on economic issues, for the government had to aid the farmers and the "little fellows."[21]

The last tour of 1931 took him to Nebraska and back to Iowa. He spoke on bimetallism to an Elks benefit in Omaha and on the economic ills of the nation at Lincoln. To an audience of twenty thousand gathered at Shenandoah, Iowa, he spoke on the Scotch-bank system. Many delegates wore Murray-for-President buttons, but he did not discuss Presidential politics. In his two-hour speech, which was carried by radio throughout the state, he demanded the restoration of credit and a protective tariff. After the Iowa Farmers' Union endorsed him for President, the *New York Times* correspondent for the Middle West reported that Murray was converting many Republican farmers who had come to jeer his speeches.[22]

His strength in Iowa became apparent in a *Des Moines Register* Presidential poll on November 21, 1931, in which Murray received 16,508 votes to 18,817 for Roosevelt, 18,764 for Hoover, and 7,693 for Al Smith.[23] A Kansas Presidential poll, published in the *Wichita Beacon* on January 10, 1932, ranked him far ahead of other potential candidates. He received 6,882 votes; Will Rogers, 984; Calvin Coolidge, 577; Franklin Roosevelt, 364; Al Smith, 364; Newton D. Baker, 319; and Herbert Hoover, 229.[24]

Next Murray began trying to build favorable sentiment in the South. R. P. Hill, executive secretary of the "4-B club" in Oklahoma City, wrote to C. W. Jones of the Southern Trade Congress in Atlanta urging him to organize Murray's campaign in Georgia.[25]

[20] *St. Louis Post-Dispatch*, Sept. 25, 26, 1931.

[21] *Arkansas Gazette* (Little Rock), Sept. 27, 1931.

[22] *Kansas City Star*, Oct. 3, 1931; *Omaha World Herald*, Oct. 3, 4, 6, 1931; *Des Moines Register*, Oct. 5, 6, 1931; *New York Times*, Oct. 18, 1931.

[23] *Des Moines Register*, Nov. 21, 1931.

[24] *Wichita Beacon*, Jan. 10, 1932.

[25] R. P. Hill, Jr., to C. W. Jones, Oct. 21, 1931, Democratic National Committee

L. J. Bugg, a lawyer in Monroeville, Alabama, wrote to Louis Howe, aide to Franklin D. Roosevelt, that Murray clubs were forming all over the South, and at the Jackson, Mississippi, cotton conference in November sentiment ran high to nominate Murray for vice-president.[26]

Now Alfalfa Bill had to put his own house in order. The Oklahoma Democratic executive committee met in Oklahoma City in December, 1931, and set February 20, 1932, as the date for the state convention. By holding the meeting this early, the home-state Democrats could endorse Murray before he entered the Presidential primaries in March. The executive committee, completely dominated by the Governor, made the arrangements exactly as he directed.[27] Not all Oklahoma Democrats favored his candidacy. The Democratic National Committee received many letters from farmers, housewives, and young Democrats endorsing Roosevelt. Tulsa publisher Eugene Lorton, labor leaders Victor Purdy and Pat Malloy, and Farmers' Union President John Simpson also favored Roosevelt. Former Oklahoma Governor William J. Holloway expressed his views in a letter to Roosevelt: "Unfortunately, we have here an old fossil as Governor who thinks he is a candidate for president."[28] But despite the efforts of these men and others, Murray held absolute control of the Democratic party in the state.

In January, 1932, his Presidential campaign got off to a fast start with a series of speeches in Washington, D.C. Arriving in Washington on the seventeenth, he was met at the railway station by a group of admirers who escorted him to his hotel. In an interview he said that potential Presidential nominee Roosevelt lacked courage and failed to "measure up to the standard." He spoke on "The Banking System and Credit" over the National Broadcasting System and told an audience at the Ingram Memorial Congregational Church that American morals needed a "housecleaning." In a

File, Oklahoma, 1928–33 (Hyde Park, Franklin D. Roosevelt Library). Hereafter cited as DNC File [state, date], Roosevelt Library.

26 L. J. Bugg to Louis Howe, n.d. [probably November, 1931], Nov. 26, 1931, DNC File, Oklahoma, 1928–33, Roosevelt Library.

27 *Panhandle Herald* (Guymon), Dec. 31, 1931.

28 William J. Holloway to Franklin D. Roosevelt, Dec. 12, 1931, DNC File, Oklahoma, 1928–33, Roosevelt Library.

speech before the Women's Democratic Club he said that if the American middle class was not to be destroyed the Democratic party had to win in 1932. Delegates to the annual convention of the Anti-Saloon League received a shock when he told them that people should be allowed to have private stills and vineyards. Murray said that morals were hard to legislate and that he favored permitting individual states to decide the prohibition question. He wanted to eliminate prohibition as a political issue in 1932 and suggested that it might have to be replaced by liquor controls. The audience, which had received him warmly, sat in cold silence throughout the remainder of his speech. It will be recalled that Alfalfa Bill had never advocated absolute prohibition and that during the first Oklahoma legislature he had urged a state-dispensary system.

Before the House Committee on Ways and Means Murray spoke in support of his favorite inflationary scheme, the Scotch-bank system, and he endorsed a bill by Oklahoma Representative Tom McKeown to repeal the 10 per cent tax on state bank notes. During his testimony he drank two pots of black coffee to sustain him while he blamed Wall Street and the Federal Reserve System for the depression. After the appearance before the committee, he went to the House cloakroom to visit many of his old friends. The Oklahoma congressional delegation presented him with a black hat to wear with his frock coat. While he was in Washington, Murray conferred with the leaders of the railroad brotherhoods and issued a statement opposing the use of injunctions to halt strikes.[29]

Nationally syndicated columnist Mark Sullivan reported Murray's appearance in Washington. Sullivan said that Murray's uncouth appearance was partly deliberate. While he displayed six inches of bony leg and white cotton socks when talking to reporters, he was all "spit and polish" two hours later when he spoke to the women's club. At their tea he was well dressed and displayed impeccable manners.[30] Bill Murray knew how to appeal to nearly every audience, both in dress and in speech topic.

[29] *New York Times*, Jan. 18, 19, 1932; *Washington Post*, Jan. 18, 19, 20, 1932; *Oklahoma News* (Oklahoma City), Jan. 19, 20, 1932.
[30] *Muskogee Daily Phoenix*, Jan. 21, 1932.

On January 20 and 21 he spoke in Charlotte and Asheville, North Carolina, and in Columbia, South Carolina. At Charlotte he spoke to a large crowd for more than an hour and received a favorable response to his attack on the banking system. The South Carolina legislature invited him to address them before he spoke at a mass rally in Asheville. In Columbia he said that the country stood at a crossroads. One road led to revolution, another led to military dictatorship, and a third led to the Constitution and the principles of the nation's founding fathers. Murray paid tribute to South Carolinians John C. Calhoun and Wade Hampton and called for increased trade with Latin America and the equalization of taxes.[31] After a brief stay at Asheville he returned to Oklahoma to make plans for the county and state Democratic conventions.

When the county organizations met on January 23, Murray's supporters won control of all but one of the seventy-seven counties, losing only Tulsa County to the Roosevelt forces. The virtually unanimous endorsement resulted from Murray's assertion of power over the party machinery at the grass roots. When the state convention met on February 22, Alfalfa Bill named the national-convention delegation, the national committeeman, and the national committeewoman, and the convention instructed the twenty-two delegates to vote for the Governor at Chicago.[32] With his own state secured, he now began to create a national organization.

The Murray-for-President headquarters in Oklahoma City was operated by his old constitutional-convention friend George Henshaw and by Ann Lord, a public-relations and advertising specialist. The organization financed itself by selling hats, combs, windshield stickers, and books. One of the volumes offered for sale was Gordon Hines's campaign biography, which appears to have been subsidized by oilmen Robert S. Kerr and James Anderson. Ann Lord opened a Murray headquarters in New York City, where visitors could hear the two campaign songs, "Hoover Made a Soup Houn'"

---

[31] *State* (Columbia), Jan. 21, 1932; *Charlotte Observer*, Jan. 20, 1932.
[32] *Harlow's Weekly*, Jan. 30, Feb. 27, 1932; *Blackwell Morning Tribune*, Jan. 9, 1932.

out o' Me" and "Bread, Butter, Bacon, and Beans." The latter
featured such verses as:

> Give us the good old days, give us the good old days,
> Give us back the old familiar scenes.
> Then we'll have money to pay the rent;
> Murray for President.
> Bread, Butter, Bacon, and Beans.

> We want no more high hatted boys to rule our native land.
> We want a man, a common man, who'll always take a stand.
> That right is right and wrong is wrong, no matter what we say.
> And all hell's demons can't stop him, Bill Murray's on his way.[33]

Two of his supporters established a headquarters in Wichita,
Kansas. In Georgia his campaign received a setback when he failed
to get his name on the ballot in that state's Presidential primary.
Georgia leader C. W. Jones had organized Roosevelt clubs in 1930
and had tried to sell memberships in the group. When Roosevelt
disavowed him, Jones switched his support to the Oklahoman. The
Governor sent Ed Seamans to work with the Georgian, but his
filing papers arrived too late for his name to be placed on the
ballot.[34]

The candidate sought support in his birthplace, and on February
18 a reception was held for him at Collinsville, Texas. It began with
a five-mile-long parade, after which a monument bearing his like-
ness was unveiled. Despite bad weather thousands of Texans and
Oklahomans turned out. W. K. Henderson, a Shreveport, Louisiana, capitalist and financial angel for Huey Long, paid for the
celebration.[35]

Murray's Presidential candidacy began to generate some interest—and concern—among national Democratic political leaders.
E. Y. Mitchell, a Missouri politician, reported to a friend, "I heard
in Washington that Governor Alfalfa Bill Murray is to be the

[33] *New York Times*, Mar. 3, 1932.
[34] *Ibid.*, Feb. 17, 22, 1932; *Durant Daily Democrat*, Feb. 13, 1932.
[35] *Collinsville Times*, Feb. 18, 1932; *New York Times*, Feb. 19, 21, 1932.

nominee for Vice President on the third party ticket, if there is one."[36] Wayne Gard wrote in the *New Republic*, "Anyone who wants to see an Eastern politician squirm needs only to mention Alfalfa Bill Murray, Oklahoma's two-gun Governor." Gard reported that supporters of Roosevelt and of Maryland's Governor Albert Ritchie were concerned about Murray's growing strength among the farmers.[37] Frank Pierce, secretary of the Iowa Municipalities League, feared Alfalfa Bill's support among Republican farmers in his state.[38] Missouri Farmers' Association President William Hirth, a Roosevelt supporter, wrote an editorial in the *Missouri Farmer* urging readers not to waste their efforts on Murray, who could not win.[39] Hirth was deeply concerned by the Oklahoman's strength in the corn belt and worked hard to combat the tide to Murray in the Middle West.[40]

The Roosevelt-for-President organization, expertly led by James Farley, recognized Murray's ability to win the hearts of rural Americans. One Roosevelt biographer has said that Murray did not give Roosevelt any cause for concern, but some Roosevelt men in Missouri, Nebraska, Iowa, and North Dakota expressed great fear of Alfalfa Bill and his platform.[41] In the preconvention fight Farley directed the New York Governor's campaign, which saw the future President use the Oklahoma Governor as a whipping boy and as a weapon against Al Smith.[42] On one occasion Smith made a speech in which he used the word "demagogue." The barb was aimed at Roosevelt, but when reporters questioned Roosevelt, he said, with

[36] Ewing Mitchell to Robert D. Johnson, Feb. 6, 1932, E. Y. Mitchell Collection (Columbia, State Historical Society of Missouri, Western Historical Manuscripts Collection). Hereafter cited as Mitchell Coll., SHSM.

[37] Wayne Gard, "Alfalfa Bill," *New Republic*, Vol. LXX (Feb. 17, 1932), 11.

[38] Frank Pierce to Morris L. Cook, Feb. 29, 1932, DNC File, Iowa, 1928–33, Roosevelt Library.

[39] *Missouri Farmer*, Mar. 1, 1932.

[40] William Hirth to Frank P. Walsh, Mar. 3, 1932, William Hirth Collection (Columbia, State Historical Society of Missouri, Western Manuscripts Collection). Hereafter cited as Hirth Coll., SHSM.

[41] Frank Freidel, *Franklin D. Roosevelt: The Triumph* (Boston, Little, Brown and Company, 1956), 245.

[42] James A. Farley, *Behind the Ballots* (New York, Harcourt, Brace and Company, 1938), 97.

tongue in cheek, that Smith had made a "terrible attack on Alfalfa Bill Murray."[43]

Murray was convinced that he was a real challenger, and from February through May he conducted a nationwide canvass for convention delegates. In late February he went to Indiana to give six speeches. Accompanied by former Hoosiers Perry Easten and Ed Seamans, he spoke in Monticello, Indianapolis, Gary, Marion, and Fort Wayne. At Monticello Murray said that the United States must avoid going to war with Japan and that President Hoover's policy was leading in that direction. He gave a "nonpolitical" speech to the twentieth-district Rotary conference in Indianapolis, demanding stronger political leaders and honesty in government. He curtly rejected a suggestion that he run as vice-presidential candidate, with Roosevelt leading the ticket. At the Gary armory he attacked Hoover and Andrew Mellon, and at Marion he added the National Chamber of Commerce and "eastern Democrats" to his list of enemies.[44] During his speech to the Democratic convention in Indianapolis, he said he was running "because I know more than any other man spoken of for the presidency."[45] He was over an hour late for his speech, but seven thousand Democrats waited to hear his "humble" address.

Alfalfa Bill's first test of strength came in the North Dakota Presidential primary. Murray relied on the strength of the Farmers' Union and the Nonpartisan League in the state to further his candidacy with a victory, and he entered the March 15 primary with high hopes. The Roosevelt organization had determined to carry North Dakota for their man to demonstrate his vote-getting power in the Middle West. Though Roosevelt had said, "I am wholly willing to trust things to a real expression by the voters even if this means I will lose a few delegates to Governor Murray of Oklahoma and some others," the Roosevelt managers worked hard to prevent a loss in North Dakota.[46] When Farley made a trip to

[43] *New York Times*, Apr. 15, 1932.

[44] *Indianapolis News*, Feb. 23, 25, 1932; *Indianapolis Star*, Feb. 23, 24, 25, 26, 1932.

[45] *New York Times*, Feb. 26, 1932.

[46] Roosevelt to W. E. Chilton, Feb. 20, 1932, DNC File, West Virginia, 1928–33, Roosevelt Library.

Seattle, Washington, in June and July, 1931, one of the states in which he had stopped was North Dakota. Farley met with the state Democratic party leaders, and all of them endorsed Roosevelt.

There was no formal Murray organization in the state, but some Roosevelt supporters feared his candidacy nonetheless. His slate of delegates and preferential-primary papers were filed by his brother George, who now lived in North Dakota and whom he had not seen for thirty-four years. A Murray club had been organized in Minneapolis, Minnesota, by two Oklahoma City ministers, R. C. Nelson and B. M. Nelson, who also established a few clubs in North Dakota towns. B. M. Nelson and George Murray spoke to these groups, urging them to come to hear Murray's speeches during the forthcoming tour.[47] Several Roosevelt supporters in Oklahoma sent frantic letters to Farley urging him not to underestimate Alfalfa Bill's ability to win the farm vote in North Dakota.[48] North Dakota politician William Lemke wrote to Roosevelt, "While I feel confident you will carry the state, yet Governor Murray appeals to the farm vote and this especially because of the situation in which agriculture finds itself."[49] Lemke was an important Roosevelt man in the state and used his influence in the Farmers' Union and the Nonpartisan League to block Murray. Missouri farm leader Hirth became alarmed by what he called "the drift to Murray" and urged Louis Howe to let him broadcast a speech to North Dakota farmers, for he feared a Murray victory would have a deleterious effect on Roosevelt's campaign in the corn belt.[50] However, Farley and Fred McLean, the Roosevelt leader in North Dakota, remained calm as Murray traveled north to enter the primary campaign.

Murray stopped in Minneapolis and St. Paul on his way to North Dakota, but he refused to attend several meetings scheduled by the Nelson brothers and canceled three radio addresses. After meeting

[47] *Fargo Forum*, Feb. 23, 1932; *Grand Forks Herald*, Feb. 24, 28, 1932.
[48] R. W. McClintock to Pat Malloy, Feb. 15, 1932, DNC File, 1928–33, Oklahoma, Roosevelt Library.
[49] William Lemke to Roosevelt, Feb. 27, 1932, DNC File, 1928–33, North Dakota, Roosevelt Library.
[50] William Hirth to Louis Howe, Feb. 29, 1932; Hirth to Ewing Mitchell, Mar. 3, 1932, Hirth Coll., SHSM.

with Governor Floyd Olson, he gave a speech in St. Paul, which apparently made no great impact.[51] His first appearance in North Dakota was at Fargo, where two thousand farmers turned out to see him welcomed by his brother. He delivered an address on economic conditions, denouncing the corporations and demanding that the wealthy pay a larger share of the tax load.[52] At Jamestown, a standing-room-only crowd heard him attack Republican rule and state, "I'm running for president because I think the people want me, that is the plain people."[53] The farmers and townspeople at Valley City listened as the Oklahoman urged higher taxes on large landowners and the end of Republican fiscal policies. To the audience in Bismarck Murray said that the Democrats should not nominate a man from New York who stood in the shadow of Wall Street, and he urged a two-billion-dollar veterans' bonus instead of the Reconstruction Finance Corporation as a means to halt the depression. At Minot Murray stated that prohibition was not an issue and that corporations should not be given federal funds.[54] He advocated the end of property taxes on homes and urged total revision of the banking system.[55] Before the tour ended, he was too tired to stand and had to remain seated to deliver his speech in Devils Lake. His organization began to encourage Republicans to vote in the Democratic primary, a move which frightened the Democratic leaders. Columnist Mark Sullivan predicted a Murray victory in the state on the basis of his warm reception in the eight-degrees-below-zero weather.[56]

Some Roosevelt supporters also felt that Murray's tour had increased his chances of carrying the state. Pat Malloy and other Oklahomans wanted to go to North Dakota to answer his speeches, but Fred McLean felt that it was unnecessary.[57] McLean also decided against a radio speech by Hirth, for the main Roosevelt

[51] J. F. Reed to William Hirth, Mar. 4, 1932, Hirth Coll., SHSM.
[52] *Fargo Forum*, Mar. 4, 1932.
[53] *Ibid.*, Mar. 5, 1932.
[54] *Grand Forks Herald*, Mar. 4, 5, 6, 1932.
[55] *Bismarck Tribune*, Mar. 3, 4, 1932.
[56] *Fargo Forum*, Mar. 6, 7, 13, 1932.
[57] *Muskogee Daily Phoenix*, Mar. 6, 1932.

answer to Murray would come from Senator Burton K. Wheeler of Montana. Speaking over a number of radio stations, Wheeler told North Dakotans that he had nothing against Murray, who had been a good governor, but that he was not a national candidate. He felt that conservatives in the Democratic party were merely using Murray as a stalking-horse, and he charged that Alfalfa Bill was a tool in the hands of "a corrupt gang in the East which, for want of a better name, might be called the 'Wall Street crowd.' "[58] Despite the Wheeler speech, some Roosevelt leaders were still concerned that Murray might win. Associate Justice John Burke of the North Dakota Supreme Court felt that the Oklahoman had made a good impression, and E. H. Mattingly of the Jamestown central committee thought he had taken the Nonpartisan League by storm.[59]

The vote in the March 15 primary came as a surprise to everyone. The normal Democratic primary vote in the state was about 10,000, but in 1932 over 84,000 Democratic ballots were cast when thousands of Republicans crossed over to vote in the Democratic primary. Roosevelt defeated Murray by a vote of 52,634 to 32,036. Murray's brother was elected a delegate to the convention, but the other nine members of the delegation were Roosevelt men. George Murray ran seventh among the twenty-one candidates, and the next Murray candidate ranked eleventh. Murray's 32,000 votes were impressive, however, and he carried a number of counties in the state.[60]

Despite his North Dakota defeat Murray continued the campaign. Before embarking on a tour of the South, he spent three days in Kansas, speaking at Arkansas City, Winfield, Abilene, Salina, Manhattan, and Emporia. The theme of his Kansas speeches was: "Civilization begins and ends with the plow, and when you junk the plow, you junk civilization." A reporter from Abilene wrote, "This man, Alfalfa Bill Murray, hitchhiking candidate for the Democratic nomination for President, roars every time one mentions a Populist in his presence, yet there is something about him reminis-

58 *New York Times*, Mar. 18, 1932.
59 John Burke to Roosevelt, Mar. 11, 1932; E. H. Mattingly to Roosevelt, Mar. 11, 1932, DNC File, North Dakota, 1928–32, Roosevelt Library.
60 *Grand Forks Herald*, Mar. 19, 1932; *Bismarck Tribune*, Mar. 18, 1932.

cent of Populist days."[61] Certainly Murray's platform of reduced property taxes, federal aid to farmers, currency inflation, and a graduated land tax sounded like populism. But it was the gospel of agrarianism that he preached.

On March 20 Murray started on a nine-day tour of Alabama, Florida, and Mississippi. In Anniston, Alabama, he told an audience at the Lyric Theater that Roosevelt could not win. In Montgomery Governor B. M. Miller introduced him to a crowd which heard him defend states' rights. The audience was extremely cold, and his scholarly address on the Constitution was not well received, even when he said that Negroes were unequal to whites in culture and morals. Small groups greeted him at Birmingham and Mobile.[62]

The Murray-for-President committee in Florida was composed of prominent Tampa businessmen formerly from Oklahoma.[63] They made arrangements for his speeches in Tallahassee, Jacksonville, Miami, Ocala, Lake City, Fort Myers and Pensacola. On a street corner in Jacksonville more than five thousand people stood in the cool air for two hours to hear him attack Roosevelt and Al Smith. At Ocala he spoke on the Scotch-bank system, and at Fort Myers he called upon the people to elect a strong President in 1932.[64] At Plant Park in Tampa, more than one thousand were present when Murray defended "the masses, the vast middle class."[65] Yet despite his extensive tour his campaign did not succeed in the Sunshine State. Linton Collins, president of the Roosevelt-for-President club in Miami, told Farley that Murray's speech to ten thousand in that city had actually helped Roosevelt, and R. H. Chapman wrote the New York Governor that the Murray boom in Lake City was of a minor nature.[66]

Alfalfa Bill went on to Jackson, Mississippi, presumably to address the state legislature. But during the week before he arrived,

[61] *Kansas City Star*, Mar. 18, 1932.

[62] *Birmingham News*, Mar. 21, 1932; *Montgomery Advertiser*, Mar. 22, 1932.

[63] D. B. McKay to Roosevelt, Mar. 12, 1932, DNC File, Florida, 1928–33, Roosevelt Library.

[64] *Florida Times-Union* (Jacksonville), Mar. 23, 24, 29, 1932.

[65] *Times-Picayune*, Mar. 26, 1932.

[66] Linton M. Collins to James A. Farley, Mar. 30, 1932; R. H. Chapman to Roosevelt, Apr. 1, 1932; DNC File, Florida, 1928–33, Roosevelt Library.

the Mississippi house declined to extend an invitation. When they finally agreed to ask him to appear, Murray spurned their belated request, speaking instead to a large crowd at the city auditorium. He called for a "square deal for the common man" and, commenting on President Hoover, said, "I agree he was a great engineer. I agree that he who can dam, ditch, and drain the country in three years is a great engineer."[67] The southern trip won Murray no delegates. In the Florida Presidential primary he ran poorly against Roosevelt, receiving only 24,847 ballots to the latter's 203,372. Most of Murray's votes came from the cities and towns where he spoke and from the central and southern rural counties.[68]

After the excursion to the South Murray began an intensive tour of Nebraska and Oregon, where he was entered in both primaries. Arthur Mullen, national committeeman from Nebraska and leading Roosevelt supporter in that state, kept Farley and Roosevelt informed of developments. A private memorandum of March 10 reported that two men from Oklahoma had visited Governor Charles Bryan, who had helped to get Murray's petitions filed for the primary contest. Bryan controlled the Nonpartisan League in Nebraska, Mullen reported, and Harry Lux, a Nonpartisan League organizer, was leading Alfalfa Bill's campaign.[69] The Oklahoma Governor planned a trip throughout the Cornhusker State, including stops at Falls City, Omaha, Norfolk, Grand Island, McCook, Hastings, and North Platte. Several thousand people attended the Falls City rally during a rainstorm, but only four hundred appeared for the Omaha speech, in which Murray repeated his themes of economy in government, increased trade with Latin America, and expanded farm credit. When he spoke at Norfolk, he charged that Mullen had received $50,000 from Roosevelt to spend in Nebraska. The committeeman called him an "unqualified liar," and Farley also denied the charge. Later Murray said that he was misquoted and had actually said that Mullen spent $50,000 for Al Smith in

67 *Daily Clarion-Ledger* (Jackson), Mar. 29, 30, 1932.
68 R. A. Gray, Secretary of State (comp.), *Tabulation of Official Vote—Florida Primary Elections, June 7, 1932*, 3.
69 Private memorandum by Arthur Mullen, Mar. 10, 1932; Mullen to Roosevelt, Mar. 21, 1932; DNC File, Nebraska, 1928–33, Roosevelt Library.

1928. But the first version was confirmed by numerous press reports.[70] In western Nebraska Alfalfa Bill attacked corporations and the Federal Reserve and called for another Lincoln in the White House.

The Nebraska primary on April 12 gave Murray 25,214 votes; House Speaker John Nance Garner, who had not campaigned, 27,359; and Roosevelt, 91,393. Murray's 17.5 per cent of the ballots came primarily from southern and western counties in which he had spoken. He ran very poorly in Omaha and the eastern counties.[71] In explaining the results to Roosevelt, Mullen said that Murray had carried some towns where he had spoken and areas like Phelps County, in which there was no "real" town. Commenting on Murray's talks, Mullen wrote, "His speech sounds like the fiery utterance of the Dantons and the Murats in the French Revolution."[72]

From Nebraska Murray went on to Oregon and was scheduled for appearances there from April 11 to April 14. At Portland he found that the state organization was for Roosevelt, though it had arranged a speaking tour for him. On April 12 he abruptly announced that he was returning to Oklahoma on "urgent business." He had received word that Lieutenant-Governor Burns was revoking some of his executive orders.[73] Though he did not campaign there, Murray actually did better in the Oregon primary than he had in Nebraska. He received 19.4 per cent of the vote, doing best in the southern and western rural counties. The vote was 11,993 for Murray, 48,554 for Roosevelt, and 1,214 for other candidates.[74]

The Governor stopped in Denver on his way back to Oklahoma and there repeated his vote-buying charge against Roosevelt. Claiming that he was in the race to the finish despite his primary defeats,

---

[70] *Nebraska State Journal* (Lincoln), Apr. 7, 8, 9, 1932.

[71] *Abstract of Votes Cast in the Democratic Primary, April 12, 1932* (Lincoln, Secretary of State).

[72] Mullen to Roosevelt, Apr. 16, 1932, DNC File, Nebraska, 1928–33, Roosevelt Library.

[73] *Harlow's Weekly*, Apr. 16, 1932.

[74] *Abstract of Votes, Democratic Party Primary Elections, May 20, 1932*, furnished by Jack F. Thompson, Director of Elections, Office of Secretary of State, Salem, Oregon.

Murray appealed to the people of the state by endorsing bimetallism.[75] When he arrived in Oklahoma City, he canceled proposed tours of Ohio and West Virginia, blaming Lieutenant-Governor Burns's usurpation of authority for his decision. On May 10 Roosevelt defeated Murray in the West Virginia primary by over 200,000 votes, but still Alfalfa Bill continued the futile campaign.

In March it appeared briefly that Murray might win part of the Iowa delegation. A *Des Moines Register* poll of Iowa voters on March 11 showed him running neck and neck with Roosevelt.[76] Missourian Hirth went to Des Moines and spoke over radio station WHO on March 22, appealing to the farmers to work for Roosevelt. Hirth commented, "I want to say that while I have great admiration for the picturesque old crusader from Oklahoma, I congratulate the farmers of North Dakota upon their fine common sense—however much they may admire 'Alfalfa Bill,' they know he hasn't the slightest chance to be nominated."[77] When the Iowa Democrats gathered in Davenport on the twenty-ninth, all twenty-six votes were finally pledged to Roosevelt.

Murray left Oklahoma only twice between April 13 and the end of June, when the Democratic convention was to meet. He went to Amarillo, Texas, on April 28, slipping secretly across the state line to prevent Burns from learning that he was out of the state. He delivered a two-hour speech to a large gathering in Amarillo, where he had led a Presidential poll in February.[78] The other trip was to Roosevelt's own New York State, where on May 20 he addressed the Hudson Valley Blossom Festival. At the festival he gave a long speech denouncing Andrew Mellon and Jacob Raskob. Going on to New York City, he was entertained at a luncheon by an executive of the Manufacturers Trust Company. At the Empire State Club, where the luncheon was held, he was called on by Al Smith and Raskob.[79] After this brief flirtation with Wall Street Murray returned to Oklahoma.

[75] *Denver Post*, Apr. 13, 1932.
[76] *Dallas Morning News*, Mar. 12, 1932.
[77] "Address over WHO, March 22, 1932," manuscript, Hirth Coll., SHSM.
[78] *Muskogee Daily Phoenix*, Apr. 29, 1932; *Amarillo Globe News*, Feb. 7, 1932.
[79] *New York Times*, May 21, 22, 23, 24, 1932.

He told the people of the state, "I'm going to name the President," but all was not well even in Oklahoma. The press had exposed Murray's supporters, who were circulating pledge sheets among state employees asking for donations of 2 per cent of their salaries to finance his campaign.[80] A number of prominent political leaders were beginning to pledge their support to Roosevelt. Mabel Bassett, commissioner of charities and corrections, told Roosevelt that he had many friends in Oklahoma and that most of the delegation, though committed to Murray, actually favored him. Robert Bretz of El Reno asked Roosevelt to come to the Sooner State, but the New York Governor replied that he was not challenging favorite sons in their home states.[81] The Roosevelt clubs of Oklahoma urged the delegation to give Murray a complimentary vote and then shift to Roosevelt, a request seconded by former Governor Holloway.[82]

As the campaign came to a close, Murray's attacks on Roosevelt became cruel and vicious. He wrote a letter to Roosevelt demanding to know how he would aid "the little man" and announced that he favored Republican Senator George Norris of Nebraska over the New York Governor. Commenting on a Roosevelt speech, Murray stated that the address was weak and full of platitudes.[83] He reduced American politics to a low level the first week in June, when the *Blue Valley Farmer* printed the following comment on Roosevelt: "How much less can a man think who has locomotor-ataxia, a nervous disease that affects the spinal column, and ultimately the brain. I know they say it is infantile paralysis, but locomotorataxia never came from that source."[84] Murray's statement with its slanderous implication brought the New York Governor many letters of sympathy. In a gracious reply to one of the letters Roosevelt

[80] *Daily Oklahoman*, Mar. 16, 1932.

[81] R. C. Garland to Roosevelt, Mar. 17, 1932; Mabel Bassett to Roosevelt, Mar. 18, 1932; Roosevelt to Robert Bretz, Apr. 16, 1932; DNC File, Oklahoma, 1928–33, Roosevelt Library.

[82] Resolution by the Roosevelt Clubs of Oklahoma, May 28, 1932, Henry S. Johnston Coll., Univ. of Okla. Library; William J. Holloway to Roosevelt, June 1, 1932, DNC File, Oklahoma, 1928–33, Roosevelt Library.

[83] *New York Times*, Apr. 16, 1932; *Blue Valley Farmer*, Apr. 21, 1932.

[84] *Blue Valley Farmer*, June 9, 1932.

said that it was best to ignore such charges.[85] In his bitterness Alfalfa Bill had allowed himself to print this calumny, using pseudo-medical lore to substantiate it.

Near the end of June, escorted by the Kiltie Band of Oklahoma City, Murray arrived in Chicago for the national convention. When Senator Huey Long called on him at his hotel room, Murray was still in his pajamas. Long offered to put on his nightwear also, but Alfalfa Bill quickly got dressed. The "Kingfish" later reported that an interesting conversation took place. A Roosevelt supporter, Long tried to get Murray to switch the Oklahoma delegation but decided it was a waste of time. The Kingfish wrote that he was "fencing with a past master in politics."[86] When Alice Murray arrived, she received much press coverage because of her Indian heritage and folksy philosophy.[87]

At the convention Murray was elected a member of the resolutions committee, a position he had vigorously sought in 1908, 1912, and 1916. His minority platform, signed only by himself, called for a cash bonus to veterans, the end of injunctions in labor disputes, a mortgage moratorium, coinage of gold and silver in equal amounts, repeal of the 10 per cent tax on state bank notes, and a conservation compact among oil-producing states.[88] He presented his platform to the convention delegates, who defeated it by a voice vote.[89]

At 3:00 A.M. on June 30 Henry S. Johnston nominated Murray for President, calling him a "sun-crowned, God-gifted gigantic man." Will Rogers took part in the parade following the speech, and Huey Long sent the Louisiana delegation to join the Oklahomans.[90] On the first ballot Alfalfa Bill received twenty-three

---

85 Hubert Bolen to Roosevelt, June 14, 1932; Frank Carter to Roosevelt, June 15, 1932; Roosevelt to Carter, Aug. 26, 1932; DNC File, Oklahoma, 1928–33, Roosevelt Library.

86 *New York Times*, June 26, 1932; Huey P. Long, *Every Man a King* (Chicago, Quadrangle Books, 1964), 303–305.

87 *New York Times*, June 27, 1932.

88 *Official Report of the Proceedings of the Democratic National Convention, June 27 to July 2, 1932*, 151.

89 *Ibid.*, 181–84, 203–204.

90 *Ibid.*, 271–77.

votes, twenty-two from Oklahoma and one, his brother's, from North Dakota. On the second ballot Oklahoma voted for Will Rogers and on the third ballot cast eleven votes for Garner and eleven for Senator James Reed of Missouri. Finally, on the last ballot, Murray permitted the Oklahomans to vote for Roosevelt.[91]

From July to November, 1932, many Oklahoma political leaders wrote to Roosevelt and Farley pledging their support and denouncing Murray. Lieutenant Governor Burns, Mabel Bassett, Frank Carter, and others worked for the New Yorker in the fall.[92] When Murray toured the state in the general-election campaign, he praised the national ticket of Roosevelt and Garner and after the election made Farley an honorary colonel on his staff.[93] Several Oklahomans urged Roosevelt to let Alfalfa Bill run the campaign in Oklahoma, but the state committee handled the effort. When the New York Governor appeared in Kansas, Murray telegraphed his regrets that he could not attend and wished Roosevelt a successful trip and a victory in November.[94] The efforts he made to woo Farley and the new administration were totally rejected.

The "Bread, Butter, Bacon, and Beans" campaign had been a fiasco. Short of funds, experienced leadership, and organizational planning, Murray's candidacy could not turn curiosity seekers into voters. His flamboyant speeches and habits attracted crowds and the press, but they came not to see a statesman but to be entertained. Murray never recognized his own failings but blamed Roosevelt, Farley, and the "brain trust" for his defeat. During the next twenty-four years his hatred of Roosevelt and the New Deal became intensely bitter and ultimately dominated his thinking on nearly every issue.

[91] *Ibid.*, 288–324.

[92] The DNC File, Oklahoma, 1928–33, Roosevelt Library, contains many letters from Oklahoma political leaders and members of Roosevelt clubs, pledging their support to Roosevelt.

[93] *Muskogee Daily Phoenix*, July 10, 1932; *New York Times*, Nov. 18, 1932.

[94] Murray to Roosevelt, Sept. 13, 1932, DNC File, Oklahoma, 1928–33, Roosevelt Library.

MURRAY SUFFERED DEFEAT not only in his 1932 Presidential race but also in the Oklahoma Democratic primary of the same year, when many of his supporters lost to anti-Murray candidates. After the July 5 primary some newspapers in the state felt that he would still be able to control both houses of the legislature, and Murray believed that all the members of the house except the Tulsa and Oklahoma county delegations were favorable to his program, but this was not the case.[1] He took the stump in the primary and general elections to help his supporters and in the process became extremely tired. As the campaign wore on, his speeches became overly long, often incoherent, and vituperative. When some children in the audience created a disturbance during a speech in Muskogee, Alfalfa Bill lashed out, "Now listen, you kids, remember that when you go to a meeting you must respect that meeting."[2] In a few instances his supporters triumphed over his foes—as when Henry S. Johnston defeated Senator Jo Ferguson—but his efforts were generally unrewarded, and the anti-Murray bloc in the legislature grew larger.

He presented the second part of the "firebells" issues to the voters at the July 5 primary. The three measures included the proposed constitutional amendment to limit the county ad valorem tax rate on real estate and eliminate the state property tax, a law giving the governor power to restrict the cotton and wheat acreage of the state to 30 per cent of the total the previous year, and a law to levy a one-cent gasoline tax to build reservoirs and farm-to-

---

1 *Muskogee Daily Phoenix*, July 28, 1932; *Harlow's Weekly*, July 30, 1932.
2 *Muskogee Daily Phoenix*, Aug. 12, 1932.

market roads, supervised by a highway commission of which the governor was to be a member. The 231 county commissioners opposed the last proposal, which would take away all their county road funds, and farm organizations attacked the proposed acreage law. Anti-Murray members of the legislature led the fight against the tax plan. The voters rejected all three measures, even the proposal to limit property taxes, which was, in essence, a tax cut. The crop-reduction plan would not have solved the farm crisis since other states would not have reduced their production. The federal government would have to reduce production nationally.

Another initiated proposal sponsored by the Governor was placed on the general-election ballot in November. This measure provided for a new income tax on individuals, savings-and-loan associations, corporations, and banks.[3] If it had passed, it would have repealed all existing income-tax laws. Murray backers had circulated petitions for this proposal and obtained 185,000 signatures, but it was defeated.[4] Alfalfa Bill had carried out part of his campaign pledge to equalize taxes by reducing the valuation of properties for tax purposes by $100,000,000.[5] However, the voters refused to carry out the rest of his program to enlarge the tax structure through a broadly based income tax.

When the fourteenth legislature met on January 4, 1933, Murray presented his budget and again asked for the enactment of his tax program. He noted that the total state debt was $12,000,000 and insisted that it had to be reduced. He requested a biennial budget of $19,912,000, which could be achieved by making stringent economies and by balancing departmental requests with revenues. Rather than issuing state bonds, he proposed to issue state warrants which could be retired by new taxes. To maintain the highway system, a new gasoline and automobile tax should be enacted to match federal funds, he said, with any excess going to the general fund. The income tax would enable local school districts to pay their warrants at par and guarantee teachers' salaries. Mur-

[3] Basil Wilson (comp.), *Directory of the State of Oklahoma* (Oklahoma City, State Election Board, 1965), 239–40.
[4] *Harlow's Weekly*, June 25, 1932.
[5] *Ibid.*, July 16, 1932.

ray said that the state must have enough revenue to pay its debts and at the same time must reduce property taxes. The only answer was a selective sales tax and a luxury tax on cigars, cigarettes, and cosmetics. He also wanted a law to require school districts and cities to obtain permission from the State Tax Commission before they sold bonds or increased their indebtedness. This procedure would prevent the enlargement of local debts and, consequently, higher property taxes.

Other features of his address included proposals to cut the cost of government, eliminate educational frills, appropriate $600,000 in relief funds, audit the books of the State School Land Commission, strengthen the oil-proration law, suspend tax penalties, and create a new highway commission over which he would have control. If a new commission was not created, he said, the legislature must take full responsibility for the highway system. He asked for a new subpenitentiary at Atoka to relieve extremely overcrowded conditions at the McAlester prison. The basis of the program was tax revision and a reduced budget.[6] The executive budget was praised by the rural press, and even the *Oklahoma City Times* endorsed it.[7]

In the first weeks of the legislative session Murray and his supporters appeared to be in firm control of the house. Tom Anglin was elected speaker, as the Governor requested, and a house resolution endorsing the administration passed by a vote of 82 to 30. However, Murray's choice for president pro tempore of the senate was defeated. In the house approximately forty-nine members were strongly for Murray, some forty others opposed him, and the balance of power rested with an independent faction.[8] Most administration measures were either defeated or amended by the senate, which continued to resent Murray's assertion of executive power.

While the legislature was debating the budget and the tax program, several banks refused to accept any state, county, or city warrants. The legislature then passed a bill earmarking 40 per cent

[6] Murray, *Memoirs*, III, 385–405; *Daily Oklahoman*, Jan. 4, 1933; *Oklahoma City Times*, Jan. 4, 1933.

[7] *Blue Valley Farmer*, Jan. 12, 1933; *Oklahoma City Times*, Jan. 4, 1933.

[8] *Harlow's Weekly*, Jan. 7, 14, 1933.

of the gasoline tax to pay state debts, with 50 per cent of the tax going to the counties to retire their warrants. This was almost the exact plan Murray had been urging for two years. The legislators continued working to cut the budget, and new revenue had to be found to replace the $30,000,000 in property taxes which had been eliminated. Murray was forced to issue almost $9,000,000 in treasury notes to pay the state warrants due in June.[9]

Throughout the session Murray appeared in the legislature and in the caucuses to urge adoption of his budget. He went to the floor of both chambers to buttonhole members and met with the leaders in a number of secret sessions to win support for his program. The new income-tax bill was finally passed, raising the rate as the Governor had requested, and a cigarette tax was adopted. He vetoed bills to levy high taxes on chain stores, establish an old-age pension system, and institute homestead exemption. He announced that the last two bills were unconstitutional, which they probably were. A sales tax of 2 per cent was enacted, but food, clothing of less value than $8.00, farm products, raw materials, and livestock were exempted from the tax. Revenue from the sales tax was earmarked for common schools.[10] The legislature appropriated $21,642,000 for the 1933–34 fiscal year, a reduction of almost one-third from the record $35,860,000 of 1931–32.[11]

On March 2 the Governor sent a "crime" message to the legislature which was something less than a request for penal reform. His proposal for a new subpenitentiary at Atoka was adopted, and over 8,000 acres of the DOK Ranch were purchased for the prison farm.[12] His other penal ideas, ignored by the legislature, included the use of the lash and the stock for male offenders. The state did put into operation a sterilization law passed by the previous legislature and endorsed by Murray.[13] At the conclusion of the session

9 *Ibid.*, Apr. 1, 15, June 3, 1933.

10 *Muskogee Daily Phoenix*, Mar. 2, 30, 1933; *Blue Valley Farmer*, Mar. 16, Apr. 13, 20, 1933.

11 *Harlow's Weekly*, Apr. 22, 1933.

12 *Ibid.*, Jan. 28, 1933.

13 "Oklahoma Puts Sterilization Law into Effect," *Literary Digest*, Vol. CXVII (May 12, 1934), 17.

the Governor praised the house as the most effective since the first legislature in 1908.[14]

A month later he abruptly called a special session of the legislature. Opponents of the sales, cigarette, and income taxes had initiated a petition campaign to force a referendum on the measures. If the special session would pass the laws again attaching the emergency clause, there could be no referendum. Murray knew that if the tax bills were voted upon they would be defeated. The same legislative officers were elected, and the legislature began deliberations on May 24. A new income-tax bill was passed, as was the sales-tax bill, but the latter was reduced to $.01, and the Governor allowed it to become law without his signature. Revisions in both taxes meant $6,000,000 less revenue than the bills passed by the first session would have provided. Murray was angered by the revisions, which the anti-Murray senators forced upon him. The sales-tax bill contained a clause for an optional referendum, and the cigarette tax was not passed again, but the new income-tax law contained the emergency clause.[15]

A special election was called for August 15, to put to the vote a constitutional amendment to limit the maximum local property-tax rate and end the state property tax. Murray endorsed the amendment, which was approved by a margin of nine to one. The voters defeated the cigarette tax passed by the regular session, as well as a bill to strengthen the State Equalization Board. Murray had won his long fight for limits on property taxes but had lost some of his equalization power.[16] No longer would the state receive revenue from property taxes. Schools, counties, and city governments would benefit from this form of taxation.

The questions of taxes and governmental economy continued to plague the Governor. On February 21 he issued an executive order directing sheriffs not to dispossess any property owner or conduct any tax sales. He wanted to give the legislature a chance to pass a

[14] *Muskogee Daily Phoenix*, Apr. 23, 1933.

[15] *Blue Valley Farmer*, May 25, 1933; *Harlow's Weekly*, July 8, 22, 1933; *New York Times*, July 9, 1933.

[16] *Blue Valley Farmer*, Aug. 10, 1933; Wilson, *Directory of the State of Oklahoma*, 240.

mortgage-foreclosure law, which it did.[17] In November, 1933, he set aside penalties for delinquent property taxes for 1931 and all prior years, but this order was overruled by the courts.

When the need for increased revenues conflicted with Murray's convictions about alcohol, the need for funds won out. When the legislature passed a joint resolution for repeal of the Eighteenth Amendment, he vetoed it, as he did a bill for a referendum on 3.2 beer. However, he later reversed himself and authorized a special election on July 11 which would legalize beer in Oklahoma and add $3,000,000 to state funds. When the last election returns came in, Murray ordered sales to proceed, but only after the National Guard had been called out to halt premature sales.[18]

The Murray–Lew Wentz fight for control of the Highway Commission finally ended on February 11, 1933. Alfalfa Bill's effort to replace Wentz with Maud Thomas in 1932 had failed, and so he turned to the legislature for a new highway-commission law. Murray allowed the Briggs bill creating a new commission to become a law without his signature. Though he wanted the bill, the price he paid was heavy, for the senate agreed to the measure only if it could dictate the names of the new commissioners. The law required senate confirmation of the governor's appointments, though no Republican representation was required. Wentz was replaced by L. V. Orton of Pawnee, and John McKeel and Sam Hawks were replaced by H. N. Arnold of Buffalo and L. B. Selman of Walters. The two last-named members and the new fourth member, Ed McDonald of Sallisaw, were closely allied with the senate. Murray had succeeded in removing Wentz, but in the process he had lost control of the Highway Commission.[19] The Governor disclaimed any responsibility for the commission after the new members took over, saying, "I did not regard the last two years of my administration as the 'Murray Commission' although I appointed them under pressure from the Senate in order to get them confirmed."[20]

In early 1933 there was a severe banking crisis in the United

[17] *Blue Valley Farmer*, Feb. 21, 1933.
[18] *Harlow's Weekly*, May 6, 1933; *New York Times*, July 12, 13, 1933.
[19] *Harlow's Weekly*, Feb. 11, 1933; *Blue Valley Farmer*, Feb. 9, 23, 1933.
[20] Murray, *Memoirs*, II, 441.

States, and Oklahoma was no exception. On March 1 Murray closed the banks in the state. His original order would have kept them inoperative until March 6, but when President Roosevelt ordered the banks closed until the tenth, Murray extended his order. Oilman H. H. Champlin's First National Bank of Enid refused to cease business, and the Governor used the National Guard to close it. The legislature quickly enacted an emergency bank law which gave the Bank Commission power to open or close banks. When Roosevelt reopened the banks, Oklahoma followed suit, and the worst part of the crisis passed.[21]

The oil question remained unsettled in 1933, and the Murray administration came under sharp attack from the senate. A special investigating committee controlled by pro-Murray senators probed the role of "proration umpire" Cicero Murray in the oil-field operations. The committee tried to keep the investigation under control, but anti-Murray senators presented so much adverse information on the senate floor that they were forced to expand the inquiry. When witnesses reported seeing Cicero accept money from oil operators, the Governor's cousin responded by submitting to the committee his tax returns for the preceding ten years.[22] On March 7 officials of the Slick-Urschel and Anderson-Prichard oil companies testified that they had given him $32,000 to pay his "expenses" as oil czar. Bank statements were introduced to show that he had deposited the money in his private accounts. On March 9 Roy Johnson testified that he had given Cicero $2,000, of which $1,200 was a loan and the rest was payment for "expenses." O. D. Hoffman testified that 10,000 to 25,000 barrels of hot oil had been produced from one well while "Colonel" Murray was in control of the fields.[23] Cicero refused to discuss his bank account of $148,000, and the committee was discharged without taking any action other than asking for his removal and a new proration law.

Governor Murray issued an executive order on March 4, 1933, closing the Oklahoma City field for violations of the oil allowables.

21 *Harlow's Weekly*, Mar. 11, 1933; *Tulsa Tribune*, Mar. 2, 1933.
22 *Harlow's Weekly*, Jan. 21, Feb. 4, 1933.
23 *Tulsa Tribune*, Mar. 7, 9, 23, 1933.

He announced that the shutdown would continue until a more stringent law was enacted. More than 150 guardsmen patrolled the properties of Sinclair Oil Company, the alleged chief violator. The legislature enacted a new proration law on April 10, which allowed the Corporation Commission to establish oil and gas production levels, with heavy penalties for noncompliance. A tax of one-eighth of $.01 per barrel paid for the enforcement. Since Murray had threatened to veto the bill if it deprived him of control of the proration commission, the new five-man body included four men who had served under Cicero Murray, including the Governor's son Massena.[24]

The Roosevelt administration acted quickly to curtail oil production nationally. The President directed Secretary of the Interior Harold Ickes to arrange a meeting of Governor Ralph of California, Governor Ferguson of Texas, and Governor Murray to set limits on oil.[25] The oil-producing states held a three-day conference and formulated guidelines for oil-production control. Murray wrote Roosevelt that as one of the "mates" he was ready to follow the "skipper" in federal regulation of oil. He told the President that the answer was a league of oil states operating under the federal police power,[26] and Roosevelt agreed that the states needed to co-operate for conservation purposes.[27] Governor Murray and Governor Alfred M. Landon of Kansas sent the President a joint telegram on May 16, calling for an act of Congress to limit crude-oil production.[28] The answer came, not through Congress, but in an oil agreement under the National Recovery Act. However, Murray's basic idea for an interstate oil compact was ultimately accepted by the petroleum-producing states.

[24] *Harlow's Weekly*, Mar. 11, 1933; *New York Times*, Mar. 5, 14, Apr. 11, 1933; *Tulsa Tribune*, Apr. 15, 1933.

[25] Harold L. Ickes, *The Secret Diary of Harold L. Ickes: The First Thousand Days, 1933–1936* (New York, Simon and Schuster, 1953), 6.

[26] William H. Murray to Franklin D. Roosevelt, Apr. 4, 1933, Official File 56, 1933–34, Oil (Hyde Park, Franklin D. Roosevelt Library). Hereafter cited as Roosevelt Library.

[27] Roosevelt to Murray, Apr. 22, 1933, Official File 56, 1933–34, Oil, Roosevelt Library.

[28] Murray and Alfred M. Landon to Roosevelt, telegram, May 16, 1933, Official File 56-A, 1933–39, Oil, Roosevelt Library.

The Governor continued to use the National Guard to carry out his wishes, despite court orders, writs, or injunctions. When Colonel Zach Miller, proprietor of the 101 Ranch, was jailed for failure to pay alimony to his wife, the guard was called out to free him. Murray announced that no one would be imprisoned for debt while he was governor. He imposed martial law on Hassman Park in Oklahoma City to prevent Negroes from using it for an Emancipation Day celebration. He said they should use Booker T. Washington Park. By December 3, 1933, he had called out the guard twenty-seven times, and in his four years as governor he issued thirty-four proclamations of martial law. In 1934 he used martial law to prevent the sale of homes for delinquent taxes in eleven counties and threatened to arrest county treasurers who tried to sell farms when the owners failed to pay their taxes.[29] Throughout his term in office Alfalfa Bill fought the depression with the National Guard.

During his last two years as Governor, Murray gained absolute control of the State Regents of Higher Education and removed still more educators. President John G. Mitchell of Central State College and the presidents of Cameron Junior College and Murray State College were replaced.[30] In March, 1933, he issued an executive order totally revising the curriculums at the University of Oklahoma and the Agricultural and Mechanical College. He ordered prelaw and geology courses transferred to the university, premedicine and engineering to the Stillwater college, and educational courses to the teachers' colleges. Although instructors of duplicate courses were ordered dismissed, he never enforced the order, and the schools carried on as before.[31] The idea of consolidating certain courses had been considered before, and in some instances has since been accomplished, but not by the executive order of a governor.

Murray also continued his free-textbook crusade. He appointed a state textbook commission which adopted a new and less expensive

[29] *Harlow's Weekly*, Dec. 9, 1933, Apr. 21, 1934; *New York Times*, Dec. 11, 1933, Apr. 15, 22, 1934; *Daily Oklahoman*, Dec. 3, 1933.

[30] *Daily Oklahoman*, Aug. 16, 1932.

[31] *Harlow's Weekly*, Mar. 18, 1933.

series of books for grades one to twelve. The move proved unpopular, since it made obsolete the secondhand and therefore cheaper books previously used. Relief funds were provided to purchase free textbooks for destitute families, and over a million books worth $300,000 were given to children from poverty-stricken homes.[32] He also organized women's groups to battle for full nine-month school terms in local districts.[33] Eventually free textbooks were provided for all Oklahoma children, and Murray saw one of his lifelong desires realized.

His pardon-and-parole policy aroused much criticism. He initiated a parole system whereby convicts were released if they agreed to leave the state. This exportation of criminals brought vehement protests from surrounding states. Between January 4, 1931, and June 24, 1934, Murray paroled 2,214 men, including 292 murderers, 290 robbers, 106 rapists, and 339 burglars.[34] He gave lifetimer Matt Kimes a six-day leave from the McAlester prison to go hunting, which resulted in the murder of two police officers.[35] However, he actually had little sympathy for criminals and did not grant a record number of paroles. There was an extremely high number of executions during Murray's four years, though the Governor refused to allow reporters to witness the executions as they had in the past.[36] His handling of paroles differed little from that of preceding and subsequent governors, and reflected the over-all backwardness of the state in penal reform.

The economic depression grew worse in 1933 and 1934, forcing Murray to become more dependent on the federal government for relief funds. He continued to use state money to give the farmers free seeds, to provide jobs on the highways, and to supply free textbooks, but state relief activities were handicapped by a lack of funds and by Murray's refusal to expand work-relief programs. He did acquire some relief money from the Reconstruction Finance

32 *Ibid.*, Sept. 23, 1933.
33 *Ibid.*, Dec. 2, 1933.
34 *Tulsa World*, June 24, 1934.
35 *New York Times*, Nov. 28, 1934.
36 *Ibid.*, July 8, 1931.

Corporation, and his use of these funds was praised by the press.[37] The Governor instituted a program of lake and pond construction with R.F.C. grants. The largest project, near Ardmore, became Lake Murray.[38]

Murray feared that the advent of enlarged relief activities under the New Deal would cause him to lose control of all federal programs. From March to August, 1933, his supporters sent a flood of letters and telegrams to President Roosevelt and Federal Emergency Relief Administrator Harry Hopkins, praising the Governor's handling of relief and urging them to let him continue in this capacity.[39] Hopkins answered the letters, saying only that his agency was striving for efficiency at all levels. When the relief agency was transferred to the National Industrial Recovery Administration, the Governor continued to administer the F.E.R.A. funds, giving his workers instructions through the *Blue Valley Farmer*. Murray became angry when John Carlock, a patronage appointee of Senator Elmer Thomas and Senator T. P. Gore, became the public works administrator in Oklahoma. Fearing that he would lose control of the federal money, Murray went to Washington to see Harry Hopkins. Several Oklahoma political leaders had written to Hopkins urging him to end "waste and graft" in the Governor's handling of the funds. Hopkins' assistant, Aubrey Williams, had visited Oklahoma in June to investigate the charges and had reported favorably on Alfalfa Bill's methods.[40] Hopkins endorsed the Governor's procedures. Then the Governor tried to obtain $10,000,000 from Harold Ickes and the Public Works Administration. Murray opposed the large dam to be constructed at Denison, Texas, on the Red River, but wanted Ickes to give him

---

37 *Blue Valley Farmer*, Mar. 23, 1933; *Oklahoma City Times*, Dec. 2, 1932.

38 *Harlow's Weekly*, Apr. 29, 1933.

39 There are many such letters in the William H. Murray Alphabetical File (Hyde Park, Franklin D. Roosevelt Library). Hereafter cited as Murray File, Roosevelt Library.

40 Frank C. Carter to Harry L. Hopkins, July 3, 1933, Official File 444, Federal Emergency Relief Administration (Hyde Park, Franklin D. Roosevelt Library); hereafter cited as F.E.R.A., Roosevelt Library; W. C. Fidler to Roosevelt, telegram, July 7, 1933, Murray File, Roosevelt Library.

money for small lakes in the dust-bowl area.[41] His plan was for the states of Oklahoma, Texas, Colorado and Kansas to build lakes throughout the dust bowl, financed by federal funds.[42] Murray used R.F.C. and F.E.R.A. funds to build farm-to-market roads and set up a three-man county unemployment committee in each county to certify the names of men eligible for relief. One member of each committee represented the Red Cross. Murray used the lists prepared by these committees in hiring the needy.[43] Some rural counties had as many as 1,300 eligible men, who received $.30 an hour for their work. Murray forbade counties and cities to issue bonds to pay for relief projects or to accept federal loans, considering both actions unconstitutional.[44]

Continued protests from Oklahoma brought Hopkins and Williams to Oklahoma City to examine relief records. They exonerated Murray of all charges and praised his administration of funds. An additional $675,000 was made available to the state, and the Governor's crony, A. L. Beckett, became a federal relief director.[45] The next month, State Senator W. C. Fidler wrote to Roosevelt that graft was continuing, and the State Federation of Labor accused Murray of using R.F.C. grants to build poor roads and pay low wages.[46]

By November, 1933, the Roosevelt administration had begun to restrict Murray's control of relief funds. In a vicious letter to Henry Morgenthau of the Farm Credit Administration, Alfalfa Bill said that he would not appoint the farm-relief committees suggested by Morgenthau. He accused Morgenthau of refusing to appoint Murray's friends but said that instead "your Wall Street bunch selected a man by the name of Shull, whom I dismissed as Bank Commissioner in this state, without consulting me, and apparently any one

[41] *Harlow's Weekly*, Aug. 5, 1933.

[42] *Ibid.*, July 29, 1933.

[43] There are a number of these county lists in the William H. Murray Collection, OHS Library.

[44] Mimeographed letter, Aug. 17, 1933, Murray File, Roosevelt Library.

[45] *Harlow's Weekly*, Aug. 26, 1933.

[46] W. C. Fidler to Roosevelt, Sept. 7, 1933, Official File 444, F.E.R.A., Roosevelt Library; *Daily Oklahoman*, Sept. 15, 1933.

else." He told Morgenthau not to bother him further about federal appointees, for he would not permit his office to be used as a "cat's-paw" for Wall Street.[47] Murray was criticized by the Civil Works Administration for hiring only 88,000 men when the state had a quota of 102,000. Some newspapers charged that federal relief workers were being forced to buy subscriptions to the *Blue Valley Farmer*. Finally the C.W.A. removed Beckett and appointed Carl Giles to handle its funds in Oklahoma, and in January, 1934, the federal relief funds were removed from Murray's control.[48]

The following month the Governor sent a letter of protest to Hopkins, claiming that state C.W.A. and F.E.R.A. workers had been denied their right to participate in the contest for the Democratic party chairmanship. Williams replied that workers could take part in politics but that administrators could not.[49] Hopkins informed Roosevelt that he had found it necessary to take personal charge of relief administration in Oklahoma on February 24, 1934. Only in Oklahoma were F.E.R.A. workers to be federal employees; the other states continued to administer their programs.[50] The federal government also refused to pay $75,000 in overdrafts accumulated during the Governor's administration of the funds. During the rest of Murray's term federal funds came into Oklahoma only through federal agencies. During his administration Murray spent only $1,200,000 of state funds for relief. By far the larger share came from the federal government. Murray's handling of the federal money was probably not as efficient as that of some states, but Aubrey Williams said that it was "eight times" better than Huey Long's efforts in Louisiana.[51]

The relief situation in Oklahoma paralleled the problem of federal patronage. As mentioned earlier, after the 1932 election Mur-

[47] Murray to Henry Morgenthau, Jr., Nov. 8, 1933, Murray File, Roosevelt Library.
[48] *New York Times*, Nov. 26, 1933; *Harlow's Weekly*, Jan. 13, 1934.
[49] Murray to Harry L. Hopkins, Feb. 2, 1934; Aubrey Williams to Murray, Feb. 6, 1934, Murray File, Roosevelt Library.
[50] Harry L. Hopkins to Roosevelt, Mar. 3, 1934; Lewis Douglas to Roosevelt, memorandum, Mar. 6, 1934, Official File 444, F.E.R.A., Roosevelt Library.
[51] *Oklahoma News*, Aug. 21, 1933.

ray had tried to establish cordial relations with Roosevelt and had made James Farley an honorary colonel.[52] Senators Gore and Thomas decided not to handle patronage through the state party machinery, because it was completely controlled by the Governor.[53] Some of the Governor's friends urged Roosevelt to allow him to dispense patronage in the state. Former Governor Robertson wrote Louis Howe that Murray was striving for the same goals as Roosevelt and was a consistent supporter of the President. Robertson said of Murray, "At times he seems to be very erratic, but never radical." His plea was echoed by Anna Kennedy Bozeman, former secretary of the Murray national Democratic club. She claimed that the President was being unfair to Alfalfa Bill, who had joined the "Roosevelt Bandwagon."[54]

Murray continued to court Farley in an attempt to gain additional federal patronage, for he realized that Farley was the chief patronage dispenser in the Administration. But he could not get along with the New Dealers. When Harry Hopkins asked Murray to appoint a commission of dollar-a-year men to control relief funds, the Governor retorted that the press considered this "a slap at Murray," which it was. He told Farley that he hoped it was not a slap but that, regardless, he planned to continue personal control over relief money. If the Administration was against him, the Governor said, he was willing to accept the challenge. He related to Farley the long history of his negotiations with Hopkins and denied using federal funds for political purposes.[55] Murray saw Farley in New York in August, 1933, but failed to win the Postmaster General to his cause. In January, 1934, Farley responded to a question about the possibility of Murray's appointment to a federal position by saying, "Bill Murray has as much a chance to be a foreign trade

[52] Murray to Roosevelt, Feb. 1, 1933, Murray Coll., Univ. of Okla. Library.

[53] *Harlow's Weekly*, Feb. 4, 1933.

[54] Monte Warner to Roosevelt, May 25, 1933, Murray File, Roosevelt Library; J. B. A. Robertson to Louis Howe, July 3, 1933, Official File 300, Democratic National Committee, Oklahoma, 1933–44 (Hyde Park, Franklin D. Roosevelt Library); hereafter cited as DNC [state, date], Roosevelt Library; Anna Kennedy Bozeman to Roosevelt, July 9, 1933, Murray File, Roosevelt Library.

[55] Murray to James A. Farley, June 23, 1933, Murray File, Roosevelt Library.

representative of the United States in South America as I have to be Pope of Rome—and I'm not even a priest."[56]

Throughout his last year as governor Murray tried to convince the Postmaster General that he deserved federal patronage. Farley sent a copy of an incoherent letter from Murray to Marvin McIntyre, Roosevelt's secretary, who often handled political appointments. Farley told McIntyre, "Bill is as crazy as a bedbug, but evidently I stand all right with him."[57] Farley visited Oklahoma City in August, 1934, and saw the Governor at the state capitol. He expressed friendship for Murray, who responded with a laudatory introduction when the Postmaster General gave a speech at the Shrine Auditorium.[58] Despite such public cordiality, the fact remained that the New Deal was making every effort to remove Murray from control of federal appointments and funds.

Nevertheless, Murray maintained tight control of state patronage and of the state Democratic organization. Rising young politicians in the Democratic party tried to maintain friendly relations with him. Two future governors, Leon C. Phillips and Robert S. Kerr, wrote cordial letters to him, and Kerr told Murray, "I just wanted you to know that so far as I am concerned I think you have been one of Oklahoma's greatest Governors, if not the best."[59] His relations with the Oklahoma League of Young Democrats were not so friendly. At their 1933 convention Murray accused them of drinking intoxicants, and they responded by heckling his speech.[60]

Democratic leaders such as J. Berry King, Percy L. Gassaway, and newspaperman Walter M. Harrison were totally opposed to Murray and worked to undermine his control of the party. Gassaway, a rancher and politician, sent Harrison an "excoriation" of Murray which the Oklahoma Publishing Company editor refused to print. It was not that the piece was too vitriolic, wrote Harrison,

[56] *Daily Oklahoman*, Jan. 15, 1934.
[57] Murray to James A. Farley, Apr. 17, 1934; Farley to Marvin McIntyre, Apr. 26, 1934; Murray File, Roosevelt Library.
[58] *Harlow's Weekly*, Aug. 25, 1934.
[59] Leon C. Phillips to Murray, Aug. 12, 1933; Robert S. Kerr to Murray, Jan. 9, 1934, Murray Coll., Univ. of Okla. Library.
[60] *Muskogee Daily Phoenix*, Feb. 23, 1933.

but "we are on the Governor's back so constantly on matters of state that I believe we are creating some sympathy for him, and since we are going into a campaign where the Governor's strength is going to be a matter of considerable importance, I do not want to be shooting at him unless the issue is vital and directly in the minds of the people at the particular moment the criticism appears."[61] King told Gassaway that federal patronage was being withheld from Oklahoma because of Murray's statement about Roosevelt's paralysis in the 1932 campaign.[62] The accusations and name calling increased in intensity as the Democratic gubernatorial primary of 1934 drew near.

Throughout 1933 it was obvious that Murray planned to endorse Speaker of the House Tom Anglin for governor, though he did not do so formally until October.[63] Murray also planned to run a slate in the primary in order to keep control of the state. Senators Gore and Thomas and the Oklahoma congressional delegation joined forces to defeat Murray's candidates in 1934 and were influential in getting federal relief funds taken away from the Governor before the primary.[64]

The primary election had two major issues: Murray and "bringing the New Deal to Oklahoma." Anglin had to defend Murray and his administration, while his leading opponent for governor, E. W. Marland, campaigned for stronger ties between the state and the New Deal. Formerly a wealthy oilman who had lost his company to Wall Street early in the depression, Marland could use his personal financial disaster to identify himself with the economically deprived voters of the state. Anglin suffered from Murray's endorsement when the latter's slate proved unpopular. Enforced contributions from state employees stirred further resentment.

When the Democratic state convention met on February 10, 1934, the Governor kept control and saw to it that his candidate

[61] Walter M. Harrison to P. L. Gassaway, Oct. 2, 1933, P. L. Gassaway Collection (Norman, University of Oklahoma Library, Division of Manuscripts). Hereafter cited as Gassaway Coll., Univ. of Okla. Library.

[62] J. Berry King to P. L. Gassaway, Jan. 6, 1934, Gassaway Coll., Univ. of Okla. Library.

[63] *Blue Valley Farmer*, Oct. 26, 1933.

[64] *Daily Oklahoman*, June 25, 1933.

for state chairman was elected. Murray campaigned over the state for Anglin, denouncing Marland and the other two leading candidates, J. Berry King and Gomer Smith, an old-age-pension advocate. King retaliated by making Alfalfa Bill the target of his entire campaign. All the candidates tried to tie Anglin to Murray, though Murray still had a strong following in rural Oklahoma.[65]

Murray was too old and tired to make a strenuous tour of the state, but he made the effort. He was extremely irritable, and his tirades against Marland often drove his audiences away in the middle of his speeches. When some small children interrupted a speech at Newkirk, Murray shouted, "Now, you little screw worms get out of here. You haven't a —— —— bit of business here."[66] He usually sat while speaking and puffed on a black cigar, now and then spitting on the stage. Wearing a suit of white cotton, with his white cotton socks falling down over his shoe tops and revealing his bony legs, Murray would launch into an abusive attack on his enemies.[67]

Marland's slogan, "Bring the New Deal to Oklahoma," proved too much for Anglin, who was defeated along with all but two men on the Murray slate. Marland led the field with 156,885 votes, and Anglin was second with 101,698. Marland failed to receive a majority, and the two men were to meet in the runoff primary, but Anglin withdrew, saying that he lacked sufficient campaign finances.[68] Murray was very bitter about Anglin's loss, for he considered it a personal defeat. He refused to campaign for his candidates in the runoff primary.[69]

After the primary Murray leased the *Blue Valley Farmer* to his cousin Cicero for one dollar per year. Cicero was to receive all profits and pay all expenses. However, Alfalfa Bill continued his

---

[65] *Harlow's Weekly*, Feb. 10, Apr. 28, 1934; "Sparks from the Record of Governor Murray," political broadside published by J. Berry King, A. N. Boatman Collection (Norman, University of Oklahoma Library, Division of Manuscripts).

[66] *Oklahoma News*, June 29, 1934.

[67] "Memoirs, Travel Incidents, Anecdotes, Etc.," Milton Fletcher Mahin Collection (Columbia, State Historical Society of Missouri, Western Historical Manuscripts Collection).

[68] Wilson, *Directory of the State of Oklahoma*, 176–77.

[69] *Oklahoma City Times*, July 7, 1934.

weekly column.[70] The paper continued to carry long articles attacking Marland and began to praise his Republican opponent, former Senator William Pine. Although the paper never endorsed Pine, its savage attack on the Democratic nominee could lead readers to only one conclusion: Bill Murray wanted the Republican to be the next governor.[71] The revolt came to nothing, for Marland easily won the general election.

The fifteenth legislature gathered in the house on January 8, 1935, to hear Murray's last general message. He urged the legislators to exempt homesteads from taxes by a constitutional amendment and advocated a ten-year state dam-building project and an enlarged state-park system. He announced the formation of the William H. Murray Educational Fund, established by friends, to provide scholarships for the poor. He denounced the New Deal bureaucrats, warning the legislators of "brain busters known as brain trusters who are trying to destroy our government."[72] His last gubernatorial message was the opening gun in what was to be a twenty-one-year attack on Roosevelt and the New Deal. In conclusion he said that during the last four years "the Office of Governor, at all times, has been where the Constitution placed it—in the State Capitol—and all knew where to locate it: and no one has ever doubted who was [Governor]."[73] With this statement no one argued.

When Governor-elect Marland visited Murray before the inauguration on January 14, he was coolly received and had the honor of sitting in one of the chairs chained to a radiator. After the ceremony was over, "Governor Murray disappeared into the crowd amid shouts of 'Good-bye Bill' and 'well done.' "[74] Murray, his wife, and daughter Jean left Oklahoma City for Tishomingo.

An evaluation of Murray's record as governor in terms of his

[70] *Harlow's Weekly*, July 28, 1934; lease for *Blue Valley Farmer*, July 12, 1934, Murray Coll., Univ. of Okla. Library.

[71] *Oklahoma City Times*, Aug. 23, 1934; *Blue Valley Farmer*, Sept. 27, Oct. 4, 11, Nov. 1, 1934.

[72] *Last General Message to the Fifteenth Legislature of the State of Oklahoma,* Jan. 8, 1935; *New York Times*, Jan. 9, 1935.

[73] Murray, *Memoirs*, III, 646.

[74] *New York Times*, Jan. 15, 1935.

desire to restore a pastoral civilization would mark it as a failure. The nation continued to move toward an urban, industrial society, and even the depression failed to halt the march. If Murray's four years are evaluated on the basis of his 1930 campaign pledges, then his term was a partial success. He accomplished major tax reforms and equalized the tax burden. Corporations and individuals with higher incomes were compelled to pay more taxes, while farmers and homeowners were relieved of heavy state property taxes. The Oklahoma Tax Commission and the equalization boards proved to be lasting accomplishments. The state system of higher education suffered drastically under Murray, who tried to make the schools into an image of College Hill Institute of the 1880's. Patronage jobs for relatives and friends, graft in the oil fields, guardsmen at the bridges, and chairs chained to radiators are the things remembered by his detractors. His supporters in the state remember higher oil prices, free bridges, payroll warrants valued at par, and hungry men fed vegetables growing on the mansion lawn. Murray summed up his term by saying, "My administration has just been one damn thing after another."[75] He had found it impossible to fight the depression by using the National Guard, but after four years he still did not realize that running a state was different from running a farm.

[75] *Tulsa Tribune*, Jan. 1, 1935.

★

THE TWILIGHT YEARS

XII

AFTER E. W. Marland's inauguration as governor, Alfalfa Bill was ready for a vacation. His son William drove him to central Texas, where he visited the towns and people he had known before coming to Indian Territory. In an address to the state legislature at Austin he gave the New Deal a thorough lashing. He went on to Corpus Christi and Brownsville, ventured briefly into Mexico, and returned to Tishomingo by way of Lake Charles—"Huey Longana" —and Little Rock.[1]

Since their return from Bolivia in 1929 the Murrays had not owned a home of their own. In June, 1935, Alfalfa Bill purchased a sixty-three-acre farm on Yashau Creek near the town of Broken Bow. When the family left Tishomingo, a thousand people gathered to bid them farewell. Murray rebuilt a four-room shack on the farm and acquired some horses, a mule, a cow, a few hogs, and some chickens. He refused to purchase a tractor, and when he wanted to go to town, he hitchhiked to Idabel, twelve miles away. Sleeping on the floor of the unpainted house, the family cooked outdoors on an open fire until improvements could be made. A Negro couple worked for them in this peaceful, pastoral existence, and they lived on the Yashau until 1938.[2] Alice was in poor health but still made jams, jellies, and peach pickles for the children. The Murray boys were deeply concerned about their mother and father, but their parents seemed to enjoy the primitive conditions.[3]

[1] Murray to Alice Murray, Feb. 3, 8, 12, Apr. 7, 1935, Murray Coll., Univ. of Okla. Library.

[2] *Harlow's Weekly*, July 6, Aug. 3, 1935; *New York Times*, July 7, 1935.

[3] There are many letters to Bill and Alice Murray from their children in the 1930's in the Murray Coll., Univ. of Okla. Library.

Alfalfa Bill's political beliefs remained resistant to change. From Broken Bow he disseminated anti–New Deal tirades and threatened to bolt the Democratic party in 1936 to "save the Constitution." He rejoiced in the Supreme Court decision which ruled the National Recovery Act unconstitutional. He declared, "The despotism of a majority is worse than the despotism of one man, because you can shoot him." Murray continued to oppose the New Deal relief program: "Relief—the dole—has broken the morale of the people. It is in the industrial centers that the greatest danger lies. If there is a breakup of the Union, the North, South and West will go along, the East will blow up."[4]

Murray kept in close contact with other New Deal opponents, and in June, 1935, met with Governor Eugene Talmadge of Georgia, and Governor O. K. Allen of Louisiana at Biloxi, Mississippi, to discuss the New Deal and ways in which it might be effectively opposed.[5] In October Murray announced the formation of the Association for Equality and Economy. He was to be national director of this organization, whose purpose was to elect an economy-minded Congress. His goal of one million members failed to materialize, and the size of the operation could never have been as large as he claimed, for its headquarters was in his house on Yashau Creek. Alfalfa Bill ran full-page advertisements in newspapers over the country demanding "tax equality" and economy in government. He announced that he was not running for office but only trying to save the Republic. He published many pamphlets denouncing the N.R.A. and the Agricultural Adjustment Administration. He opposed the growing federal debt and "runaway inflation," which he claimed were destroying the middle class. New Dealers were impoverishing the country and using federal funds to buy the votes of the poor, he said.[6] Despite his statement that he had no

4 *New York Times*, June 9, 1935.
5 *Harlow's Weekly*, June 22, 1935.
6 *New York Times*, Oct. 18, 1935; James A. Farley to Roosevelt, Jan. 3, 1936, Official File 300, DNC, Oklahoma, 1933–44, Roosevelt Library; "Remember Children: Oppressive Government Is Fiercer than Tigers!" pamphlet of the Association for Economy and Tax Equality, Murray Coll., Univ. of Okla. Library.

plans to run for an office in 1936, some Democrats feared that Alfalfa Bill would oppose Senator T. P. Gore's bid for renomination.[7]

Murray continued to threaten to bolt the party unless Democratic candidates advocated tax equality and decreased governmental expenditures. When his old friend Governor Alfred Landon of Kansas received the Republican Presidential nomination in 1936, Murray sent him a telegram saying: "Sincere congratulations. Now for Liberty, law and Landon opposed to Russian red revolution."[8] He visited Landon and said he was capable of being a good President. He stopped short of a formal endorsement of the Kansan, since he wanted to retain his position within the Democratic party, although some party members were ready to read him out of the party anyway.[9]

When Landon visited Oklahoma City to make a campaign address, he asked Murray to introduce him. Murray did so with a very complimentary speech but again refused to cut his ties to the Democratic party. He claimed to have known Landon for many years and said that John W. Davis, James A. Reed, Alfred E. Smith, Bainbridge Colby, Lewis Douglas, and other "real" Democrats were for Landon. Governor Marland reacted quickly and stated that Alfalfa Bill was no longer a Democrat.[10]

Murray toured Oklahoma and neighboring states in the fall of 1936, attacking Roosevelt and praising Landon. He spoke in Springfield, Sedalia, Moberly, Nevada, and Trenton, Missouri, before going on to Iowa, Nebraska, and Kansas. An "association of friends" paid his expenses, but he still refrained from openly endorsing Landon. On October 29, 1936, a group of Tulsa Republicans purchased time on a national radio network for him to speak against the New Deal. The thirty-minute speech appeared in book

[7] Eugene Lorton to "Mac" [probably Marvin McIntyre], [n.d.], Official File 300, DNC, Oklahoma, 1933–44, Roosevelt Library.

[8] *Harlow's Weekly*, June 13, 1936.

[9] *New York Times*, June 16, 1936; Scott Ferris to James A. Farley, July 27, 1936, Democratic National Campaign Committee, Correspondence of J. A. Farley, 1936, Oklahoma–Oregon (Hyde Park, Franklin D. Roosevelt Library).

[10] *Harlow's Weekly*, Oct. 24, 1936; *New York Times*, Oct. 24, 1936; manuscript of speech, Oct. 23, 1936, Murray Coll., Univ. of Okla. Library.

form in 1937 as the *Rights of Americans*. Publication was probably financed by the same Tulsa group.[11]

The *Rights of Americans*, Murray's second literary effort, was the first to deal with politics. An earlier book, *Murray's Essays on Pocahontas and Pushmataha*, had been primarily concerned with Indian lore and genealogy.[12] Dedicated to Justices John Marshall, Roger B. Taney, Edward D. White, William Howard Taft, and Charles Evans Hughes, the second book drew primarily on his experiences and his reading of Claude Bowers, Alexander H. Stephens, Edward Gibbon, Adam Smith, and John Stuart Mill. The author propounded an extremely narrow interpretation of the Constitution and condemned the Fourteenth Amendment for giving corporations the same rights as individuals. Murray argued that human and property rights were inseparable and defended the concept of states' rights. He claimed that the entire New Deal program violated the rights of Americans and was unconstitutional. From his bibliographical sources he drew evidence substantiating his opposition to expanded governmental activity. A lonely, defeated man, he began to publish vicious attacks on individuals and groups whom he blamed for his defeats.

Although his friend Landon was thoroughly routed in 1936, Murray continued to assault the New Deal. When Roosevelt proposed to enlarge the membership of the Supreme Court, Murray warned, "If they succeed in this the control of the press is the next step."[13] In the summer of 1937 he went to California to deliver ten speeches and made some "nonpolitical" tours of Oklahoma.[14] That summer a "Draft Murray" group organized to support him as a candidate for governor in 1938. On August 10 he delivered a long radio speech attacking the legislature, arguing for a reduction in its membership and for shorter sessions. Although the press had never strongly supported him, many papers praised his attack on the legislature.

[11] *Oklahoma City Times*, Aug. 19, 1936; Murray, tape-recorded interview of Nov. 20, 1952, OHS Library.

[12] William H. Murray, *Rights of Americans* (Boston, Meador Publishing Company, 1937); William H. Murray, *Murray's Essays on Pocahontas and Pushmataha* (Ardmore, Paine Printing Co., 1924).

[13] *New York Times*, Feb. 12, 1937.

[14] *Harlow's Weekly*, July 17, 1937.

He toured the state during September and October, giving a speech entitled "What of the State?" which castigated the legislature and Governor Marland for making large appropriations and adding to the growing state debt.[15]

Murray formally announced his candidacy on November 17, 1937. The *Blue Valley Farmer* was resurrected on the eighteenth. At this time the paper was owned by Cicero Murray, Alice Murray, and Anson B. Campbell. Cicero was the editor, and Campbell was his associate. Through the paper Alfalfa Bill promised a strenuous campaign on a platform of governmental economy, an end to bond issues, reduction of the state debt, and two-year terms for state senators.[16] The press began to take sides in the primary, and Murray received endorsements by newspapers in Blackwell, Atoka, Weatherford, Sallisaw, and Poteau. Papers in McAlester, Frederick, Wagoner, Bartlesville, and Norman opposed him.[17]

His candidacy presented a problem to other contenders, for the elimination of the runoff primary had made it possible for him to be nominated by a minority of all the votes cast. This probability became a dominating feature of the campaign. He made an interesting about-face on the question of the runoff primary. On January 6, 1938, he said he wanted it restored. If he could not win a clear majority of votes, he said, he did not want to be governor. Just four days later he denounced those supporting a runoff, saying that they were trying to defeat him.[18]

Murray's campaign organization resembled the one that conducted the 1930 campaign. Oklahoma City headquarters was managed by Joe Neely, his friend of forty years, and Mrs. Jessie Moore, former clerk of the supreme court, headed the women's division. The *Blue Valley Farmer* served as Murray's voice, and little use was made of other media. The *Blue Valley Farmer* had several press runs of over 350,000 copies and seems to have been well financed.[19] He had a rather small organization, though he received

[15] *Ibid.*, July 24, Aug. 14, 21, Sept. 25, Oct. 2, 1937.
[16] *Blue Valley Farmer*, Nov. 18, 1937; *Harlow's Weekly*, Nov. 20, 1937.
[17] *Harlow's Weekly*, Nov. 27, Dec. 25, 1937, Jan. 8, 1938.
[18] *Oklahoma City Times*, Jan. 6, 1938; *Oklahoma News*, Jan. 10, 1938.
[19] *Harlow's Weekly*, Mar. 17, 24, 1938; *Daily Oklahoman*, July 3, 1938.

backing from a number of conservative lawyers and businessmen.

Oklahoma's financial condition became the key issue in the 1938 campaign. The state was in fiscal disarray, and the state debt had increased in spite of record tax receipts. The sixteenth legislature, at Marland's urging, had spent money far in excess of available revenue. All the major candidates opposed Governor Marland and pledged to restore the state to fiscal stability.

The leading candidates were Murray; Leon C. Phillips, a member of the state House of Representatives; William S. Key, head of the Oklahoma Works Progress Administration; Hubert L. Bolen, a leading Democratic politician; Jack Walton, corporation commissioner and former governor; and Ira Finley, organizer of the left-wing Veterans of Industry of America. Phillips, a former Republican, took an ambivalent position on the New Deal, pledging only to restore financial responsibility. He was supported by organized labor; by Henry Bennett, president of the Oklahoma Agricultural and Mechanical College; by most members of the legislature; and by a rising young politician, Robert S. Kerr. Key, the candidate of the New Dealers, had been state adjutant general and warden of the penitentiary before heading the state W.P.A. Former governors Martin Trapp and Robert L. Williams and Senator Josh Lee were supporting him. After protracted negotiations, Key and Phillips talked Bolen into retiring from the race. Walton and Finley divided the radical vote and were never serious threats to Murray, Key, and Phillips. Efforts were made to persuade either Key or Phillips to withdraw, but the battle remained a three-way conflict.[20]

As usual, Murray received the support of the farmers. His record as governor in reducing their taxes kept them loyal, as did his opposition to crop limitations established under the New Deal. A poll of farmers by the *Farmer-Stockman*, which was hostile to Murray, showed a strong majority for him. Murray considered Key his major opponent and emphasized his spending on W.P.A. projects to "prove" his inability to put the state's financial house in order. Murray's proposed constitutional amendment to forbid the creation of any state debt received widespread support. Throughout

20 *Daily Oklahoman*, May 13, 1938.

the spring and summer he made two or more speeches a day. After he advocated repeal of the sales tax, a group of Republicans openly began to work for him.[21]

Key lacked editorial support and was hurt by the ineptness of W.P.A. administrators who encouraged those receiving aid to engage in political activity and who raised the W.P.A. minimum wage just before the election. The wage increase did not help Key, since Senator Elmer Thomas took credit for it, and voters were irritated by "federal intervention" in the primary. A speech by Phillips endorsing the New Deal also cut into Key's support. The *Daily Oklahoman*, the *Oklahoma City Times*, the *Tulsa Tribune*, the *Tulsa World* and the *Oklahoma News* supported Phillips in an attempt to defeat New Dealer Key. The metropolitan press did not attack Murray as they had in 1930, but reprinted his charges against Key.[22] Political columnists thought that Murray's chances were very good, and many predicted he would win.[23]

In June the Roosevelt administration sent Charles A. West to Oklahoma to work for Key and for Senator Thomas, who was running for re-election. West said that he came to "stop Murray," but some New Dealers felt that more help was needed. Senator Josh Lee, believing that Key was in serious trouble, begged Roosevelt to come to Oklahoma and attack Murray for supporting Landon in 1936.[24] Roosevelt responded with five speeches in Oklahoma. His main address was given at the Oklahoma City fairgrounds on July 9. Cheering crowds greeted the President along the parade route and in the grandstand at the fairgrounds. In an address entitled "America Needs a Government of Constant Progress along Liberal Lines," Roosevelt called for more liberal officials. He did not want more "yes, but—" people, he said, only those totally committed to the

---

[21] *Tulsa Tribune*, June 26, 1938; *Daily Oklahoman*, Apr. 17, 1938; *Harlow's Weekly*, Feb. 5, Apr. 23, May 7, 11, June 11, 1938; *Enid Morning News*, May 4, 1938; *Oklahoma News*, Jan. 16, 1938.

[22] For the role of newspapers in the campaign, see Briscoe, "The 1938 Oklahoma Gubernatorial Campaign as Presented by a Group of State Newspapers."

[23] *Daily Oklahoman*, June 26, 29, 1938.

[24] *Tulsa World*, June 19, 1938; *Harlow's Weekly*, June 25, 1938; Josh Lee to Roosevelt, June 28, 1938; Lee to Roosevelt, telegram, June 28, 1938, Official File 300, DNC, Oklahoma, 1933–44, Roosevelt Library.

liberal cause. Then the President digressed to a marginal, hand-written note, and proceeded to destroy Murray's gubernatorial chances: "Of course, some are not even 'yes, but'—people for I note that one of the candidates for a place on the Democratic state ticket in Oklahoma this year is nationally known as a Republi-can."[25] The obvious reference to Murray removed him from the front-running spot in the race. Both local and national observers commented on the damage to his candidacy, and estimates of his loss of votes ran as high as 75,000. Widespread defections occurred among rural citizens, most of whom appear to have voted for Key. Both Walton and Finley offered to withdraw in favor of Murray, but he was afraid their votes would go to Key or Phillips. It is possible that Murray might have won if he had accepted their offers.[26] In his *Memoirs* he later wrote of the Roosevelt appear-ance, "As a result of that speech, all the Negroes and Jews (except half a dozen) voted for Key," and estimated his loss at 60,000 votes.[27]

A record 594,695 ballots were cast on July 12, 1938, and the pri-mary was the most closely contested in twenty-four years. Phillips received 179,139 votes; Key, 176,034; Murray, 148,395; Walton, 45,760; and Finley, 37,107.[28] Five other candidates received ap-proximately 7,000 votes. Phillips carried twenty-eight counties, mostly in the western part of the state, including populous Okla-homa, Tulsa, Garfield and Kay counties. Key's strength came from twenty-eight eastern counties, while Murray carried twenty-one, all but two of which were in the southern half of the state.

Several factors contributed to his defeat. Though the *Blue Val-ley Farmer* had been widely circulated and his platform had ap-pealed to rural voters, his campaign probably reached a peak too soon. Moreover, he was sixty-eight years old, and many voters felt that he had become too eccentric. However, it was those twenty-

25 *The Public Papers and Addresses of Franklin D. Roosevelt, 1938* (New York, The Macmillan Co., 1941), 445.

26 Neal Barrett to Roosevelt, telegram, July 11, 1938, Official File 300, DNC, Oklahoma, 1933–44, Roosevelt Library; "Washington Notes," *New Republic*, Vol. XCV (July 13, 1938), 279–80; *Harlow's Weekly*, July 16, 1938.

27 Murray, *Memoirs*, III, 16.

28 Winters, *Directory of the State of Oklahoma*, 56.

three words in the Roosevelt speech that defeated him. Written on the train before the President's arrival in Oklahoma City, approved by Senator Thomas, Senator Lee, and congressmen Lyle Boren, Wilburn Cartwright and Jed Johnson, the marginal note had served the purposes of the New Dealers.[29]

Murray tried to play a role in the general election. A group of friends urged him to enter the senatorial race as a nonpartisan candidate against Senator Thomas. His name would be placed on the ballot by petition. The Murray organization sought to obtain 150,000 signatures before September 1 to get him in the race. The *Blue Valley Farmer* continued publication, and Murray issued a senatorial platform opposing the federal farm policy and New Deal relief agencies. Only 36,775 voters signed the petitions; his rural friends began to desert him, especially when he began touring the state to campaign for Republican congressional candidates.[30] The petition effort suffered from insufficient funds, for Murray had spent $2,000 running for governor and hesitated to go into debt for the senatorial contest.[31] When the State Election Board solved his problem by ruling that his petitions were illegal, he appealed to the Oklahoma Supreme Court, which ruled that his name could not be placed on the November ballot.

The two political defeats in 1938 were not as crushing to Murray as Alice's death on August 28, at Saint Anthony Hospital in Oklahoma City. Her body rested in state in the blue room of the capitol before burial at Tishomingo. From over the state came messages of sympathy, and eulogies filled the editorial pages of Oklahoma newspapers. His own "Adios, Alice, Adieu," written a week after her death, revealed the depths of his love for his wife. He wrote of her faith, sincerity, and modesty. She was his ideal of a good wife— one who managed the home, reared the children, and always remained apart from the husband's public life. He praised her for the way she had brought up the children and kept the mansion while he was governor. Alice had been a steadying influence all of their

[29] *Oklahoma City Times*, July 16, 1938; *Harlow's Weekly*, July 16, 1938.
[30] *Harlow's Weekly*, Aug. 6, 13, 20, 1938; *Blue Valley Farmer*, Aug. 18, 1938.
[31] Murray to Ewing Mitchell, Oct. 6, 1938, Mitchell Coll., SHSM.

married life, and he was unable to accept her death, later referring to her as though she were still alive.[32] From the time of Alice's death until his own, he usually lived by himself at his own insistence. His accelerated mental and physical decline can be dated from the fall of 1938.

In 1939 Murray received an invitation from the Colston Leigh Speakers Bureau to make a seven-month speaking tour. These arrangements were never completed, but Murray agreed to a six-speech tour for the Redpath Bureau. He spoke in Illinois and Ohio, but his last four appearances were canceled. He blamed Washington "bureaucrats," but the truth was that he was simply too decrepit to be effective.[33]

He spent the next year crusading against the New Deal. In February, 1940, he addressed a meeting of the Southern Coalition of Conservative Democrats and Republicans at Houston, Texas. He spoke to law classes at the University of Oklahoma and to a number of dinner groups in the spring, always damning the New Deal. In September he called a reunion of delegates to the constitutional convention, and twenty-three elderly men gathered, this time to reminisce, not to organize a campaign.[34]

Almost blinded by cataracts, he dictated his next two books to Anson B. Campbell, who also did the proofreading and compiled the indexes. He would lie down in the evening, think out the narrative, and then dictate it to Campbell the next day. The first volume was called *The Presidency, the Supreme Court and Seven Senators*; the second, *Uncle Sam Needs a Doctor*.[35] The book on the Presidency compared the seven Democratic senators who defied the Roosevelt purge of 1938 with the seven Republican senators who

[32] Murray, *Memoirs*, III, 647–63; Johnston Murray, interview of Dec. 29, 1965; Burbank Murray, interview of Feb. 10, 1966.

[33] W. Colston Leigh to Murray, Jan. 30, 1939; C. E. Beckman to Murray, Jan. 21, Mar. 17, Mar. 20, Apr. 21, 1939, Murray Coll., Univ. of Okla. Library; Murray, *Memoirs*, III, 11.

[34] *Harlow's Weekly*, Feb. 11, 25, Sept. 23, 1939.

[35] William H. Murray as Told to Anson B. Campbell, *The Presidency, the Supreme Court and Seven Senators* (Boston, Meador Publishing Company, 1939); William H. Murray as Told to Anson B. Campbell, *Uncle Sam Needs a Doctor* (Boston, Meador Publishing Company, 1940).

voted to acquit President Andrew Johnson of impeachment charges after the Civil War. Murray wrote that both battles revealed the importance of the principle of separation of powers in the American government. He contended that Roosevelt's attempt to remake the Supreme Court demonstrated the continuing need to preserve the integrity of all three branches of the government. The small volume concluded with a plea to return to states' rights and the philosophy of John C. Calhoun. It was a rambling discourse designed to prove the political and philosophic corruption of the New Deal. The book sold for one dollar a copy and appeared to have had only limited circulation.

Uncle Sam Needs a Doctor was another assault on the New Deal. Murray wrote that in 1932 he had thought Roosevelt would be a good leader, but the New Deal had simply become a political machine. In his opinion, Rexford Tugwell's Resettlement Administration contained twelve thousand "Pinkies," and the President was guilty of unconstitutional acts, favoritism, and fraud. His concern with "Communists" in government caused him to praise Congressman Martin Dies and the work of the House Un-American Activities Committee. Feeling that American liberties were being subverted, he urged voters to defeat Roosevelt and the New Deal in 1940. *Uncle Sam Needs a Doctor* had a greater circulation than his book on the purge of 1938 and also appeared in a paperback edition.

Murray stood in the forefront of a group of well-known Democrats throughout the country who tried to elect Republican Wendell Willkie in 1940. Missourian E. Y. Mitchell also became a rabid anti–New Dealer, and often wrote to Murray about a proposed coalition of conservative Democrats and Republicans. Mitchell sent letters to Landon, Thomas E. Dewey, and Charles P. Taft urging them to give Murray the vice-presidential nomination on the Republican ticket.[36] The Oklahoman wanted Vice-President John Nance Garner to head the Democratic ticket and decided to bolt the party when Roosevelt won a third nomination. He sent Willkie

---

[36] Ewing Mitchell to Murray, Feb. 3, 1940; Mitchell to Thomas E. Dewey, Charles P. Taft, and Alfred M. Landon, June 17, 1940, Mitchell Coll. SHSM.

a telegram announcing his support of the former Wall Street executive.[37]

In the summer and fall of 1940 Murray campaigned for Willkie and issued a press release describing the Republican nominee as a real Jeffersonian Democrat. Alfalfa Bill criticized Roosevelt's precedent-breaking campaign for a third term and welcomed speaking engagements under the auspices of various Democrats-for-Willkie clubs. Five years later in his *Memoirs* he wrote that he was glad Willkie was defeated in 1940 because the former candidate was actually a "front-man" for the "world government crowd."[38]

Murray made a political race of his own in 1940, campaigning for the Democratic nomination for congressman-at-large. Running against incumbent Congressman Will Rogers, a schoolteacher not related to the famed humorist, and fifteen other Democrats, Murray campaigned as an anti–New Dealer. Alfalfa Bill traveled by bus from town to town in a pathetic effort totally lacking in finances and organization. What the country really needed, he proclaimed, were more small, independent, home-owning farmers, his solution to all problems for the past fifty years. Murray opposed American entry into World War II on the grounds that such action was being advocated by "Jews and Communists." Small crowds heard him denounce Rogers, who, he said, had been elected on someone else's name.[39] He claimed to be running mainly against Roosevelt, and his speeches bear out this claim. He gave Rogers a vigorous contest, but Rogers won with 148,416 votes to Murray's 115,302, while the third man in the race, Paul Jones, received 14,000 votes.[40]

Murray's defeat and Roosevelt's third victory thoroughly disheartened him. To his fellow "Jeffersonian Democrat," E. Y. Mitchell, he wrote: "The man [Roosevelt] who takes the last word

[37] Cancelled check for $10.00 to the Garner-for-President Club, Feb. 29, 1940; Wendell Willkie to Murray, telegram, July 21, 1940, Murray Coll., Univ. of Okla. Library; *New York Times*, July 21, 1940.

[38] "Why I Will Vote for Willkie," manuscript of a press release, and political broadside, Aug. 31, 1940, Murray Coll., Univ. of Okla. Library; Murray, *Memoirs*, III, 30–31.

[39] Political broadside, Apr. 25, 1940, Murray Coll., Univ. of Okla. Library; *Oklahoma City Times*, Apr. 25, 26, June 18, 20, 1940.

[40] Winters, *Directory of the State of Oklahoma*, 53.

—on the Potomac is a bit disturbed. . . . When the boys return from training camps, etc., no jobs will be open for any of them. . . . Little hope for the future—providence alone can save the republic."[41] He told Mitchell he was thinking seriously of going to South America. Even now when he was defeated he looked to a new frontier.

Still listing his occupation as "farmer," Murray filed income-tax returns reporting his pitiful earnings of $925.30 in 1940 and $1,648.35 in 1941.[42] For the rest of his life he lived on money earned from the sale of his books, which many Oklahomans generously helped to finance through gifts and purchases.

In 1941 he published a book on manners, scholarship, grammar, and morals. *The Finished Scholar* included chapters on sentence construction, numerals, poetry, word usage, and language.[43] Murray appealed to his friends for money to help him publish the book. He paid $600 to Dorrance and Company to publish it and planned to sell the copies he was required to purchase.[44] Murray and his publisher failed to maintain harmonious relations. The author accused W. H. Dorrance of acting like a "Jew." Dorrance replied that Murray's letter smacked of Hitlerism and said that the manuscript contained many misspelled words.[45]

Written while he was living in an Oklahoma City hotel, *The Finished Scholar* was Murray's answer to the decay of morality and manners among young people. He praised his College Hill Institute training and his teachers, John W. McCracken and D. P. Hurley. He urged young people to read "strong" literature, such as Shakespeare's plays, Ralph Waldo Emerson's essays, Quintilian's rhetoric, George Bancroft's and Alexander H. Stephens' histories of the United States, and John Richard Green's or David Hume's histories of England. He also recommended the works of Plutarch, Edward Gibbon, and Adam Smith and his own books. In 1936 he

[41] Murray to Ewing Mitchell, May 21, 1941, Mitchell Coll., SHSM.

[42] Federal income-tax return, 1940, Oklahoma income-tax return, 1941, Murray Coll., Univ. of Okla. Library.

[43] Murray, *The Finished Scholar.*

[44] "Governor Murray's S. O. S. Call to His Friends," Mitchell Coll., SHSM; Dorrance and Company to Murray, Aug. 13, 1941; contract between Dorrance and Company and Murray, July 24, 1941, Murray Coll., Univ. of Okla. Library.

[45] W. H. Dorrance to Murray, Jan. 9, 1942, Murray Coll., Univ. of Okla. Library.

had suggested a longer list, which included the writings of Sir Walter Scott, Robert Burns, Sir Francis Bacon, and Alfred, Lord Tennyson, but *The Finished Scholar* recommended more works of history and law, less fiction, and fewer classics.[46] A potpourri of homespun philosophy and erroneous information, *The Finished Scholar* demonstrated Murray's self-education, his faith in that process, and his vanity.

In 1941 he became an active member and leader of the America First organization. Totally opposed to United States entry into World War II, Murray joined Charles A. Lindbergh, General Robert Wood, and other isolationists who favored total neutrality. When Lindbergh appeared in Oklahoma City, Murray praised the son of Congressman Lindbergh, with whom he had served in Congress. Alfalfa Bill spoke for returning to the "traditional" American foreign policy and hemispheric defense. He toured northern Texas in October, speaking in six towns near Dallas. In Montague he claimed that Communists had telephoned him before the meeting and threatened his life. To sparse crowds he presented his message opposing the war.[47] General Wood invited him to become a formal member of America First and to serve as a member of the national committee.[48]

In the 1940's Alfalfa Bill began to correspond with members of extremist groups, and by the 1950's he was lending his name to anti-Semitic and anti-Negro organizations. In September, 1941, Gerald B. Winrod, leader and organizer of a number of racist groups, wrote him: "The Jews have us on the brink of war. International Jewish banking is crumbling. Roosevelt put in by the Jews, is obviously carrying out their mandate, in trying to rehabilitate losses sustained by the reactions gathering momentum in all parts of the world against the damnable conspirators."[49] Murray began

[46] *Harlow's Weekly*, Mar. 28, 1936.

[47] Manuscript of speech, Aug. 29, 1941; schedule of speaking dates, Murray Coll., Univ. of Okla. Library; *Dallas Morning News*, Oct. 7, 8, 1941.

[48] Robert E. Wood to Murray, Sept. 22, 1941; minutes to the America First National Committee Meeting, Nov. 28, 1941; Murray to Wood, Dec. 4, 1941, Murray Coll., Univ. of Okla. Library.

[49] Gerald B. Winrod to Murray, Sept. 12, 1941, Murray Coll., Univ. of Okla. Library.

to repeat such nonsense and became an avid reader of Winrod's publications.

In 1942 he wrote an article for the Atoka, Oklahoma, *Indian Citizen Democrat* called "Essays on Forms of Government from Theocracy to Foolocracy," which was reprinted in pamphlet form and in his *Memoirs*. Murray stated that the only real democracy had been that of ancient Athens and contended that the New Deal, fascism, and nazism were modern names for despotism and regimentation. The New Deal combined state socialism and communism and was similar to nazism, he claimed.[50] Murray repeated these remarks in a campaign for the Senate that year.

He ran against Senator Josh Lee and Judge Orel Busby in the Democratic primary of 1942. Murray said later that he ran only to defeat Busby. Lee easily won renomination with 188,279 votes, Busby was second with 96,647, and Murray ran a dismal third with 36,925 votes.[51] He was too old to be taken seriously as a candidate, and only a small band of his devoted followers voted for him. After his defeat he wrote to E. Y. Mitchell saying that he feared there would be no elections in 1944, for by then Roosevelt would be a dictator. Former Republican Senator William Pine won his party's nomination but died before the general election. The Republican State Central Committee named Tulsa oil millionaire Ed Moore to replace him. Moore, a lifelong "Jeffersonian Democrat," switched parties, and with the active support of Murray and other conservatives he defeated Lee to become Oklahoma's third Republican Senator.

To save his failing eyesight, Murray underwent a series of operations at Saint Anthony Hospital.[52] The operations helped the seventy-three-year-old Murray, but during the remainder of his life his vision, both physical and political, remained extremely limited.

After the operations he spent six months in Oklahoma City and Tishomingo hotels writing his three-volume *Memoirs*, dictating

[50] Murray, *Memoirs*, III, 664–88.
[51] Winters, *Directory of the State of Oklahoma*, 50.
[52] Murray to Ewing Mitchell, Oct. 5, Nov. 10, Dec. 1, 1942, Mitchell Coll., SHSM.

much of the material to a stenographer, Nell Reaves.[53] The project was financed by prepublication sales to friends and businesses. Ironically, his old enemies the utility and oil companies, railroads, and banks made large purchases or donations. J. G. Puterbaugh of the McAlester Fuel Company helped him raise the $5,450 paid to the Meador Publishing Company to print the volumes.[54] The books were published in 1945.

Murray's *Memoirs* provide interesting insights into the man and his lifetime. He wrote of his life, his friends, and events in Oklahoma and the nation from the vantage point of the mid-1940's. He always presented his views as the "correct" ones and traced his defeats to the treachery or thievery of others, never to his own inadequacies. Many of the 1,731 pages of the *Memoirs* contain historical inaccuracies, religious digressions, fancied occurrences, prescriptions for home remedies, phrenological nonsense, and bizarre ideas about diet. But many of his stories and recollections are clear and concise and can be supported by other sources. The first volume is the most important, for there he describes his early life, his education, and those experiences which shaped his thinking and personality. The third volume consists primarily of appendixes containing speeches, letters, and fiscal information about the state of Oklahoma.

The *Memoirs* show Murray's mental deterioration during his twilight years. In 1907 he had expressed revulsion at the mistreatment of Jews in Russia, and in 1917 he had urged an immigration law allowing Jews and members of other religious minorities to enter this country without having to pass a literacy test. Yet in the *Memoirs* he established himself as a racist of unbounded hatred. He claimed that Franklin Roosevelt was a Jew and that Bernard Baruch was the creator of the New Deal, a program which was actually written by "Israel Moses Sieff." "The Negro is the White man's burden," wrote Murray. Yet Negroes had some virtues, he

---

[53] Murray, *Memoirs*, I, 7; III, 102.
[54] The Murray Collection, Univ. of Okla. Library, contains order blanks and a record book of the sales. See also J. G. Puterbaugh to W. A. Delaney, Jr., Oct. 4, 1944; contract between Meador Publishing Company and Murray, Nov. 15, 1944; Murray Coll., Univ. of Okla. Library.

wrote, but Jews had none. He called Luther Burbank the "best of the white race" and in the horticulturist's writings he found "scientific" support for his racism. Murray's twelve-volume set of Burbank's writings is heavily marked and annotated. Oddly enough, most of the sections to which he referred were ghostwritten by men working for Burbank.[55] He praised Americans of British, Scandinavian, German, and French descent but said that the "low-grade races" of southern and southeastern Europe were a threat to civilization.

Even in his old age Murray continued to defend his agrarian philosophy. He told fellow Oklahomans to keep their state agricultural, free from the taint of manufacturing. "America is an agricultural nation," and the virtues of agriculture must be preserved, he wrote.[56] Just as he failed to examine critically the bases of his racism, he simply ignored evidence that the nation had become urban and industrial. All his life Murray sang the praises of agrarianism, and he never creased to formulate his beliefs and judge the actions of others within its narrow framework.

When World War II ended, Murray was living in a motel in Tishomingo. His landlady reported that he neglected to bathe, chewed tobacco constantly, and spat on the floor. From his sanctuary he announced that President Harry Truman was a "damn fool," that the United Nations was a Communist plot, and that oilman Roy Turner, the next governor, was the "best governor money can buy."[57] Two years later, still in Tishomingo, he published *Palestine*, an anti-Semitic pamphlet attacking Jewish immigration to the United States and arguing for Arab control of Palestine. He quoted long passages from a spurious "Talmud" and from "The Protocols

[55] Marginal notes in Murray's twelve-volume set of *Luther Burbank: His Methods and Discoveries and Their Practical Application* (New York, Luther Burbank Press, 1915), now owned by Burbank Murray. A Burbank biographer contends that the horticulturist wrote little contained in these volumes. See Walter L. Howard, *Luther Burbank: A Victim of Hero Worship* (Waltham, Chronica Botanica Co., 1945–46), 370–71.

[56] Murray, *Memoirs*, I, 91–94, 260–66, 308–10; II, 556; III, 35, 50, 131, 109–16, 280.

[57] *Oklahoma City Times*, June 11, 25, 1946.

of Zion," which had been proved a forgery many years before.[58]

In 1948 the bolt by southern Democrats against President Truman's civil-rights platform led to the formation of the Dixiecrat party. Meeting in Birmingham, Alabama, on July 16, the Democratic bolters created the new party, cheered on by Alfalfa Bill. Seated in the convention-hall balcony, Murray, then seventy-nine-years old, was ragged, half-blind, and deaf. A piece of gauze was wrapped around his neck. He had traveled from Tishomingo for two days on a bus and had rented a tiny room without a bath. He declared his opposition to any form of civil-rights legislation. When he was called to the speaker's platform, he said, "This country became great through Christian principles and the white man's brains."[59]

Returning to Oklahoma, he met with a handful of Oklahoma Dixiecrats in an unsuccessful attempt to get their ticket on the November ballot. Lawyer Ross Lillard, politician John Steele Batson, Charles N. Haskell's daughter Frances, and Murray endorsed the Dixiecrat candidates and demanded the continuation of segregation. Like many other conservative Democrats, including his old friend T. P. Gore, Murray could not remain in the Democratic party which had evolved out of Franklin Roosevelt's New Deal coalition.[60] He blamed the New Dealers, the Negroes, and the Jews for all his defeats and the decline of his beloved rural America.

In 1948 Murray published his most viciously racist book, *The Negro's Place in Call of Race.*[61] Written in the early 1940's but unpublished until the year of the Dixiecrat campaign, the book became a best seller in the extremist bookstores of Gerald L. K. Smith, Gerald B. Winrod, and their organizations.[62] Subtitled *The Last Word on Segregation of Races Considered in Every Capable Light as Disclosed by Experience*, the book was as anti-Semitic as it was

58 William H. Murray, *Palestine* (Tishomingo, William H. Murray, 1947).

59 *New York Times*, July 18, 20, 1948; *Atlanta Constitution*, July 17, 1948; *Courier-Journal* (Louisville), July 17, 1948.

60 "Platform of the States Rights Democratic Party," Aug. 14, 1948, Murray Coll., Univ. of Okla. Library.

61 William H. Murray, *The Negro's Place in Call of Race* (Tishomingo, William H. Murray, 1948).

62 Ralph Lord Roy, *Apostles of Discord* (Boston, The Beacon Press, 1953), 66–67.

anti-Negro. Though Murray disavowed any opposition to racial or religious groups, his written words revealed a bitter and bigoted mind. He argued for segregation, for the deportation of all Russians from the United States, and for the abolition of the United Nations. He wrote, ". . . only the Christian, blue or grey-eyed races can govern themselves, under universal suffrage, and not all of them —now or at any time of recorded history."[63] He repeated all the myths about Reconstruction and the Ku Klux Klan and said that the "yellow" Negroes resulted from "Sherman's march to the sea." Negro towns were the only answer to the racial problem, he wrote, for integration was both communistic and anti-Christian. He urged President George L. Cross of the University of Oklahoma to invite Winrod and Smith to address the student body. He wanted Cross to fire Professor Laurence Snyder, a world-renowned geneticist, who, Murray said, taught the "Communist line"—that is, the biological equality of the races. His sources were the Patrick Henry Order of Columbus, Georgia; the *Cross and the Flag*, published by Smith; Winrod's *Defender Magazine*; and other hate literature. Almost incoherent, the book reflects the depths to which Murray had sunk in his last years. Despite his sons' pleas to stay away from such extremists, he maintained his correspondence with them and used their publications to bolster his views.[64]

He continued to eke out a small living from the sale of his books. On his eightieth birthday he was given a party at the state capitol. The Chickasaw Squirrel Rifles had been reorganized, and offices were sold in the group to raise money to repay Murray for part of the $4,000 he claimed he had spent during the constitutional convention of 1907.[65] A total of $1,476.94 was raised. Almost totally deaf and blind, the Alfalfa Statesman continued to refuse to live with his sons.

In 1950 and 1952 Murray wrote his last two books, *Christian Mothers* and *Adam and Cain*.[66] *Christian Mothers* was actually a

[63] Murray, *The Negro's Place*, 14.
[64] Burbank Murray, interview of Feb. 10, 1966.
[65] *Daily Oklahoman*, Nov. 21, 22, 1949.
[66] William H. Murray, *Christian Mothers* (Boston, Meador Publishing Co., 1950); William H. Murray, *Adam and Cain* (Boston, The Meador Press, 1952).

group of selections from a book by phrenologist O. S. Fowler, published in the late nineteenth century under the title *Science of Life*. Murray dedicated his book to Christian mothers—in contrast to Communist mothers—and repeated his idealized view of Victorian women as homemakers, mothers, and dutiful wives. *Adam and Cain* was another racist tract. A compilation from a number of sources, the volume was based upon the "Protocols of Zion," the writings of racist Arnold Leese, old travel books by Laurence Austine Woddell, and the works of John H. Harvey, an Englishman. Murray praised the Roman Catholic church as the only moral organization in the world which could hold back the march of communism. He repeated his old charges against the Jews and the Negroes and told a bizarre tale about Adam, a king of Troy who founded a Gothic civilization. According to the story, Adam and Eve were the parents of Cain, not of Abel, who was the bastard son of Woden. This fantasy is almost impossible to read and wholly impossible to understand.

In 1950 Alfalfa Bill watched his son Johnston become the second Murray governor. Running on a platform of "Just Plain Folks," Johnston led the field in the first primary and won narrow victories in the runoff primary and the general election. Alfalfa Bill sent out a campaign letter urging his friends to vote for his son but did not take an active part in the campaign.[67] As Uriah Dow Murray had sworn in his son, so the Sage of Tishomingo administered the oath of office to his son. From 1951 until January, 1955, Johnston and his second wife, Willie, provided a home for his father in the mansion. Visitors to the weekly open houses often saw the elder Murray being helped in and out of the house by the staff. Though Johnston had campaigned much as his father had, giving many speeches in small towns, his gubernatorial term was very quiet in comparison with his father's.

Murray's last effort to return the nation to "constitutional" government came in 1952, when he went to New York City to present a plaque to General Douglas MacArthur. The award, for Mac-

---

[67] Mimeographed letter to "Friends," Jan. 9, 1950, Murray Coll., Univ. of Okla. Library.

Arthur's service against communism, was presented at the Waldorf Astoria Hotel. The hotel management received a shock when Alfalfa Bill shuffled across the lobby, carrying his meager belongings in a brown pasteboard box tied with a hemp rope. That fall he voted for MacArthur for President by pasting a picture of the General on his ballot.[68]

After the Murrays left the governor's mansion in January, 1955, Alfalfa Bill went to live with his son Massena. In October, 1956, he suffered a paralytic stroke, followed by pneumonia. He was taken to Saint Anthony Hospital, where he sank into a coma and died on October 15. He was buried at Tishomingo beside his wife.

William Henry David Murray's life extended from Reconstruction to the first Eisenhower administration. The story of his life from 1898 until the 1940's is also in many respects the political history of the state of Oklahoma. Always the proponent of the rural life and all its virtues, Alfalfa Bill had only one goal: to maintain the state and the nation as the home of Thomas Jefferson's yeoman farmers. When the nation moved toward urbanization, industrialization, and governmental centralization, Bill Murray saw his dream shattered. His narrow vision of America meant that he could not accept the changes made necessary by an advancing civilization. He died still cherishing the life he had known on the farm in the Washita River bottoms, where he had studied constitutions, raised his family, and cultivated alfalfa.

[68] *Daily Oklahoman*, May 4, 5, 7, Oct. 24, 1952.

✪

A NOTE ON SOURCES

MOST OF THE citations in this book are to manuscript collections and newspapers. The William H. Murray collections in the Division of Manuscripts of the University of Oklahoma Library at Norman and in the Oklahoma Historical Society Library at Oklahoma City were invaluable for this biography. The university collection contains significant letters, speeches, memorabilia, and newspaper clippings. Despite its size, the collection has both topical and chronological gaps. The Historical Society collection is much smaller.

The Charles N. Haskell collections at the university and the Historical Society and the massive Robert L. Williams collection, also at the Historical Society, are important for the period 1906 to 1916. The P. L. Gassaway, Claude Weaver, Henry S. Johnston, Campbell Russell, J. B. A. Robertson, and Oklahoma State Federation of Labor collections at the university contain a limited number of pertinent manuscripts. Other than the Murray collection, the Marion Unger collection is the most important one on the subject at the university, since it contributes considerable information about the years Murray spent in Bolivia.

Manuscript collections outside Oklahoma were important for some phases of Murray's life. The Franklin D. Roosevelt official files and the Democratic National Committee collection, both at the Franklin D. Roosevelt Library in Hyde Park, were valuable for information about the election of 1932 and Murray's relationship with the New Deal from 1933 to 1945. The "Murray Colony," File 824.52 in the Diplomatic, Legal, and Fiscal Branch of the National Archives, provided a wealth of material on Murray's Bolivian colony. The Woodrow Wilson and William Jennings Bryan papers in the Library of Congress, Division of Manuscripts, were of marginal value, as were the papers of James S. Hogg and O. B. Colquitt at the University of Texas Archives in Austin. The William Hirth and E. Y. Mitchell collections in the Western Historical Manuscripts Collection of the State Historical Society of Missouri at Columbia were helpful for the years 1932 to 1945.

The vast newspaper files at the Oklahoma Historical Society proved to be the most important source of journalistic references. The sizable index to the newspapers facilitated research. The Murray collection at the University of Oklahoma contains many newspaper clippings which are important for the 1890's and for the gubernatorial campaigns of 1910 and 1930. The university has an almost complete file of the *Blue Valley Farmer*, Murray's campaign newspaper. The Oklahoma Publishing Company Library in Oklahoma City contains clippings of the *Daily Oklahoman*, the *Oklahoma City Times*, and the *Oklahoma News* for the years 1920 to 1956. Copies of newspapers published outside Oklahoma were found at the Library of Congress, the University of Missouri Library, and the Texas State Archives in Austin.

The author conducted a number of interviews. The most important were those with Murray's sons Johnston and Burbank. Both related many personal stories and described life in the Murray family. Burbank Murray was particularly helpful. The two-hour tape-recorded interview of the elder Murray by B. B. Chapman, in the Historical Society Library, proved very interesting. The question-and-answer session revealed a spritely Murray who, though eighty-three years old, was still in possession of his oratorical gifts.

Among popular and scholarly journals, *Harlow's Weekly* was particularly helpful because of its extensive coverage of political news. The *Congressional Record* provided the necessary details about Murray's congressional career.

Secondary works were also employed to some extent. The most important of these, Gordon Hines's campaign biography of Murray, was used with caution. The histories of Oklahoma by Edwin C. McReynolds, Edward E. Dale, Morris L. Wardell, J. B. Thoburn, and Roy Gittinger were, of course, extremely useful.

278

INDEX

MacArthur, Gen. Douglas: 275–76
McClaren, William: 178
McClintock, R. M.: 177
McCool, R. M.: 177, 209
McCracken, John: 5–7, 10, 14, 268
McCurtain, Green: 37
McDonald, Alva: 203
McDonald, Ed: 242
McDonough, D. C.: 161
McDougal, D. H.: 147
McElroy, Mat: 208
McGuffey's Readers: 5, 187
McIntyre, Marvin: 251
McKeel, John: 26, 202, 212, 242
McKellar, Rep. Kenneth: 123
McKeown, Tom D.: 140–44, 222
McLean, Fred: 227–28
McLemore, Jeff: 134
McNeal, J. W.: 98
McReynolds, James C.: 113
Mallory, Pat: 221, 228
Malthus, Thomas: 131
Marland, Gov. E. W.: 252–54, 256, 258, 260–61
Marshall, Chief Justice John: 259
Marshall, Thomas: 102, 152
Martin, Gabriel: 166
Masséna, André: 29
Mattingly, E. H.: 229
Meador Publishing Company: 271
Mellon, Andrew: 226, 233
Memoirs of Governor Murray and True History of Oklahoma: 270–73
Memphis, Tenn.: 205
Messenger, E. F.: 65
Mexia, Tex.: 16
Mid-Continent Oil and Gas Association: 197
Milburn, George: 215–16
Mill, John Stuart: 131, 259
Miller, Gov. B. M. (Alabama): 230
Miller, Zach: 245
Mills, Roger Q.: 9, 66
Minneapolis, Minn.: 227
Mississippi Basin Unemployment Conference (Memphis, Tenn., 1931): 218–20
Missouri Farmers' Association: 225
Mitchell, Cap: 147
Mitchell, E. Y.: 224, 266–67, 270
Mitchell, John G.: 245
Montague, Tex.: 4

Moore, Charles: 51
Moore, Sen. Ed: 270
Moore, Jessie: 260
Moore, Thomas: 111
Moreno, Mogro: 160
Morgenthau, Henry: 248–49
Mosley, Palmer S.: 32
Mullen, Arthur: 231–32
Murphy, Charles: 102
Murray, Bertha Elizabeth Jones: 3
Murray, Cicero: 199, 212, 216, 243–44, 253, 260
Murray, Clive: 29, 209
Murray, George Thomas: 3, 18, 107, 227, 229
Murray, Jean: 88, 211, 254
Murray, John Shade: 3–4, 6, 29, 74, 88, 107
Murray, Gov. Johnston (Oklahoma): 29, 160, 167–68, 171, 235
Murray, Gov. William Henry: birth of, 3; childhood of, 3–5; education of, 4–7, 10, 19; Farmers' Alliance activities of, 6, 11, 13–14; enters politics, 6; as traveling salesman, 6, 7, 14; as reporter, 7, 11, 14; as schoolteacher, 7–8, 10, 16–17, 19; religious views of, 8; on Populist party, 8–9, 12–13, 19; sources of political views of, 11–12; on alien landownership, 11, 41; on regulation of railroads and business, 11, 41, 54, 62–63; on tariff, 11, 108–109; on states' rights, 12; on immigration, 12, 112, 119–20, 134; on national banks, 12; first political campaign of, 14; on coinage, 14, 17; relations of, with Pres. Grover Cleveland, 16; early romance of, 17; as newspaper publisher, 18–19; on Negro, 18, 20, 55–56, 63–64, 94–95, 187–88, 269–70, 273–74; second political campaign of, 18; on direct primary, 18; sources of political strength of, 19; studies law, 19, 33; legal practice of, 20; moves to Indian Territory, 21; in Chickasaw politics, 26–27, 32; legal practice of, in Chickasaw Nation, 27, 30–31; marriage of, to Mary Alice Hearrell, 27–29; physical appearance of, in 1899, 29; moves to farm on Twelve Mile Prairie, 30, 32–33; and origin of

283

286